WITHDRAWN
NDSU

HAWKES
A Guide to His Fictions

HAWKES
A Guide to His Fictions

FREDERICK BUSCH

SYRACUSE UNIVERSITY PRESS 1973

Copyright © 1973 by Syracuse University Press, Syracuse, New York
ALL RIGHTS RESERVED   FIRST EDITION

Library of Congress Cataloging in Publication Data
Busch, Frederick, 1941–
Hawkes: a guide to his fictions.

Bibliography: p.
1. Hawkes, John, 1925–
PS3558.A82Z6   813'.5'4   72-7765
ISBN 0-8156-0089-5

Excerpts from *Cannibals and Christians* and *Why Are We in Vietnam?* by Norman Mailer, are reprinted by permission of Norman Mailer.

Excerpts from the poetry of T. S. Eliot are reprinted from his *Collected Poems 1909–1962* by permission of Harcourt Brace Jovanovich, Inc.; copyright, 1936, by Harcourt Brace Jovanovich, Inc.; copyright © 1963, 1964, by T. S. Eliot.

Excerpts from *Brighton Rock*, by Graham Greene, copyright 1938, © 1966 by Graham Greene, are reprinted by permission of The Viking Press, Inc.

Excerpts from the following works by John Hawkes are reprinted by permission of New Directions Publishing Corporation: *Charivari* and *The Cannibal*, copyright 1949 by New Directions Publishing Corporation; *The Beetle Leg*, copyright © 1951 by John Hawkes; *The Goose on the Grave*, copyright © 1954 by John Hawkes; *The Lime Twig*, copyright © 1961 by John Hawkes; *Second Skin* and *Lunar Landscapes*, copyright © 1963, 1964 by John Hawkes; *The Innocent Party*, copyright © 1966 by John Hawkes; and *The Blood Oranges*, copyright © 1970, 1971 by John Hawkes.

Excerpts from *Portrait of the Artist as a Young Dog*, by Dylan Thomas, are reprinted by permission of New Directions Publishing Corporation, copyright 1950 by New Directions Publishing Corporation.

Manufactured in the United States of America

To Joseph Locke Slater

FREDERICK BUSCH, a novelist and short-story writer whose work has appeared in England and America in such journals and collections as *Penguin Modern Stories 9, New American Review, Fiction,* and *The Quarterly Review of Literature,* received the A.B. degree from Muhlenberg College and the M.A. from Columbia University. He is assistant professor of English at Colgate University, Hamilton, New York. A collection of Busch's short stories, *Breathing Trouble,* is scheduled for publication in 1973.

CONTENTS

PREFACE ix
INTRODUCTION xi
1 *Charivari* 1
2 *The Cannibal* 17
3 *The Beetle Leg* 39
4 *The Goose on the Grave* 61
5 *The Lime Twig* 87
6 *Second Skin* 107
7 *The Innocent Party* 123
8 *The Blood Oranges* 139
AGENDA 171
NOTES 175
BIBLIOGRAPHICAL NOTE 183
INDEX 187

PREFACE

The work of the American writer John Hawkes has been available for more than two decades, but readers have not met his language with the eye and ear it requires. Many writers, though, have received nourishment from Hawkes's words, and energy, and have taken him for example and solace. They have seen that such a wordsmith, so long misunderstood by critics and other readers, survives; if he can, so can other lesser writers—and because of him, some do. Writers indebted to Hawkes continue to tell us his name and to urge his work upon us. And so it seems that this time is right—with Hawkes at the height of his powers—for a declaration of sides, a statement about Hawkes's importance and about how earnestly we must approach his writing. John Barth says in "A Tribute to John Hawkes," *The Harvard Advocate,* October 1970: "When the literary ornithologists write a Field Guide to Hawkes I'll read it gratefully, but as one already rapt in his flights, to learn not how to love them but how perhaps to account for their hold." This book looks closely at Hawkes's novels and plays and attempts to suggest interesting paths into the works' strange woods. My overriding concern is to show how Hawkes creates whole worlds of imagery in which even his most monstrous characters can hold us, often against our will.

Thanks must go to John Hawkes, of course; to Professor Joseph Slater, for whose wisdom and friendship I am grateful; to Marshall Olds, who worked himself myopic assisting me with

PREFACE

bibliographical details; to the Colgate University Research Council for its support; to Albert J. Guerard for his courtesies; to Chester Anderson, who once told me that my interest in Hawkes might result in a book; to Edward Tayler, who demanded right language of me; to Harold L. Stenger, Jr., and William Kinter, who taught me to love the word with respect.

Judy: most of all.

Poolville, New York FREDERICK BUSCH
Summer 1972

INTRODUCTION

"I am a monster of the solitudes," declares Beckett's noncharacter in *How It Is*. He speaks for the characters of John Hawkes. Whether in a surrealistic England, a mythical American West, a wandering island on which the protagonist finds peace by inseminating cows artificially, or in a place named Illyria where there are no seasons, Hawkes's people are monsters of the mind; they are possessed by their dreams, their imaginings. Initially in Hawkes's work their dreams are poison, and the monsters die of unnatural causes—themselves. In the later novels, the imagination has come to be a haven—or at least a cove in a storm of acid waters—and we see characters like Skipper in *Second Skin* and Cyril in *The Blood Oranges* hanging on by the sound of their language, the grip on living which their words can offer them, and surviving—perhaps.

Hawkes's characters inhabit a world of word-weavings—no real place. Hawkes's western America in *The Beetle Leg* might stem from his experiences in Montana; whether it does or not, it is not that American state; it is a state of mind. Like Henri Matisse's "Egyptian Curtain," a fabric of visual metaphor which both is and is not a glimpse through a window of a strange green tree (for it is also a curtain in the foreground and a window in the background, and it is also the tree seen through the window, the curtain before it, the window between them—all on one level of a two-dimensional picture), Hawkes's worlds are metaphoric ones with enough of our world adduced—a wicked verisimilitude —to keep us suspended between what we have thought to be real and what Hawkes causes us to really care about in his monstrous worlds.

INTRODUCTION

John Hawkes writes narratives of prisoners of their dreams. Although he shuffles time, place, and voice, his works nevertheless display the sequence of narration: somewhere, always, there is an event that begins things and something that—for the moment, at least—ceases them. For Hawkes is concerned with the human cycles of response to the self. And if his work seems insular, slow to yield to our hunger to know *What is going on?* it does yield, finally, and in terms of how people respond to their own cries of *What is going on?* In that sense, Hawkes's work is like life: unfair, damaging, often lovely (as a bruise's colors can be), and as savage as we who experience it.

Hawkes has written that "for me the writer should always serve as his own angleworm—and the sharper the barb with which he fishes himself out of the blackness, the better."[1] In his work—the short novel *Charivari*, the novels *The Cannibal*, and *The Beetle Leg*, the novellas *The Owl* and *The Goose on the Grave*, the novels *The Lime Twig*, *Second Skin*, the plays in *The Innocent Party*, the stories collected in *Lunar Landscapes*, his latest novel *The Blood Oranges*—since 1949, Hawkes has been such a fisherman, angling for himself in those eddying waters where one's past (Hawkes's past, civilization's old days) rushes into the present. As he says, "I too believe in fiction—hard, ruthless, comic—and I myself believe very much in the sack of the past slung around our necks, in all the recurrent ancestral fears and abortive births we find in dreams as well as literature."[2]

So we find ancestral fears, abortive births, and the self-fishing dreamer recurring in the works. In the play *The Undertaker*, the son of a suicidal father cries to him: "All this time you've been the rusty fishhook lodged inside my brain."[3] In *The Beetle Leg*, fishing for a drowned brother, the protagonist "lifted the huckleberry pole and there, biting the hook, swung the heavy body of a baby that had been dropped, searched for, and lost in the flood."[4] And, finally, in *The Blood Oranges*, the narrator Cyril, speaking perhaps for Hawkes, says "if my world has flowered, still flowers, nonetheless it stands to reason that even the best of men and the most quiet and agreeable of lovers may earn his share of disapproval. There are those who in fact would like nothing better

INTRODUCTION

than to fill my large funnel-shaped white thighs with the fish hooks of their disapproval."[5] The fisher is himself fished up; his search yields himself.

Hawkes was born in 1925 in Connecticut. His studies at Harvard were interrupted near the end of World War II by his work with the American Field Service, for whom he drove an ambulance in Italy. After spending some time in Belgium and Germany, he returned to Harvard, enrolled in Albert J. Guerard's creative writing class, and began producing—although he had come to Guerard as a writer of verse—*Charivari*, his first novel, and, soon afterward, his second, *The Cannibal*. His classmates were as shocked by his work as his first public readers. Even now, seven novels, four plays, and six stories later, while Hawkes is an esteemed professor at Brown, his readers still are shocked or even repelled. To many of them—and one wonders how many have read his books all the way through—he is a "writer's writer," that nasty bouquet we throw to authors whose works are structurally or stylistically difficult, whose reviewers equivocate, whose admirers are said to be only other writers. The phrase is our excuse for including them in lists of Important Writers but for excluding them from our shelves. As a result, they are on the edge of our vision, but we too frequently fail to promote them from this peripheral exile. We use the rumors of other writers' affection for their work as excuses for not confronting their dangerous visions head-on.

We are the losers, of course. We know that, even as we do not order their books or do not take them from the library or do not teach them in our courses—or, after ordering, borrowing, or assigning them, do not go on to read them on their own terms. Thus we make writers and what they care about into a society separate from ours. There are *our* books—accessible, "relevant," "teachable"; they are books that can be "worked out," "'cracked," "solved." And then there are *their* books—difficult, frightening, maddening, filled with wordknots.

But we do, finally, know that our failure to read these "writers' writers" is an act of bad faith with the life of the mind, and so

INTRODUCTION

they never quite disappear from sight: we hold them on our vision's edge as offerings to our displeased conscience. After all, we are not stupid: we are more often lazy, more often scared. And so Hawkes, whose first novel was published in 1949 when he was twenty-four years old, has never been embraced as have other major American writers, although he has been—ugly child one cannot disown—held at a stiff arm's distance.

His commonality with our other valued writers is more clearly seen when we consider the terms of his rejection. We frowned at Updike for *The Centaur*—bizarre, complex, risky—but embraced him for the more accessible *Bech: A Book*. We bought Nabokov's *Lolita*, then didn't read the massive and arrogantly complex *Ada*. We praised Mailer for his good journalism in *The Armies of the Night*, but spanked him for his linguistic hubris—he captured the American diction—in *Why Are We in Vietnam?* We applauded Reynolds Price for *A Long and Happy Life* because we felt for Rosacoke Mustian; we reviled his *A Generous Man*, though, because—true to Hawthorne and Irving—it was a genuine thorny American romance. How long did Walker Percy, celebrated for *The Last Gentleman*, have to wait for an understanding reception of his first novel, *The Moviegoer?*

Hawkes is as important a writer as Updike and Nabokov. As difficult as they sometimes are, he is difficult consistently. He has not yet written a book the reading public has found as accessible as, say, *Couples* or *Pnin*. And so he has remained out of sight—almost. Of late, though, the writers whose writer he once seemed to be have told us that he is not only theirs; he is ours. Now, they say, we must expose our difficult child to the whole neighborhood. And so this complex, lyrical, bold, often verbally arrogant writer has slowly become more of a presence with whom we must deal. He is a geographer of the impossible, and we do not want to live there. Hawkes, however, is slowly proving to us that we *are* there. We are his characters. And what follows is an attempt to say with Walt Kelly's Pogo that we have met the enemy—those strange characters in their strange home grounds— and the enemy is us.

This study will rely heavily on Hawkes's own comments about

his writing, and certainly such procedure may be questioned. Why should we believe a writer's remarks? Why may the works not stand alone? Whatever became of our fears of the Intentional Fallacy?

Those questions are useful to literary scrupulousness, and let it be said that they surge in this writer's bosom. But the belief in their tutelary values should force us to another consideration—that of missing out on something that will help us. Should we not take advantage of the life in our living artists? All too often we wait until they are dead before reading and studying them; we cannot wait until they are dead to interview them. The work of such interviewers as John Enck and those who performed valuable service for the *Paris Review Writers at Work* series—as well as the brave performance by Norman Mailer, who interviewed himself for *Cannibals and Christians*—cannot be praised too highly. They have provided us with information. Like all information, it may be wrong. But it is potentially right. And we are therefore given a new dimension in which to work. Remembering that literary examination is always, at best, only possibly correct, we are in a position to learn something more about the language and structures and moral perspectives we examine.

The use of Hawkes's own comments is restricted to what he has said about how he writes and what he writes. There is no interest in presuming to examine Hawkes himself. As for what he has said about his works, we are at liberty to disbelieve him. We are also at liberty to hold it possible that what he says does apply. And, in light of the passages quoted above, we are at liberty to wonder—if we wish to think of such nonfictional material—about the application of statements such as this: "It seems to me that fiction should achieve revenge for all the indignities of our childhood; it should be an act of rebellion against all the constraints of the conventional pedestrian mentality around us."[6] If we choose to attend to it, we may then be in a position to make—always tentative—assumptions about Hawkes's psychic fishing expeditions. We may wish to see how oriented his work is to the intrusion upon the present person of his past; such a sense of Hawkes's work becomes instructive when we watch him deal

INTRODUCTION

with cultures and their past, as in the America of *The Innocent Party* or the Germany of *The Cannibal*. We may wish to muse upon how, though he is always studying the individual psyche and its ghosts, he is also dealing, as an American, with the concern which has absorbed so many American writers—the cultural past which haunts us. How like Hawthorne and Melville and Faulkner (and Robert Coover and Philip Roth) he then may seem. We might even care to assess the kind of "revenge" Hawkes's own characters and even forms of fiction take, as we recall that his novels assault traditional forms while his narrators rework what we assume to have happened to them in the books and confuse us by weaving an imagistic picture that, finally, is different from what we assumed their past to have been.

Hawkes's description of the fiction he believes in—"hard, ruthless, comic"—is evident in the writers he admires: Céline, Faulkner, Nathanael West, Djuna Barnes. Of Céline Hawkes has said in an interview: "Yes, Céline is an extraordinary writer, and his *Journey to the End of the Night* is a great novel. His comic appetite for invented calamities suggests the same truth we find in the comic brutalities of the early Spanish picaresque writers, which is where I locate the beginnings of the kind of fiction that interests me most."[7]

Hawkes's work abounds in "invented calamities," and we find a comic brutality in his work that reminds us (and Hawkes) of the techniques of Nathanael West. Denying "the pretension of the sweet spring of E. E. Cummings," Hawkes claims that "the true purpose of the novel is to asume a significant shape and to objectify the terrifying similarity between the unconscious desires of the solitary man and the disruptive needs of the visible world"; he suggests that West makes this objectification: "for Nathanael West love is a quail's feather dragged to earth by a heart-shaped drop of blood on its tip."[8]

> Miguel freed his bird and gave the other back to the dwarf. Abe, moaning softly, smoothed its feathers and licked its eyes clean, then took its whole head in his mouth. The red was finished, however. It couldn't even hold its neck straight. The dwarf blew away the feathers from under its tail and pressed the lips of its

INTRODUCTION

vent together hard. When that didn't seem to help, he inserted his little finger and scratched the bird's testicles. . . . The dwarf groaned with anguish, but no one else said anything.[9]

A grotesque creature—one of the world's wounded—grotesquely expresses his love unashamedly for another of the wounded; the rest of the world says nothing, and the dwarf's anguished groan is not only a true call of love, but a revelation of how pitiless the healthy world is and, therefore, how truly wounded. This is the sort of love Hawkes writes about, and this is the sort of grotesquerie—unsentimentalized and tangentially revealing of profound emotions—in which he engages. In that sense he is kin to Flannery O'Connor, of whom he has written with admiration.

In Hawkes's work we find many echoes of T. S. Eliot's poems, Nathanael West's ironies, the dry flatness of Flannery O'Connor's characters, the moist confession of Ford Madox Ford, and Djuna Barnes's lofty music. And while we may guess that Hawkes is sensitive to the touch of what he reads and is influenced by what he cares about, we might also leave room for the possibility that what he cares about echoes tones of who he is and how he writes. As Hawkes himself says, Faulkner "is still the American writer I most admire—though at this point I ought to insist again that in general my work is my own."[10] Certainly we do find in Hawkes's work the ongoing sonorousness of Faulkner—the connected fragments of vision and experience that glide past like cars on an endless fast train—but a return to Faulkner suggests that, when Hawkes runs long sentences on, they are only similar to Faulkner's and are in fact generally devoid of the syntactical balance and latinate polysyllables which Faulkner introduces in order to speak with history's voice. The gliding sinuousness of Faulkner is present in Hawkes, but it is the sinuousness of present experience; when Hawkes wishes to introduce the past, he does so—not by changing his rhetoric—by introducing a body in a dam, a chastity belt into a grotto: he uses images and objects and events. The prose of his past and present are the same, and therefore more difficult, often, than Faulkner's. When Faulkner pushes the past into view (or hearing) the style changes, and we are signaled—as when Quentin in *Absalom, Absalom!* stops talking

INTRODUCTION

realistically and switches into what is virtually a new dialect, the diction and syntax of what happened a hundred years before. When Hawkes introduces the weight of the past—and in this sense he is related to Djuna Barnes—the past is upon his characters and is working to destroy them, sometimes, before we notice.

One cannot help but remark how frequently, in essays and interviews, the questions of influence come up. Influence is an important matter—in this age of university-supported writers (men and women who are paid to subject themselves to literary influences) the question becomes ever trickier—and we should not ignore it. But it is interesting to speculate that one reason for the particularly heavy influence-snooping in the case of Hawkes is that critics and general readers are looking for his trouble. They do not ask How do the books work? They seem to be saying, rather, Perhaps if I know who's behind you, I'll get a hint of what's wrong; tracing from them to you, maybe I'll know why you're so strange. As in the case of many of our difficult writers who may not be ignored, critics search for literary pathologies— all too often to "cure" the writer or themselves of what he has been writing. They view his strangeness as a kind of disorder, and they try to treat it as such—instead of treating as the real hospital zone the tidy world of pat symbolisms in which most of us work.

In Hawkes we find an invented prose that qualifies him to be thanked for being a poet. Here is what the poet Hawkes says of his art:

> Between poetry and the "longer form" of experimental fiction there exists a kinship, a seedling intemperate spirit, within which may be found the climate of the imaginative process. . . . Like the poet, the experimental fiction writer is prompted to his narrative only by the vision which exclaims above him, or is driven to it from below; like the poet he enters his created world . . . with something more than confidence and something less than concern over the presence of worms in the mouth. Like the poem, the experimental fiction is an exclamation of psychic materials which come to the writer all readily distorted, prefigured in that inner schism between the rational and the absurd. And the relationship between the sprightly destructive poem and the

experimental novel is not an alliance but merely the sharing of a birthmark: they come from the same place and are equally disfigured at the start.[11]

The "exclamation of psychic materials" comes in this way:

> I've never outlined a novel before starting to write it—at the outset I've never been aware of the story I was trying to handle except in the most general terms. The beginnings of my novels have always been mere flickerings in the imagination, though in each case the flickerings have been generated, clearly enough, by a kind of emotional ferment that had been in process for some time. . . .
>
> . . . In each case what appealed to me was a landscape or world, and in each case I began with something immediately and intensely visual—a room, a few figures, an object, something prompted by the initial idea and then literally seen, like the visual images that come to us just before sleep.

More often than not, it is the visual image in Hawkes's work which strikes us. Although the sounds of the characters—their calmness in the midst of nightmare or their nightmare in calm day, the music their language is—are crucial to the prose, Hawkes's visual strokes loom as most important, as in the case of the animal imagery that runs through his work from beginning to end. Interestingly, Hawkes connects this dependence on image with his "feeling for dreams and . . . interest in exploiting the richness and energy of the unconscious."[12] We are not dealing here with automatic writing; we are concerned with a prose that is dominated by imagery which in turn is fed—the author apparently *wants* it fed—by the buried memories, moments, fears, and desires we have learned from Freud to recognize are within us. Hence, Hawkes writes of fishing for dead infants (as so many seventeenth-century Puritans must have probed in their minds for the ghosts of the unwanted children they had buried in the earth); he writes of a past crawling up the drain—in a house haunted by negritude—although each day it is buried in a swamp near the sign that says COLORED ONLY; his Nabokovian narrator in *The Blood Oranges*, who feels threatened by fishhooks, becomes what

xix

INTRODUCTION

we fear to fish up within ourselves. Hawkes is the poet of our dread.

As Hawkes speaks of "these envisioned worlds," and elsewhere in the interview of how "I want to try to create a world, not represent it,"[13] we come back again to the notion of Hawkes as a maker of worlds. He makes worlds with words. This study is concerned with the nature of Hawkes's worlds and, therefore, with how he drives, pumps, rolls, chants, bends, hurls, and juggles his language. There is no separate section here on Hawkes's language because this book-by-book engagement with his work (a chapter on each major writing, in order of publication) deals with the specific language of each novel or play or, sometimes, story. But it is the language that must always be kept in mind, for Hawkes is a poet, not a purveyor of information or case histories.

He is a poet as the metaphysicals were poets. When Dr. Johnson castigated them in his life of Cowley he might have been summarizing a block of attitudes that has worked against Hawkes's fair reception by a world of letters that sorely needs him:

> their thoughts are often new, but seldom natural; they are not obvious, but neither are they just; and the reader, far from wondering that he missed them, wonders more frequently by what perverseness of industry they were ever found. . . . The most heterogeneous ideas are yoked by violence together; nature and art are ransacked for illustrations, comparisons, and allusions; their learning instructs, and their subtlety surprises; but the reader commonly thinks his improvement dearly bought, and, though he admires, is seldom pleased.[14]

Hawkes makes a satyr insist upon virginity, a cat call for a kiss, a German nobleman carve a small child into chunks, thinking of him as "the fox"; he calls a character Cassandra, names a nonexistent place after one of Shakespeare's nonexistent places, tattoos a protagonist with a green lizard crawling on his chest; a suicide by hanging is termed an accident, and the German worlds of the First and Second Wars leapfrog over one another in the same book. Time and again—as Donne with his bracelet of

INTRODUCTION

bright hair about the bone—he shocks the reader into a new look at what words do; his is the *frisson* of the metaphysicals, the shudder they engender, the shock we receive from biting an apple to discover the presence of worms in the mouth.

Hawkes's lyrical and baroque language, his often opaque events, elusive settings, and chimerical characters, have prompted our own critics and reviewers to call him "mediocre and unrebellious,"[15] a writer who "creates suspense to squander it in rhetoric,"[16] one whose "plots play themselves out in patterns of chiaroscuro and mock seriousness."[17] As Albert J. Guerard sums it up, speaking of the response of his creative writing class at Harvard in 1947 and 1948 to Hawkes's work,

> The fact is that older and professional readers, with a few honorable exceptions, did not like Hawkes's work at all. They incorrigibly looked to those elements of fiction Hawkes saw as his "enemies" at the beginning of his career—plot, theme, character, structure. (I am not sure Hawkes was as conscious of these enemies as he was to be in retrospect; he was from the start one of the small company of absolutely original writers, without models and largely without theories.)[18]

But if they wait long enough (often in their graves) good writers surface to sympathetic public response. Hawkes has not had to wait that long. He has always enjoyed the support of critics as perspicacious as Leslie Fiedler and Albert J. Guerard. He has won grants and has been gradually recognized by the powers in publishing, and so he is now reviewed on the front page of *The New York Times Book Review*, he is asked to be visiting professor at large and small universities, his novel *The Blood Oranges* is excerpted in *TriQuarterly* and *The Dutton Review*, and a compendium of criticism wholly on *Second Skin* is published in the Charles E. Merrill Program in American Literature. In that volume, Albert J. Guerard says that Hawkes "offers the consoling example of a major writer rather than an eccentric innovator: one determined to explore both the inherited resources of the novel form and those he has, in some sense, invented himself."[19]

The goal of this book is to elucidate ways of approaching an important writer's work—no more. I do not hope to have said the last word on Hawkes; I hope, in fact, that this book, along with John Graham's admirable *Studies in Second Skin*, will show readers that there are rich vineyards to harvest—that call us to labor—in the complex writings of this contemporary master.

HAWKES
A Guide to His Fictions

1 Charivari

Charivari, Hawkes's first novel, appeared in 1949.[1] It was completed in Albert Guerard's creative writing course at Harvard after Hawkes had returned from driving an ambulance for the American Field Service in Germany and Italy.[2] It is a thin tale—the few events of a day in England—which offers acerbic comment on a sort of waste land, its unsexual inhabitants and their utter fear of life. Although the characters are stereotypical, they are also caricatures, parodies. The element of parody becomes a key feature of Hawkes's work—both enhancing and, to some readers, at times detracting from their receptiveness to the book. Furthermore, the novel introduces a hallucinatory narrative, one that refuses to accept limitations of time or place or sane action—and such elements of interior adventure, along with a grotesque imagery (often bestial) that represents interior events in the external world, become hallmarks of Hawkes's work.

In this early book there is little evident ratiocination. There is experience, palpable and frightening, conveyed in a prose that takes on the nightmare qualities of the events it renders. One opens the book to find no assurances, no assumptions of certain ways to live that offer order or hope. The reader opens the novel to find himself fascinated—in the way that he would be fascinated if he opened his medicine chest one morning, prepared to shave, and looked down to see a giant centipede rushing up at him from the drain of his familiar sink.

Henry and Emily Van, the novel's protagonists, expect to have a child soon. Henry is troubled and Emily is in trouble with Henry: pregnancy is an imposition on "these forty-year-old Jackdaws" (365). Indeed, proximity would seem to be an imposition too, and we are shown how nearness is avoided, and how Hawkes violates realistic expectations: "They slept in separate rooms. A massive dog patroled the space between. His big eyes glimmered in the darkness, sniffing from door to door, a weak growl." Beasts patrol the length of the book.

While the dog mounts watch—either as a real dog or as extension of the Vans' psyches—Henry has a nightmare in his room. He converses with an "Expositor," himself, his buried fears, about Emily whom he sees in the dream with an infant in her arms. The Expositor asks Henry what must be done about the baby and Henry replies, "I have to put it in a bucket of water and keep it there." The baby becomes a threat, a snapping beast. Fertility must be drowned:

> *Expositor:* Do you think you can keep it from jumping out and biting you?
> *Henry:* I can't. It's going to bite, It's going to bite! I'll run away. I'm going to run, run. . . . (365)

As the dream continues through the night the dog howls, supporting an air of bestiality begun with the first sentence. With the approach of dawn a cock starts to crow and the dog leaves off howling. The sight or sound of an animal is never absent from the human scene in this book.

The day begins as Emily and Henry say good-morning near the dog, which is "always chained up in the daylight" (366). The dog, then, is intentionally loosed, we may infer, to keep the Vans unnaturally apart. Together and, yet, apart, they share a sullen, silent, somehow sordid breakfast among "a few locks of greying hair, butter melting on the already hardening toast, crumbs caught in a trouser cuff, and a soft perfume suggestive of many bygone springs" (367). They are measuring out their lives with coffee spoons, and their half-thoughts and half-hallucinations will soon show that what they share as man and woman is no more than greying hair and fear.

These people are decadent; all springs are bygone. All communication, too, is gone: after their speechless meal Emily tacks a piece of paper to the wall; the note says, "dinner at one" (367).

Charivari

It already is fair to wonder whether, at lunches, Henry asks himself whether he dares to eat a peach.

Then, as if they had been together, Henry and Emily separate to be alone with their unnamed fears and repressions. Henry goes to his room, which is decorated with stuffed animals, and Emily goes to her room to ruminate on "the incriminator in the other room." Henry longs to "go into her room and make it up" (367). The cause of this accusation, reproval, and guilt is the child they are to have—Emily's transgression by process of her body.

The world of the Vans is one of spiritual death, reminiscent of the nightmare world of Section II ("A Game of Chess") in Eliot's *The Waste Land*. Hawkes delineates a lifeless life that Eliot characterizes with

> 'What shall I do now? What shall I do?'
> 'I shall rush out as I am, and walk the street
> 'With my hair down, so. What shall we do
>   tomorrow?
> 'What shall we ever do?'
>   The hot water at ten.
> And if it rains, a closed car at four.
> And we shall play a game of chess,
> Pressing lidless eyes and waiting for a knock
>   upon the door.[3]

That knock comes, for Henry and Emily Van, when their dinner guests for "dinner at one" arrive. All order will now be reversed: the spiritually dead will live and nightmare will be the routine of the English gentry Hawkes scrutinizes. And the animals' dance will begin.

Note, for example, Hawkes's description of the dinner guests (including the Vans' parents) whom Henry greets: "the dapples, piebalds, greys, and blacks who streamed pretentiously past his outstretched hand" (368). For the duration of the party (which is the duration of the novel) the guests are described in animal terms, and animals haunt the background of the gathering: the book is a vast metaphor made of animalisms, in which, for example, when one guest is refered to as "mousey," in the next sentence, to complement this description of that guest, we see that "the butterflies flapped violent wings" (369).

One of the guests, called "the adventuress," "lolled complacently in green on a kitchen chair. She raised her head in a devouring gesture" (372). And, while her character is offered in animal terms—she evokes the Sweeney poems—Hawkes creates a background of animal activity: "Henry heard the buzzing bees, the long-billed tapping of a kiwi bird. . . . In the growing darkness, people tittered back and forth from crevices to kitchen, broke glasses, soiled the rug, and made lewd exclusive demonstrations. *Two unclaimed canaries were fighting in a gilded cage* [italics added]" (373).

Hawkes's suggestion of character through description of people in animal terms is apparent—Henry's father turned, "bristling with effort" (375); Emily's father and mother, dozing through the party, "clawed to life" (376)—and so is his creation of environment and mood through animal images made vivid. In a passage suggestive of bestial or inhuman behavior (such as the one offered above) Hawkes uses, as in the italicized sentence, a sudden pointing-up or apprehension of a particularity—the canaries in their cage. This technique, which relies almost invariably on named animals, grounds the often surrealistic narrative in fact, strengthens suggestions that people are more or less than just people, and permits Hawkes (and the reader) to metaphorize with a foundation of realism. One can never quite dismiss a Hawkes passage as only fantasy.

As the party progresses we see that the guests are, indeed, bestial; that Emily's and Henry's parents are ineffectual in the roles of comforters or guides they are expected by tradition to fulfill; and that Emily is regressing from womanhood, Henry losing all vestiges of masculinity.

Henry, for example, "found his own room and set to weaving his tapestry, methodically preserving odds and ends, awaiting the return of his warrior soul" (381). In his most recent novel, *The Blood Oranges,* Hawkes uses the figure of the tapestry as a metaphor for the fictional structure that the main character's narrative is, thus presenting the whole novel as a tapestry. Recognizing his having become Penelope to himself, Henry says "Why must I always play a feminine role?" (381). He writes a gentle note of goodnight to Emily—"They wrote notes like this to each other all the time" (382)—and, though he walks away, reacts to the fact of his impending fatherhood and the fact that his walking away is futile—"My home is a microcosm of the world to me" (380)—by running away from both his baby and his home. We may recall that Henry screamed in his early nightmare, "I'm going to run, run . . ." (365).

Emily, unable to bear the contumely of her guests' knowledge of her somehow shameful pregnancy, also flees—"quickly as an angry water-fowl rushes into the air." She runs, as an animal does, to "lick her wounds alone" in her room where "She had a kewpie doll for every happy party" (382). When a guest breaks into Emily's solitude to congratulate her for pregnancy Emily further displays her regression to childhood, her escape from the symbol of life that pregnancy is, by replying only with, "Go get Mother." As she says this, "The cat's jaw broke the wings of the thin bird" (383). The inhumanity and carnivorousness of this novel's world are once again brought sharply to our attention.

Emily further runs from life by falling asleep in her room—"young and round . . . smiling her prettiest reward, a tumble-stomach little doll" (384). She dreams a discourse with an Expositor who tells her that "It is time for you to leave too." But Emily, who flees into childhood, cries, "No. Please let me stay, please. I don't want to go away" (385). Henry has fled by physically running away. Both have somehow left. And the rest of the novel is concerned with Henry's and Emily's flights and fears, described in animal terms and rendered dramatic through a background of animal images.

It is raining as Henry leaves a life he loathes and which terrorizes him. The rain is as inhospitable as his own house or his own life. Even the bus he travels on becomes animal and threatening: "Its yellow eyes bore down in the mist" (386).

In a seashore town Henry seeks lodgings, reminiscing as he does so of his childhood and of Emily, to whom he "almost wanted to go and speak." At Mrs. Mahoney's boarding house, Henry hears "the cries of a few scattered gulls" (387)—of no importance now, but soon to take on heavy significance. In his decaying room (ironically, Mrs. Mahoney indicates that it is a "bridal chamber" [389]) in a decaying house Henry hides as regressively as Emily does: "He pulled the lumpy quilt up over his head, brought his knees up to his stomach and fell asleep" (389); he retreats to a proximate womb.

When he awakens the rain has grown to an ocean-side storm of sun and thunder. But rain is no longer so inhospitable as it was. Appropriately for his manner of sleeping, Henry feels a sense of rebirth that is partially signified by an animal traditionally indicative of peace: "he felt a sense of exhilaration—in the pitch of love and in the face of death. The weeds beat around the bottom of the house, doves cowered in the belfry of the church" (390). Hawkes takes the sea—traditional symbol for life, birth, and renewal—and makes it, for Henry, at once love and death: life is sought in terms of love by Henry, but love is also death. It is possible that for Henry Van life and death are inseparable. We should note, too, that Hawkes renders the sign of peace, the dove, as one that cowers—in a belfry, no less. We have a gothic scene, then: bats inhabit belfries, and there is a metaphorical transfer in Hawkes's figure of bat-qualities to doves: peacefulness is still somehow linked to creatures of the night.

Henry renews himself by washing and dressing scrupulously, ceremoniously, rinsing his mouth many times. He reminds us of his departure from any coherent view of life by echoing Emily's childishness: he says, "go out, go out to play" (391).

But then he sees someone he had seen on the bus and in the streets near his lodgings, a young woman who sat in the corner of the bus, holding a wet bundle: "Her eyes were shaded by a little black hat, a hat above the pointed skull of a Jezebel" (386). When Henry sees her on his morning of renewal, it is as a "phantom bride-elect" (391). Henry thinks that, very soon, he will speak to this shaded woman sitting, Circe-like, among the slimy rocks of the spitting shore, watching the rain.

After tea with the gin-swilling old ladies who run the house, Henry shouts, "This is one of the happiest days of my life" (392), and it probably is. Henry has fled a life of gardens and weeds and has come to the sea for renewal. There is in the air for him "the pitch of love," "the face of death," and perhaps they are both embodied in the "phantom bride-elect," a mermaid beckoning.

Henry goes out and the storm suddenly swells: wind and blown water shoot down the street and rotted wood is torn from buildings; cobblestones are covered with "a running slime." Henry "lost his nerve" (395). As the true rough forces of life rise to meet this Prufrock, who perhaps thought to walk the beaches with his trousers rolled, he flaps in the middle of the street, tries to return to the house, but cannot.

Then: "The door opened and she came out and walked easily into the storm. . . . He could almost see the features of the face, oh, Emily, yes, yes, the howling wind, the shadowed mouth open to gasp for air behind that wind, the eyes covered by a constant veil, the hair beating upon the open throat. For one brief moment his hope and desire came together, to walk up to her, hold her, speak to her, hold the blowing hair. . . . Then he turned and was blown off down the street" (396). As Henry's encounter develops with the demi-creature, demi-woman, Circe—the almost-held idea of love—so does Hawkes's use of animals. Henry is blown down the street "happier in each dolphin-winged spasm, careening along with pillaging, battling black birds." He thinks, incoherently, "To catch fish," almost as if he is a sea-bird; Hawkes's metaphor here is implicit and typical: the background of animals represents the interior worlds of the characters.

He runs through "hurling starfish" (396) to an inn filled with sailors and no women, a place in which he finds great relief from the woman-thing to which he was drawn and which we now see to be a cause of great fright: "Absence of long hair, pale skin, tapering legs, and Piccadilly voices . . . no Eve dressed in leaves or slinking in spangles, no perfume, nothing for the bees to buzz about" (396–97).

From the storm and sexuality and unwanted thrill of life Henry, like Prufrock, retreats. He finds himself a place "of stags," "stained jowls," paintings of fish, "the old bucks grumbling. Stags," "claws" on chairs, an old black dog. In the all-male and animalistic environment Henry recalls the stag party given for him—before his wedding and the presumed beginning of sexual activity, vitality—at which he was toasted with, "'Here's to Henry as he starts out on the sea'" (397). Now that he has reached the sea the toast is ironic: his environment at the sea is asexual, he is surrounded by "stags," old seamen, "Survivors of the sea, a little group of Ulysses' men with albatrosses around their necks" (398).

Thus, Hawkes has rather gently, with no straining at or for myth, led us through referents of parodied fertility-heroes (Prufrock and the *Waste Land* denizens) to see Henry as an evader of life forces. It is interesting here that Henry, a voyager of most unmythical proportions (he "voyages" by bus and, as a potential Ulysses, never gets into or onto the water) is blown in the wind with flapping fish nets—symbols of a savior, fertility, or a life force—that do not catch fish. And he seeks refuge among "stags," commonly men who are together to celebrate an instinct for and pleasure in ribaldry and rutting but are here defunct fishers, noncatchers of fertility, mere grumbling old beasts.

Henry—Penelope and Prufrock, voyager to the sea, married man—is stranded in what he sees as a refuge with men who have come through what the sea brings (sex, life) to stay dry, free of life and its demands. Yet as the albatross reminded the Ancient Mariner of those demands, so is Henry reminded. His confusion between Homer's epic and Coleridge's points up his lackluster mind, but it may suggest to us as well the quality of Henry's own adventure, his life: no heroic epic, but an ironic perversion of epic in which heroic voyagers become men shackled to mementos of denial of others and denial of the spiritual. We are told all this through the albatrosses and their meaning in the context of Coleridge's poem, and we are reminded again how Hawkes uses animal imagery to color and characterize the people in his books.

As Henry revels in the stag-party atmosphere, a messenger calls to the men at the inn that a girl has drowned. The men, in oilskins, turn out to the beach amid "sea animals and fish" (398), human motion "obscured by the flapping skins" as if the men themselves were merely beasts.

The party climbs down from a pier to survey the corpse an outgoing tide has left behind. The wind dies, permitting a presence of rot and animal stench to rise—as it so frequently does when Hawke creates an encounter with death: "A dark underground world, and here the smell was overpowering; dead marine life, carbuncles, blue jellyfish in pools, mounds and mats of congested seaweed, huge silver fins and dark green tongues. . . . Shivering species and dead bones" (399).

There is "A sweet-sour stench," "an acid smell," "Smell of fish." And the gulls, previously unsymbolic, "circled overhead and cawed unmercifully" (399), signifying death. The fertile sea spawns death for Henry; woman is death for him: his Venus—the girl on the bus—is a corpse. Just as the characters and incidents in Hawkes's novels take on the atmosphere of the always-present animals, so, too, do the animals take on the nature of the books' characters and events. The transfer takes place frequently, smoothly, and so, as a result, it often becomes difficult to tell one from the other; this attribute of difficulty may account for some critics' judgment that Hawkes is difficult to read clearly; for others, however, the metaphorical transfer of characteristics may serve as excellent example of how metaphor should work most effectively.

Death and bestiality are now everywhere; Henry's "phantom bride-elect" is dead, drowned, and so is his phantasmagoric impulse to sexuality; vitality is denied Henry in his flight to the stags.

Like J. Alfred Prufrock, Henry has "squeezed the universe into a ball / To roll it toward some overwhelming question"[4]: "Henry thought he would go back home. First to the room and then home. It was his own decision; he would go home." Henry's father, a parson, comes for him and he rides back in his father's car, curled on the back seat like a child, to the rhythm of placid enormous cows, "No people. A lonely bird" (401), harmless beasts, emblems of Henry's emasculated inhumanity.

HAWKES: A Guide to His Fictions

Though he says nothing upon his return, Henry might chant, with Prufrock, that

> I have heard the mermaids singing, each to each.
> I do not think that they will sing to me.
> ....
> We have lingered in the chambers of the sea
> By sea-girls wreathed with seaweed red and brown
> Till human voices wake us, and we drown.[5]

In the section entitled "THE WEDDING" we are exposed to Hawkes's most dense and tortuous use of animals for the sake of characterization and metaphor, and to what his proponents call poetic writing, his detractors, confused prose.

In what is obviously a flashback, a collier's wife, part-time seamstress, is in her hovel at work on what we learn will be Emily's wedding gown. From the outset of this view of the past a background tapestry of animals creates a mood of vicious and mad bestiality. As the hag works, singing crazily, a turtle moves his arms in a porcelain dish, "Horns clattered in the cold smoky air" (reminding us, perhaps of stags), blackbirds scream, "a prize porker grunted behind mud-spattered boards and stared out at the passing feet [outside the old woman's window] with murderous red eyes" (402): the reader finds himself in a kind of hell populated by animal demons.

As the collier's wife works, Henry, husband-to-be, is fitted by a tailor for his wedding suit: the tailor's "fingers were insect's wings in the crotch of his trousers, hummingbird wings in the crotch of a young tree" (403). The tailor describes Henry not as a man, but as an animal: "and a fine specimen it is" (404).

When Henry and his future father-in-law leave, the seamstress enters the shop to buy cloth and, not surprisingly, canaries sing overhead. The old woman addresses the tailor as Mr. Beetle, the shop is called "the Beetle's shop," and we are told that the tailor's "shell was covered with black and purple spots" (405). While the metaphors encountered by the average reader of fiction are verisimilitudinous in varying degrees, it is probably safe to posit that none quite achieves the degree of completion (save Kafka's *The Metamorphosis*) which Hawkes reaches here: a man who is like a beetle *is*, simply, a beetle. The reality of the book, whatever "realism" it had, suddenly vanishes; we are in a world of people-made-animal—and, as will become apparent shortly, of animal-made-human. Surrealism and hallucination prevail, and the madness that seems to dominate the characters of the book is objectified for us in the exposition of these characters; language itself becomes a touchstone for the nature of that which it describes.

Hawkes does not create characters here in the sense that we might call Hardy's Tess a character—a flesh and blood person with whom we sympathize, identify, mourn, or rejoice. Rather Hawkes isolates his characters—"figures" might be more apt for the sake of contrast—from emotional communication with his readers. However, he does free his fiction here from the demands that traditional character-making places on a writer's work: realistic behavior. He is free to have his characters behave according to *his* vision and not according to that of his readers or to the tradition of behavior in novels to which they may have become accustomed. Once he shatters his readers' expectations, the readers are Hawkes's captives. He can demand of them at his will by deciding how *his* characters (not the readers' traditional notion of characters) will act; he can enflesh his ideas and weave his world. He is freed of his readers' demands. Thus, his stereotypical characters are, here, little more than avenues for his prose, gambits for his larger strategies.

The narrative then returns to Henry who, at a nearby fair, watches a dancer. Henry unwittingly glimpses his fate:

> The veils fluttered; round rough thighs were taut. The woman's hocks sank in the mud. Her eyes strained. The driver flecked her with a switch of brush. Her nostrils were red, the horns lowered. Henry heard the clanking of chains, the suck of hoofs covered with water. The haunches swayed, moved forward and stopped. She mooed. . . .
> . . . for a moment, [he] saw the old woman behind the men.

Using his arms, his head, his chest and elbows, he pushed and squirmed, and free of the straining faces, he ran. (406–407)

As Henry runs, the old seamstress disappears, the carnival dancer retreats to the stage curtain, and the narrative of this bizarre epithalamion returns to the inside of the seamstress' house. But, before following the narrative, we ought to heed Hawkes's method in his animal description above; the pattern of this image's construction is a key to what one critic calls Hawkes's "hallucinated vision."[6]

The metaphor of the dancer is entirely in keeping with Hawkes's tendency to describe people as animals. And so the dancer's "hocks" sink, she is flecked by a (cattle) driver's whip, *"the* horns" (italics added) lower, her "hoofs" suck, her "haunches" sway—she moos! But if this figure were to be complete metaphor, it would have to be completely inhuman: no reference to *woman* would be made, nor to *her* following *woman,* nor to *she; it,* instead, would make the metaphor complete.

But Hawkes, here, does not create a realistic metaphor. Instead, he offers one in which bestiality is obvious but only almost complete; the cow is still a woman, the woman is still a cow; each is itself, each is the other. People in this novel are, indeed, animals—but so are they animal-people. By manufacturing such a sense of simultaneity—a sense perhaps caught by some characters themselves—Hawkes creates a netherworld, a vision of hallucination, a place where our referents of space and time are useful only in that they show us that the "real" of our experience no longer wholly pertains. These are a new kind of people in a context that, though tinged with a touch of the familiar, is startlingly new.

The old woman who works now on Emily's gown drapes it on a bust, "cellophane-satin doll, half-made faceless bride" (407), and, in her mad house, she chants madly. As she sews, her cat comes through the window into the room and speaks with her:

'How are ya doing tonight, 'ooman?'
'Healthful, Mr. Cuddles. But I've lots of work.'
'It's a lame old sufferer you are.'
'Mind your tongue, or you'll find yourself back outa the winda.'

'That's all right, now, you'll hear from me later on tonight. I might do a bit of singin', ya know. There's poisonous people who comes to hear me sing.' (407)

The cat continues to speak teasingly as the old woman sews faster and faster. There is an acid smell in the room; in the presence of death, Hawkes places an animal stench. A bug creeps from his lair and the "wife chased him with her stamping foot, monstrous beastie" (408); the idea of "wee, tim'rous beastie" is displaced, suggesting that all animal roles are reversed and that there is monstrosity in the tiniest creature of this novel's world.

The cat wakens, walks "across the room on his hind feet" (408) and reaches to the cupboard shelf, drinks the seamstress' wine. She chases the cat, trying to punish him with her needle, but he escapes. She returns to the gown which, in the breeze through the window, flutters as if it were alive. She notices that she has pricked a finger in her pursuit. She looks at the bust: "Then she leapt. The pin plunged in and out of the abdomen, quicker and quicker, in and out above the things. Small drops of blood appeared on the satin" (409). We see Emily's marriage in effect "blessed" pervertedly as the locus of her sex is attacked.

It is no wonder, in the logic of the book, that Henry (who was "blessed" by the Beetle's hands on his groin) and Emily feel cursed by Emily's pregnancy. A common event, the prenuptial well-wishing and expression of hopes for fertility, has been replaced by malediction. The old woman seems nearly a witch, the cat her familiar. The marriage begins under the auspices of a voodoo reversal of human and animal roles. At the Vans' wedding, the reversal is carried to its furthest extreme, the curse of the old woman and Beetle are spoken aloud: the parson intones, "*Maledicat illum sancta Dei genetrix et perpetua Virgo Maria*" (414). The couple is joined in a virtual black mass.

The final section of the book, called "RHYTHM," abounds in animality. But its nightmare drama is really told in terms of one animal and Freudian image: the snake.[7]

Emily dreams that she sees her child. She looks at its mouth: "It was like a bird's." Its voice is frail and "peeping" (415). The roses in Emily's room are "frozen huddled pigeons." Then she wakes and rejoins the party downstairs. A woman's necklace "flicked its tail and collected itself to squeeze"; "the white chandelier hanging from the ceiling swayed to and fro, its feet lifeless and still"; "Long sharp wires ran under the rug"; "The doctor played with the string dangling from his monocle" (416). Inanimate objects are alive and serpentine, everywhere. This imagery creates an atmosphere of wriggling and crawling, a sense of nervousness, a literal snakepit.

Henry (who is somehow at the party again) feels at his neck as his necktie "grew tighter"; a long wire catches a woman's feet; the music of a harp "and its long vibrating strings filled the room, plucked strings and struck strings, wires" (417). The house is alive with snakes. A man's shoelaces float in spilled water "like strangling water-moccasins" (418). In this madness, Emily is seen in animal terms: "she spun around once more and sat down amid waves of applause, her tail wagging" (419).

The revelry grows more drunken and hallucinated, and then we are with Emily in a car that roars through space. She is being kidnapped by three old women, each wearing a black veil. Her hands are pinioned and she is blindfolded; she wears a black hat very much like that of Henry's "phantom bride-elect." From a house of snakes, danger, entrapment—penises, of which Emily would certainly be terrified—Emily experiences a car ride characterized by linear shapes, snakelike shapes, seen through twisted trees and rotting fence rails: "thin line of heavy smoke," "the long electric wire that ran, like a fat hose," a smoke stack (426), "the knotted cord" that binds her feet (427).

Emily is taken to a mysterious hospital along the sides of which grow "a few thin strips of vine." At the reception desk is a nurse with "a black rubber tube dangling from her pocket" (428), who admits her for an examination that is described in a scene worthy of the Kafka of "In the Penal Colony":

> [A doctor] lit the sputtering burner, twisted dials, spun plastic knobs, watched needles jump, marked six crosses on her scalp, and laughing wildly, swung the machine into position. . . . After

fastening a piece of garden hose around her arm and poking needles into each of the crosses on her scalp, he hunched over and wrote rapidly with his chicken quill, blinking at the faces on the dials. An assistant kept hitting the back of her head with a mallet. (429)

Emily faints and is revived. She sees, in rows of canvas hammocks, "the new babies" (430). Her hallucination is of birth—a terror of abduction, forcing, torture, and ignorance.

She runs through the hospital, seeing more snake facsimiles, and is captured by a doctor and two riveters. Strapped on a table near a hellish furnace, she hears a riveter scream, "Drive the damn thing in" (432), voicing what seems to be Emily's own reaction, her resignation to and fear of such acts as begot her child.

Henry, meanwhile, is at home with the guests. Hawkes has Henry's ears twitch, spaniels cry (433), the guests (as they did at the book's beginning) clatter by like horses, and mules pull at tethers; Hawkes creates a symphony of animals that characterize the world to which Emily returns from her nightmare, running across the lawn, as if she had really been away. She may have been in her room, actually. But Hawkes is unconcerned with objective actuality. His concern is the mind in nightmare waking —*how* it perceives, not *what* it perceives. As with the dancer metaphor, Hawkes shifts dream to physical substance and the physical to dream. The reader is hard put to separate one from the other; and, in the context of the novel and its hallucinated characters, dream and a possible physical actuality are inseparable.

As Emily returns—whether from a real abortion, a visit to a doctor, or a nightmare—Henry looks at her and "he knew she was not going to have a child" (435). A guest ends the book, summarizes the life of the unsexual, infantile Vans, and emphasizes the feeling of hallucination which the novel creates, by calling, "it's time to play" (436).

This is where Hawkes publicly begins—with incisiveness, malice, a subordination of sensual imagery to his ideations. The start is auspicious, and we can trace his later imagistic achievements, the enactment of his searing moral vision in a prose of high brilliance, from this taut work.

2 The Cannibal

The Cannibal, published in 1950, has been called Hawkes's "real first novel." In an interview with John Graham, of the University of Virginia, Hawkes had this to say about his book:

> I suppose in general, that novel is an hallucinated vision of a neo-Nazi rise. The contemporary part of the novel is dated 1945 but that date is supposed to be taken as a something to disregard. The time of that novel is simply in the future—remember it begins with all of Germany coming out of an insane asylum into a devastated landscape. And it ends with the success of the neo-Nazi movement which in turn results, positively and ironically, in the return of the whole country to an insane asylum. And this . . . is posed against the literally historical period of 1914, the first World War. I suppose this juxtaposition at the outset is intended to try to suggest that perhaps we don't move so much in cycles as repetitions or that we have always had these particular problems of violence, destruction, sadism and so on.[1]

It should come as no surprise that the novel is "an hallucinated vision" or (after experiencing *Charivari*) to learn that *The Cannibal* warps time, takes liberty with historical facts, and is concerned with "violence, destruction, sadism." In varying degrees, all these elements are present in Hawkes's first work. In the second novel, however, it becomes clear that experimentation with narrative method is more controlled, as is Hawkes's use of stereotyped characters. Hawkes says, "I began *The Cannibal* after reading a brief notice in *Time* magazine about an actual cannibal discovered in Bremen, Germany (where I had been, coincidentally, during the war)."[2]

The scene of the action is post–World War II Germany in 1945—defeated, debris-ridden, a waste land. Central figures are Madame Stella Snow, who spans the gap from the Germany of 1914—pompous, jingoistic, assured of glory—to the decadent ruin of 1945; her mad servant, Balamir; her younger sister, Jutta; Jutta's daughter, Selvaggia; Zizendorf, the land's new political "leader," lover of Jutta and narrator of the story; the Duke, remnant of early Germany, a mad cannibal; Jutta's young male child, who flees the length of the book, pursued by the Duke; Cromwell, an English sympathizer of the 1914 Prussians and admirer of Stella; Ernst, the epitome of World War I Germany, who tends toward father-worship and is insane; Leevey, the lone American motorcyclist who patrols and oversees conquered Germany.

The novel is ostensibly a narration by Jutta's lover, Zizendorf, the neo-Nazi leader; it opens with his statement that "I have told our story. The things that remain to be done weigh heavily on my mind, and all the remarkable activity of these foreign cities cannot distract me. At present, even though I enjoy it here, I am waiting, and at the first opportunity I will, of course, return."[3] Since we soon learn of Zizendorf's efforts to revive a Nazi brotherhood, we may infer, in the absence of further clues, that he is now in exile after having either failed in his efforts or having succeeded and, for some reason, gone abroad. We can infer further that the Nazism we are to learn about is moving through the world, dangerous by nature, despite its success or failure in the narrative.

The book traces Zizendorf's political efforts, the history of a local insane asylum near the edge of the town that is the book's locus, and the pursuit of Jutta's child by the Duke. Woven into the narrative is the story of Madame Snow's life in an earlier Germany.

And that, skeletally, is all. The plot, though confusing and tortuous, is once again thin. It is absurd as history is absurd. But through it Hawkes's grotesque characters begin to flower, and his poetic prose comes to majority. And we see the essential elements of this short novel created largely in terms of animals-as-humans and humans-as-animals.

Perhaps his American Field Service experience in Italy and

The Cannibal

Germany during World War II contributed to Hawkes's obsession with Europe and with war. *The Cannibal, The Goose on the Grave, The Owl,* parts of *The Lime Twig,* and much of *Second Skin* are concerned with the Second World War; all but *Second Skin* are set in Europe. The Germany of *The Cannibal* is that of Kaiser, Hitler, and the Third Reich. But it is also a fictive Germany, not unlike the Mexico of Malcolm Lowry's *Under the Volcano,* of which William Gass says:

> We shall never verify this history. It rests nowhere in our world. . . . And the real mountains of Mexico, those two chains which traverse the republic, exist despite us and all our feelings. But the Popocatepetl of the novel is yet another mountain. . . . Lowry is constructing a place, not describing one; he is making a Mexico for the mind where, strictly speaking, there are no menacing volcanoes, only menacing phrases, where complex chains of concepts traverse our consciousness, and where, unlike history, events take place in the moment that we read them.[4]

The same may be said for the Germany of this novel; the book is concerned with actual place and with a history of real decline as well as with a nation made of menacing phrases and traversing chains of concept.

The narrative begins with Balamir, Stella Snow's servant, walking among the unnamed town's ruins past "the institution" which dominates the countryside. Though the war is over, "the population had not grown, the same few brown forms prowled in the evening, the same tatters of wash hung for weeks in the same cold air, and the Census-Taker sprawled, thin and drunk, blue cap lopsided, behind his desk" (3). The town, in other words, is evidence of living death. Of the all-important institution, which seems almost to possess the town, the narrator says: "the institution had become empty, officials and nurses gone for distant lands, their eyes tight and faces drawn, and over the high narrow buildings no sound could be heard. Every day from the hill, thin children looked down on the empty scorpion that was all that was left of the ordered institution" (4). If the institution is an analogy for something unstated—and it seems to be, if we may judge from the frequency of its reference in the novel—it probably is symbol for Germany itself. It is apparent, then, that Hawkes creates an animal analogy for a building that is analogy for a nation; he renders Germany a scorpion and from the outset maintains an attitude toward his subject matter that is so very effective because the novel is told by a neo-Nazi. The narrator knows that his Germany is a scorpion; and Zizendorf's use of the metaphor virtually makes of the fact that he uses it another metaphor: he, himself, is portrayed by himself as the scorpion's keeper —the caretaker of a deadly pet.

Zizendorf goes on to locate the action further: "A single spire of notched steel hung high above the town, devoid of banners, un-encased by building walls, sticking up above them in all the cold blue evening. Steel rungs hung crookedly exposed all the way up the spire, and steel slabs were driven across the narrow open cellar window where Balamir paused, his white skin wet in the still evening light" (4). It is here, where the stone of a church is replaced by battered steel—a nightmare crafted by Albert Speer —that the events of the novel take place.

Madame Snow, whom Hawkes describes as "the life-force, the life-drive," would have been a grandmother had not her son's child "no bigger than a bird" (5), died in an explosion. Her son, who carries the burden of a stump and steel canes as a result of wartime injuries, "worked with the black machine in the hot projection room" of the movie house, "showing each day the same blurred picture to no audience" (5). She busies herself as janitor of her building or sits in her large gilt chair "tying rags together and infrequently pulling the heads from small fowl" (6). Also in Madame Snow's house live her sister and her children, the drunken Census-Taker who, by having no work to do, marks the death of Germany, and Herr Stintz, who "played his tuba late into the night, and the notes fell on the cobblestones recalling the sound of fat marching feet." The Duke lives there too, and he completes the family of madness in Madame Snow's house.

Amid the stinking canals and smoldering dung heaps of the town is the background of animal imagery that Hawkes customarily employs: the ceiling is "spidery black" (6); the town is "roosting" on charred earth (7); it "gorged itself" on beggars; the town, "without its walls and barricades, though still a camp-site of a thousand years, was as shriveled in structure and as decomposed as an ox tongue black with ants" (8). The horses of the town, "dull-eyed monsters of old force" (8), "had been commandeered from the acre farms for ammunition trucks, and all were gone but one grey beast who cropped up and down the stone streets, unowned, nuzzling the gutters. . . . Children took rides on the horse's tail and roamed in small bands, wearing pasteboard Teutonic helmets, over the small confines of the town, their faces scratched and nails long" (9).

The Mayor, "too blind to tend the chronicles of history" (8), may well be frightened because the horse is a *memento mori* of the Germany that produced the wreckage he starves in. Again, Hawkes uses an animal figure for an analogy of something large (a nation's past), just as, at the outset, he used an animal as metaphor for the nation itself. This frightening horse is important because there is a parallel figure—another horse—that serves as metaphor later in the narrative and that, in terms of what it represents, stands in opposition to this starving beast.

Not unusually, for Hawkes, in the presence of death there is fetid odor: "The damp smell of the river rolled over soldiers' leggings and trousers that had been left in doorways, and a cow lying dead in a field looked like marble" (10). Insane Balamir, who sees himself as Madame Snow's Prince, tender to Germany's spirit, "longed to tend the sheep and be a gangling black dog racing at the herd over green slopes"; "He remembered photographs of vicious tigers"; "he thought of a pigtailed donkey" (11). In the air is the smell of goose feathers and damp wood. The Duke, like an animal, catches the smell because, as he chases Jutta's child through the ruins, "his eyes were sharp and he was keen on the scent" (14). He is an animal and, in one degree or another, so are his fellow-denizens of the wasted town.

Once we see these characters established, largely in animal terms, for what they are, the narrative moves to focus on Zizendorf, Jutta, and her mad daughter—and the institution that holds such importance for these carnivorous and hungry defeated.

Zizendorf says that Jutta "was just now reaching the turn in the road [of her life] where nakedness seemed to hang like a hundred apples, pink, wet, and running with sweet stiff worms" (20). The Census-Taker lies drunk in Jutta's room as she and Zizendorf make love and the globe light overhead burns "at the end of a current without direction," displaying a light "through the wings of moths, yellow, soft" (21). Zizendorf sees in Jutta, as she pleases him, "the nibbling lips of the goat" (22).

The narrative momentarily leaves Jutta and her lover for the Duke, who "poked with his cane into the dark crevices, hoping to stick the crouched body of his prey, to light upon the little fox" (24). While the animal dance goes on, and while the heart of Jutta's daughter beats under her "narrow fish-bone chest" (26), Jutta and Zizendorf leave her room for a dance in the institution. With the portrayal of this dance, Hawkes thoroughly establishes the tone of his novel of grotesqueries.

Zizendorf describes the weak and dispirited revelers:

> They swung out of the mist and appeared with pocketed cheeks and shaven heads. They seemed to dance with one leg always suspended, small white bodies colliding like round seamless pods, and *fingers entwined were twice as long as palms* [italics added]. They danced continuously forming patterns, always the same, of grey and pale blue. The beauties were already sick, and the word *krank* passed from group to group over devious tongues, like the grapevine current of fervent criminal words that slide through wasted penal colonies. (31)

This is dying Germany: an exhausted performance of custom, a "clockwork" of action done by dancers who forget that there is neither cause for revelry nor excuse for joy. This scene, in effect, is the movement of the novel: a continuous dance in which patterns are always formed—Hawkes's "repetitions" of "problems of violence, destruction, sadism" "that we have always had." This dance, metaphor for the character of a nation, is subtly rendered in animal terms. The dancers have fingers twice as long as their palms, and they are likened to monkeys. Such monkeys are used later by Hawkes in a scene in which the spirit of sick Germany

The Cannibal

runs amok—and in which that spirit is characterized by the presence of gibbering monkeys.

As the dance of the dead goes on, Zizendorf feels for the pistol hidden in his clothes and speaks with his friends of *"der Tod"* (the death that will occur), when Zizendorf and his henchmen will leave the dance and, hidden by the side of a dank canal, assassinate their overseer. And, as they plan their renaissance of slaughter, Jutta's son flees the Duke, his knees whirling "like the uncoordinated thrashings of a young and frightened fox," and Jutta picks her way home through rubble "in the thick deserted kingdom of crumbling buildings and roosting birds" (36).

In the midst of the human dance—defeated, automatic, futile, psychotic—Jutta's son, "the fairy" (36), is hunted, the American is hunted, Germany itself is hunted by itself. Stench, debris, ruin, and a sense of preying pervade these early pages which flow into the second section of the book, so mockingly entitled "LOVE."

"LOVE" takes place in 1914 and is illustrative of Hawkes's tendency to warp time by turning his narrative back upon itself. Without prelude or explanation, Hawkes *insists* the two eras into juxtaposition, and historical investigation becomes a crucial concern which is maintained in the novels that follow. Hawkes disrupts time in order to investigate it. His concern is where events flow from, causalities (or causal illusions); his concern is one of narrative, and his works, no matter how complex, inverted, or bizarre, thus deal with *story:* from a mad "once-upon-a-time" to a horrific "The End." Stella Snow is encountered at the start of this portion, so the reader may assume that she is to provide the narrative with a continuum, a sense of that which is abiding in Germany. The narrative is somehow to be built around her, and yet she is more than a focal point. The events for which she is the center are metaphor for the events of modern Germany; modern Germany is, too, metaphor for the Germany of World War I. Like animals in their relationship to people in Hawkes's works, the analogue and its object (1914 and 1945) are reflective of, and influential upon, one another.

Stella, singing in the *Sportswelt Brauhaus* before stiff-uniformed soldiers, moves "as if she could draw them sailing on a sacred lake, and first a crackling chicken, then a duckling" (42) fall under her gaze. These "undecorated chests" (43) are birds prepared for an eating; the Germany of 1945 will be the remains of that dinner for which they will serve. At the novel's end, Germany's future will be devoured.

The *Sportswelt Brauhaus* is Germany in 1914. Stella, who "caught her breath and flung herself at the feet of her horned and helmeted kinsmen" (soldiers and horned bucks simultaneously) (43) while she sings, is the history of Germany, its spirit, the blood-song of its fate. Ernie, or Ernst, son of the *Brauhaus* owner, is Germany's ruler-to-be; he has a face covered with dueling scars, "pockets stuffed with hundred mark notes," a tongue "thick and numb with beer" (43), a hand from which two fingers have been chopped, and an association with homosexual activity. He is pursued by "the Merchant" (as "the fairy," in 1945, is pursued by the Duke) who may well be something of the middle-class spirit that, rising, will dominate Germany. Like Zizendorf, Ernie has dreams for a future in which he and Germany, the ruled and the ruler, are one: "He would sit on a worshipped pile of granite, a small duelist in the hall of kings" (44). Germany will in fact—as has already been seen in the first section—be a pile of granite, a rubble-heap.

Then, surrealistically, Ernie is inside the beer hall, sitting with his father; Herr Snow, the Merchant, is reported "fallen" somehow; there is a hint of death against "the background of summer nightbirds." That hint is usual for Hawkes—an animal smell, a "pea-green pit of stench" (45). The moon over the canal that smells of death is described as "loaded like a sac with water" (44): this Germany is the embryonic sac, the seedtime for the mature Germany that will go to its death stillborn.

At the finish of her song, Stella goes to sit with Herr Snow as "the tide of conversation rolled in the lion cage" (46). She meets Cromwell, an expatriate Englishman, and Ernie, who excites her

The Cannibal

—his eyes between "web-like tissue," his bestial aura that causes her to wait "for the three claws of the left hand to close talon-like just above her knee" (47).

But it is Cromwell who takes Stella home and who rides in his carriage "as an Archduke" (48). Ernie, following the carriage in the rain—Ernie, whose father "loved him with the passionate control of a small monarch gathering and preening his . . . army" (51)—thinks of the Merchant he has killed (but whose ghost will rise for Germany) "sprawled out in the alley . . . sprawled like a murdered Archduke" (53). He begins to run frantically, "raced to coincide with Princip in Sarajevo" (54). Suddenly Ernie is no longer only a budding Kaiser; he is, too, the incipient assassin who precipitated the war and, ultimately, Germany's decline. He is both at once, Germany's future. Ernie runs madly, thinking, " '*love, Stella, Ernst, lust, tonight, leader, land*' " (55–56). When Zizendorf, contrapuntally, rushes to assassination, his thoughts are little different—except "Ernst" becomes an American Jew, Germany's watchdog. And, while Ernie chases Stella and Cromwell, Stella has a vision of Germany's fate: "Francis Ferdinand lay on the seat of the carriage, his light shirt filled with blood, his epaulettes askew and on the floor lay the body of his departed wife, while the assassin, Gavrile Princip, ran mad through the encircling streets" (56). But Ernst falls behind, and though Stella's dream is true, it is not enacted physically in the course of the narrative. Hawkes's history is spiritual.

In a detailed examination of Stella and Ernie, we see Stella's mother killed by a crashing airplane and we see her wooed by Ernie, or him by Stella. Their match is the beginning—this wedding of fierce ambition, prophecy, and spirit to cowardice and a lust for *leader* and *land*—of Germany's end. It is a courtship and match in which animal imagery plays a large part.

The house in which Stella lives with her parents is, "like the curving dolphin's back," "more monstrous than the fattest shark" (61). Stella's father stares from "a skull like a bird's" (66) and is descended of a line of males "alike as brother eagles" (68). Jutta runs through the house with "thin legs apart as if she were riding a horse" (69). Birds outside the house sing and fall silent, a swallow dips, Stella and her mother, shopping, pass a man "slumped over a table scratching the fleas" while "dogs barked and howled" (71). As they walk, "a huge dog with black and white spots" (72) trots by. Stella's father, a retired general now sought for advice since war has been declared, is besieged by callers "seeking on their padded feet to scale these, her walls . . . flies over the white sheet . . . the cannibals" (75). While Stella shops, the grocer "flapped his apron at a pink-nosed dog," and "flies hung over the blue meat"; "live fowl in a dirty cage were silent" (77). It is to this background imagery that Stella and Ernst are joined. It is an imagery, thus far, of no system or pattern whatsoever; it is an imagery that, simply, is metaphoric in terms of the beastliness of the land and the people on whom the narrative focuses.

Then—Hawkes bends time to his narrative ends—Stella is in mourning, her mother dead, and "the birds twittered in angelic surmise, reeled high and low, fed, nested, called beyond the curtains in gentle mockery." A "perpetual afternoon clawed about her knees" (79). As Stella sits near the funeral bier, "the orchestra rose up and glided over the empty avenue, the old woman in starched collar leading, tripping" (80); this is reminiscent of the earlier dance of the living dead and of Herr Stintz, who plays his tuba to no one at midnight, evoking the ghosts of ancient military parades. While she envisions this dance, Stella hears "the perpetual scratching feet of insects who walked over the coffin lid with their blue wings, their dotted eyes" (80). When the coffin is finally taken away, Ernst comes to sit at Stella's feet, and "the birds buried their heads in the shade under their wings" (81–82). Ernst and Stella court until the winter comes: "The leaves turned heavy on the branches, birds coursed away, forgotten, and the cold chill of a new season descended on the city with rain and late fever" (83). The bestial imagery, the sense of disease and unrest, constitute the *leitmotiv* for what the conjuction of Ernst and Stella will produce for the world.

The narrative then moves to Stella and Ernst on their honeymoon at an ice-ringed and isolated mountain resort that, in its distance from everyday society and its atmosphere of supernatural

The Cannibal

strangeness, is evocative of the Sanitorium Berghof in *Magic Mountain*. The couple is witness to an animal figure that plays an important role in this section of the novel: "Every afternoon the old horse stood wheezing by the porte cochere, trembling slightly with head lowered from the terrible exertion of the long climb. . . . The horse appeared blind, so limply hung the head, so blank the closed lids, and little drops of frost grew in his nostrils and on the bit, clung embedded in the sparse mane. . . . 'Ah, the poor beast,' Ernst would say, looking over the sucked-in tail and fragile hocks. . . . The black horse stumbled down the hill, and the couple continued their honeymoon, two golden figures in the setting sun" (85).

It is with this animal always present that Stella and Ernst cavort "in the midst of healthy guests, the men giants, the women tanned with snow, even the old venerable and strong because they were not too old." Here, Ernst is "nearer God" (84) in "the upper world" from which the guests occasionally descend until "their enjoyment dropped, until it was too low to bear" (85). Ernst and Stella are in a Teutonic kingdom of the gods, a dreamworld whose illusion is shaken only by the presence of the horse —a carrier of intimations of death—or by descent to the real world below, where "snarling dogs ran under foot" (85).

It is in the lowland, not the world of supreme illusion, where the horse is healthier: "The black horse thrived better in the lower world. He was the same horse the students rode, shivering with the cold, tied alone to suffer the night. And yet he carried them, their switches flicking in the wind" (86).

Ernst and Stella encounter an old man near the lodge who carves crosses and crucified Christ-figures. Ernst buys one, "a terrible little demon with bitter pain curling about the mouth no larger than a bead" (87). Then he begins to collect them, filling his bedroom with them, praying aloud, forgetting the *Sportswelt;* he no longer thinks of Stella's singing, "and particularly did not want to hear her sing" (88–89). What identifies him as Germany, her future, begins to fade, and the Valhalla in which he thrives begins to pall: "The altitude made him faint, he breathed heavily, and could not stand to think of pain. . . . Then the old man, the Christ-carver, began to visit the hotel regularly, bringing with him each day a basket of those crucifixes that he could not sell, so that the black ugly Christs hung upon the walls of their rooms along with the bright new ones. . . . Stella began to have him lean on her arm as they walked and knew that the most beautiful bird holds tightest before flying straight upwards" (89).

After Ernst has "given up the sword" and "lost the thread of the war's virus" (90), Cromwell, the expatriate and follower of war, arrives. He speaks with relish of the war's progress, says, "'No nation has the history of ours'" (94) in speaking of Germany. His name, of course, suggests that Cromwell who by killing a king threatened monarchies across Europe. Hawkes's Cromwell, an exaggeration of the ferocities often imputed to the seventeenth-century Cromwell, may be a representation of the Anglo-German brotherhood felt by so many Englishmen before World War II. Hawkes, who appears to be fascinated by England, seems often to detest it and, here, he appears to accuse the English of sharing—firing up—Germanic war-lust. As Cromwell speaks, we are shown the battlefield at Cambrai where the Merchant, dead once and now, fantastically, dead again, "without thoughts of trade, dressed in grey, still fat, had died on his first day at the front and was wedged, standing upright, between two beams, his face knocked backwards, angry, disturbed. In his open mouth there rested a large cocoon, protruding and white, which moved sometimes as if it were alive. The trousers, dropped about his ankles, were filled with rust and tufts of hair" (94).

Above is one of the more stunning images in the novel, the white moving cocoon in the mouth of a corpse. Whether or not the animal-figure about to be born, resting in the mouth of the dead, is a metaphorical comment on Germany's fate (and, in the context of this metaphor-laden novel, it would seem to be so), we must nevertheless note how Hawkes typically renders his images with sensuous specificities. The image itself is deeply moving; it is nauseating, in fact, and illustrative of Hawkes's imagistic power. As metaphor, it is most effective in showing the sluglike horror of what is to rise from the Germany of 1914, that earlier nation's corpse, a parody of the crucifixion.

The Cannibal

The next morning Stella wakens, looks to Ernst's bed, and sees only "a small black-haired Christ on the pillow, eyes wide and still, who trembled, and with one thin arm, motioned her away." Simultaneously, a child's voice outside cries that " 'the old horse is dead!' " (94).

Thus Hawkes brings many concerns of this section together in his image of the horse. In its suffering and service in the real world (the world "below") it becomes a kind of Christ-figure. Ernst, in his pity for the horse, his growing religious depth, and his incessant collection of crucifixes and Christ dolls, moves away from war to a height above his Germany's dream. But he is brought down by Cromwell's arrival with news of the war, which deals its blows in terms of crucifixion. The pity and suffering which Ernst comes to feel are symbolized by force of context through the horse. When it dies, we see that history has moved beyond its figures: the war, once Ernst's dream, will continue without him; history will work without individuals shaping it. Hawkes's "repetitions" will dominate. Dreams of war—of *lust, leader, land*—will occur again. Germany will continue mystically and terribly on her course, although her leader, Ernst, begins to die once the symbolic horse has died. When the Mayor sees a decrepit horse in 1945, he is frightened—and appropriately: he sees the ghost of Germany's tragedy. (The horse as a figure of death sired partially by the Second World War will appear in *The Lime Twig.*)

Ernst and Stella descend to the lowlands. There is no heaven anymore. The honeymoon is over indeed. As the couple rides in a dark, damp, and cold train, "Ernst could hear the howling of the dogs out in the passing fields and by the rails." These are the dogs of death and destruction, the dogs of war. They grow more and more human as humanity leaves Germany and as the people in the land come more and more to be inhuman puppets, creatures blown about by time:

> His face pressed against the glass, Ernst heard the cantering of their feet, the yelps and panting that came between the howls. . . . These dogs ran with the train, nipped at the tie rods,

snapped at the lantern from the caboose, and carrying on conversation with the running wheels, begged to be let into the common parlor. . . . As paying passengers, they would eat and doze and leap finally back from the unguarded open platforms between cars into the night and the pack. . . . When she helped him down the iron steps, her face red with the frost, he knew things had changed, that the dogs had beaten them to the destination. That train would certainly never run again, he felt sure, and he knew that its journey was over. (95–97)

Ernst, like the rest of Germany's people, like their dreams, is now small before the history that is moving as the train moved: "He was a puppet" (114). Stella begins to realize that he is "a fencer in the clouds, stuck through, finally, with a microscopic flu" (115)—the virus of war he has come to want to elude. Ernst asks for a carving of Christ and Stella puts it on his pillow, beside his head. He dies and, soon afterward, Stella bears their son who is destined to show the same film endlessly to an empty theater as a crippled purveyor of meaninglessness to no one. Stella survives; she is flexible; her dreams return to the singing Ernst came to loathe and which she threw—as spirit, the ambitions of Germany—at the feet of Prussian warriors. Not surprisingly, Stella is reminded of her singing when she hears dogs howl near Ernst's grave. She notes unemotionally that Ernst's Christ-carving has disappeared with Ernst; God seems to have died with the innkeeper's son. Nothing has changed. The dogs dominate. Death is overrunning Germany to Stella's singing, to the tune of time.

The narrative returns to Germany's present with images of animality and filth. The villagers burn pits of excrement, "breathing off their odor of burned flesh and hair and biddy," and this stench floats to the *Autobahn*, where Zizendorf and his followers await their American overseer and his murder; as usual, where there has been or is to be death, Hawkes creates its smell. The plotters hear ghosts, and "a wasted mongrel" (125) pawing leaves.

The Cannibal

Contrapuntally, the narrative returns to Jutta's daughter, a representative victim of Germany's history, watching the window, "eyes darting this way and that, among the shadows, hands folded in her lap, knees drawn together, small and wide awake as children who follow the night very long after the usual time to sleep, quickened and tense with the unexpected hours, wretched small keepers" (127). And another victim returns, too, a puppet in the time Germany ticks—"the fairy" who, out of sight, "was running for his life" (128). But it is the daughter here, the fairy's brother, who now engages the reader. She is quickly and deftly rendered pathetic by Hawkes as she waits in the boarding house and hears a roomer "walk the length of his cage and unlock the door" (128). As the murderers wait, the observations of the victims of it all remind the reader that war, hatred, *lust, leader* are again being set loose.

The assassins wait, the dancers in the asylum automatically jig, children tense or flee, and, not unexpectedly, "A cow with its eyes shut clawed at the empty board walls of a barn with teeth like a hare but found no straw" (132). In this perverted world even the animals change their animal roles, even cows have rabbit-teeth and claws. Stella holds Balamir's hand as he sleeps— Balamir, the servant who, in his dreams of Germany, his worship of Stella, is reminiscent of Ernst—and she recalls, while the assassins wait, the closing days of the war, when the doctors and nurses left the asylum and the patients rioted: "It snowed for nights on end, but every morning the monkeys appeared uncovered . . . misshapen, clutching in their hands and feet . . . dead rats" (152). She remembers how, just before the riot, she stood holding a stolen chicken, and how—Germany destroying itself—she killed the fowl:

> The feathers, bitten with mange, trembled and breathed fearfully. The soft broken claws kicked at her wrist. For a moment the Kaiser's face, thin, depressed, stared in at the cell window, and then was gone, feeling his way over a land that was now strange to the touch. . . . Carefully she straddled the convulsing neck with two fingers, tightened them across the mud-caked

chest, and with the other hand seized the head. . . . Madame Snow clenched her fists and quickly flung them apart so that the fowl's head spurted across the room, hit the wall and fell into a heap of shavings, its beak clicking open and shut. (153-54)

Certainly, this grotesque scene—grotesque partially because of the wealth of detail Hawkes offers; his care of description extends an air of ritual, a tense deliberateness to killing—is effective as part of the novel's imagery, part of the atmosphere of preying-on that is so pervasive. But we might recall, in addition, that Ernst, the dreamer-of-Germany and then its penitent, who died when the symbol of pity and suffering (the horse) died, was seen by Stella as the beautiful bird who is held tightest just before he flies away. Ernst's spirit, his Germany, is the chicken; Stella's murder of the bird is surely a metaphorical murdering of the land and its people as well.

The mad monkeys gibbering about, Stella leads a brigade of women to quell the inmates of the institution. The scene of the uprising is of Germany rising, mad, to kill itself. If we remember that the dancers described earlier have monkey hands, we may see that the uprising, and its quelling, is Germany hurling itself upon itself:

> During that hour the monkeys were so underfoot that the patients were saved from worse injury by the clumsiness of the women who shouted and tore and pelted everything in sight. As these women in the midst of changing years ran to and fro beating, slashing, the stiff tails and hard outstretched arms and furry brittle paws smacked against black puttees and were trampled and broken in the onslaught. . . . The barrel-staves broke on unfeeling shoulders, the rats' bodies were driven deeper in the snow. . . .
> Suddenly the deputized women found themselves alone and standing on the mutilated carcasses of little men. (156-57)

The little men are the monkeys, who are, in turn, the inmates. The people of Germany are animals, and the land is purged of them, supposedly, through murder and mayhem. But at the war's

The Cannibal

end, the weird night of the dance shows that purgation was futile; the beasts still cavort; the cycles still gyre.

As Madame Snow's revery concludes, Leevey, the overseer, is killed by a log placed on the highway. As the murderers go through his possessions, we read "It was no drunken lark. A difficult hour they had of it at that time of night, the worst time of night for odds and ends and order, especially after killing a man" (166). "A difficult hour they had of it" strongly suggests Eliot's adaptation of Lancelot Andrewes' Christmas sermon:

> 'A cold coming we had of it,
> Just the worst time of the year
> For a journey, and such a long journey:
> The ways deep and the weather sharp
> The very dead of winter.'[5]

Hawkes's continuing reference to Eliot here takes the form of obvious (and effective) parody: the murderers are the Magi; this land's witnesses to the Epiphany are witnesses to and doers of murder; the country is born dead as the Jew is killed—just as the Jew born before the eyes of the Wise Men was to be murdered. Hawkes creates the crucifixion and Epiphany as a simultaneity. The Jewish overseer Leevey is an ironic reminder of the six million Jews who were murdered; their "crucifixion" informs Leevey's: the killing of the six million suggests the killing of Christ; the killing of Leevey suggests the killing of the six million. Zizendorf's new Germany is born as Leevey dies. Hawkes seems to comment on the birth of the postwar world, civilization's final hope, in Eliot's voice—this from the conclusion of "The Journey of the Magi":

> Birth or Death? There was a Birth, certainly,
> We had evidence and no doubt. I had seen birth and death,
> But had thought they were different; this Birth was
> Hard and bitter agony for us, like Death, our death.

(We can look ahead to another parodistic echo of the Eliot poem, which will occur in *The Goose on the Grave*, when three monks will come riding over a hill to seize a small child's mother, bear her off, eventually burn her.)

As the murder is committed, the Duke catches up with Jutta's son in the movie house, the palace of non-sense, home of fantasy, owned by Stella's son, and, because there is death everywhere, "a gaunt bird settled on the throat of the headless horse statue in the center of the town" (168)—perhaps the ghost of Ernst's regrets settling on, perhaps, the horse that, in dying, showed us that Germany and concern for individual life were dead.

Zizendorf and his followers make plans to publish on Zizendorf's press a proclamation of defiance to the Allies and of hope to neo-Nazis, for "the initial blow was struck, the enemy unseated" (169). Zizendorf's dream for Germany is not only symbolically played out in the microcosm through the death of Leevey; Hawkes portrays this dream with sufficient specific detail to create a sort of verisimilitude that serves to reveal, in terms of the actual world of occupying armies and defeated nations, how small and puny is the dream and the present spirit of Germany. There is a terror in vast dreams built on a foundation so small as to be almost ludicrous; the terror derives from the detailed realism of the portrayal and enactment of rebellious ambition.

While the plotters work and while the other denizens of the town (of Germany, in other words) sleep, the Duke performs an animal action, described in animal terms, that once again shows us mankind destroying itself, Germany snapping like a gutted jackal at its own steaming viscera:

> He hacked and missed the joints, he made incisions and they were wrong as the point of the blade struck a button. The fox kicked back and he was horrified. He hated his clumsiness, detested himself for overlooking the bones. . . . It was necessary to struggle, first holding the pieces on his lap, then crouching above the pile, he had to pull, to poke, and he resented the dullness of the blade. The very fact that it was not a rabbit made it hard to dissect; its infernal humanness carried over even into death and made the carcass just as difficult as the human being had itself been. Every time a bone broke his prize became

The Cannibal

mangled, every piece that was lost in the mud made the whole thing defective, more imperfect in death. . . . It lost all semblance to meat or fowl, the paw seemed like the foot, the glove the same as the shoe, hock and wrist alike, bone or jelly, muscle or fat, cartilage or tongue, what could he do? (180–82)

The Duke returns to his room to boil "the fox" while the intriguers work. Madame Snow, the abiding soul of Germany, is invited to dine with the Duke, and she does. Zizendorf returns to Jutta, while his cohorts labor, and lies down beside her. The two "shut our eyes against the sun" and, when asked by Jutta's daughter— "more thin than ever in the light of day, wild-eyed from watching the night and the birth of the Nation"—whether anything has happened, he tells her to draw the blinds and sleep. Says Zizendorf, "She did what she was told" (195). And so, on a note of military obedience and mole-like refuge from the light, from whatever sense of reality is available to its characters, Hawkes ends his tale of mankind's cannibal soul.

There are several interesting comparisons to be made between *Charivari* and Hawkes's "real first novel." For one, there is the matter of point of view. *Charivari* has, essentially, no narrative focus; it is told by a voice as all-knowing and acidic as that of the third-person narrator which runs through *The Waste Land*. Consequently, attention in *Charivari* runs parallel to the narrative line; that is, we are interested in what the narrative voice guides us to—no more, at any given moment. In *The Cannibal*, however, there is a more distinct focus of attention. Says Hawkes:

> *The Cannibal* was written in the third person, but in revision I found myself (perversely or not) wishing to project myself into the fiction and to become identified with its most criminal and, in a conventional sense, least sympathetic spokesman, the neo-Nazi leader of the hallucinated uprising. I simply went through the manuscript and changed the pronouns from third to first person, so that the neo-Nazi Zizendorf became the teller of those absurd and violent events. The result was interesting, I think,

not because *The Cannibal* became a genuine example of first-person fiction, but because the "narrator" naturally possessed an unusual omniscience, while the authorial consciousness was given specific definition, definition in terms of humor and "black" intelligence.[6]

The Cannibal is told by Zizendorf, who somehow has knowledge of Germany's past and present in terms of Stella Snow, Ernst, and the other characters not always in direct association with him. His voice becomes the voice of Germany, if Madame Snow's soul is the soul of Germany. Although he speaks for a nation and for history, he also speaks specifically for himself; he narrates his personal events always in the context of the larger story of which he has intimate knowledge.

The effect of this narrative voice is twofold: first, Germany is personified through his voice as effectively as it is personified to greater and lesser degrees in the other characters—we know something of Zizendorf, are witness to his lovemakings and acts of murder and, so, hear Germany as a murderer talking about itself; secondly, we are affected by the sardonic ease with which Zizendorf's story is told: the murder of Jutta's son by the Duke does not serve only as symbol for a people gone mad, an act of cannibalism; it serves to shock us because of its understatement, its description of cruelty and insanity couched in conscience-salving and deluded terms; for if Zizendorf is narrator, he *knows* that he describes the corpse of a hapless, if unpleasant, child as "the fox."

The fox itself is fascinating. It appears in probably the most horrifying scene in the novel; certainly its potency and terror outweighs anything in *Charivari*, and it is different from any animal scene in that novel. It represents a concentration of metaphor that should, for us, be a benchmark in Hawkes's development of his technique.

Hitherto, Hawkes has represented animals as people, people as animals; he has portrayed each as sharing characteristics of the other, and this technique is continuous in the novels. In *The Cannibal* and in his other novels, he creates an impressive and

The Cannibal

affecting background imagery that incites us to see how bestial his characters are, how their lives are surrounded by death and nightmare. But in *Charivari*, Hawkes does not at any point concentrate a metaphor—work with it for so long a time in such chimeric detail—as he does the fox scene in *Cannibal*. A fruitful comparison is the section called "RHYTHM" in *Charivari*, where snake-images abound; hints of snake-figures run frighteningly through the latter pages of the novel. But they are not tied together or placed in one small scene and used, totally, to frighten and influence the thoughts of the reader. This, however, is precisely what Hawkes does with the fox scene. As if all his other images of self-consumption and bestiality in *The Cannibal* were insufficient (which they are not), he injects an overwhelming blackness into this one scene that might well be symbol for the world of the novel, and for the novel itself.

It is worth noting how, beside such a ghastly imagery as that discussed above, the animal imagery of so sensual a writer as Dylan Thomas pales. In the short story "The Peaches," the narrator's uncle is described as showing "his long, red, drunken, fox's face."[7] Later, the narrator, thinking of his uncle killing pigs, says: "I could see uncle, tall and sly and red, holding the writhing pig in his two hairy hands, sinking his teeth in its thigh, crunching its trotters up; I could see him leaning over the wall of the sty with the pig's legs sticking out of his mouth."[8]

This is hardly inestimable writing. It generates a *frisson* that is quite effective in suggesting the horrific dreams of a young and imaginative child. The image of the pig's legs sticking out of the uncle's mouth comes near to the awfulness of Bosch's representations of men devoured by demons. But this writing is about excitement, told excitedly; the Duke's actions are described calmly, with a technical and systematic grace, and with sufficient references to the fox's humanity to suggest that the narrator knows full well how human the "fox" really is.[9] That calm tale of roaring, yet meticulous, madness ranks higher on our arbitrary scale of horror than does the pre-adolescent nightmare told by Thomas. The Hawkes is a Jacobean triumph, as is the novel a triumphant merging of brilliant stylistics and social concern.

3 The Beetle Leg

The Beetle Leg seems to be a working-out of the water-god myth, a rather systematic enactment of the myth of the god-in-the-water whose death renders crops barren and whose resurrection means life for his wasted land. This novel's hero is a man "who lay buried just below the water level of the dam . . . embedded in the earth and entangled with a caterpillar, pump engine and a hundred feet of hose, somewhere inside the mountain."[1] The man is Mulge Lampson, who was accidentally buried in a landslide that took place during the construction of a huge irrigation dam in the American West. Somehow this novel revolves about Mulge, though he enters the book through a recalled conversation for only part of one chapter. Mulge seems to be a contemporary rendition of the water god, expected traditionally to help the people of his land cope with and control their environment.

Of the Fisher King, crucial to the water-god myth, Jessie L. Weston states: "He is not merely a deeply symbolic figure, but the essential centre of the whole cult, a being semi-divine, semi-human, standing between his people and the land, and the unseen forces which control their destiny."[2] Certainly in desert country such as that in which the book is set, construction of a dam constitutes effort by man to control his land and its "unseen forces." Once the narrative is under way there is evidence that hard times—emotional and agricultural—are upon the land. For the Fisher King cannot resurrect that god of the book; that god is dead—buried in water. Says Miss Weston: "The King must not be allowed to become old or feeble, lest, with the diminishing vigour of the ruler, the cattle should sicken and fail to bear increase, the crops should rot in the field and men die in ever growing numbers."[3]

But there is hope for surcease in the myth, and a reason for the burial of the god. In relating Adonis rituals and other Fisher King antecendents to medieval romance Miss Weston points out that "the presence of water, either sea, or river, is an important feature in the Adonis cult, the effigy of the dead god being, not buried in the earth, but thrown into the water." In a footnote to this statement she adds that "throwing into, or drenching with, water is a well-known part of 'Fertility' ritual; it is a case of sympathetic magic, acting as a rain charm."[4]

Sir James G. Frazer sums up this idea behind Mulge-as-water-god-and-talisman:

> Strange, therefore, as may seem to us the idea of a god incarnate in human form, it has nothing very startling for early man, who sees in a man-god or a god-man only a higher degree of the same supernatural powers which he arrogates in perfect good faith to himself. Nor does he draw any very sharp distinction between a god and powerful sorcerer. . . . As the gods are commonly believed to exhibit themselves in the likeness of men to their worshippers, it is easy for the magician, with his supposed miraculous powers, to acquire the reputation of being an incarnate deity. Thus beginning as little more than a simple conjurer, the medicine-man or magician tends to blossom out into a full-blown god and king in one.[5]

The thought, then, is that Mulge, somehow sacrificed to his desert people's effort to control their environment and make their crops fertile, is extension of his people's talismanic urge, their good-luck piece and god-in-the-water at once. (*Lampson* can be rearranged as *son of Lamp*. Perhaps Hawkes parodies *Son of Light*.) His land, now that he is gone (as Tammuz was gone during the barren months, before his talisman emerged from the waters when they spilled over in spring), is a waste land. His wife, Ma, is of the weeping women who traditionally mourn aloud for the vanished god. She is also a kind of earth mother. His brother, Luke, a central actor in the narrative, is the teller of

The Beetle Leg

Mulge's story (as was the New Testament Luke teller of the most extended biblical chronicle of a God who, drenched with water, or baptized, was buried and then rose).

The doctor in the novel is revealed as the father of both Mulge and his brother, Luke. The doctor may be considered to be the Fisher King himself, deliverer of the god from the waters —if he is capable of doing so for the sake of the waste land.

When Eliot, in *The Waste Land*, echoes *The Tempest*—

> While I was fishing in the dull canal
> On a winter evening round behind the gashouse
> Musing upon the king my brother's wreck
> And on the king my father's death before him.
> White bodies naked on the low damp ground . . .[6]

—he might well be speaking for Luke, who so evidently muses upon his brother's "wreck." It is well to remember, moreover, the imposition of Christian mythos upon the water-god story—the archetypal muser-upon-the-god become the Christian Luke. There is much in the book that suggests this superimposition: that the Fisher King is a Jehovah-like God; that Ma is something of Mary; that the waste land is a somehow wasted Eden.

The novel begins with a sheriff reading a horoscope: "Aquarius is poor. Sagittarius is poor. Virgo is a Barren Sign, it will produce no growth. The first day the Moon is in a sign is better than the second and the second better than the third. Seed planted when the Earth is in Leo, which is a Barren, Fiery Sign, will die, as it is favorable only to the destruction of noxious growth. Trim no trees or vines when the Moon or Earth is in Leo. For they will surely die" (7).

The animals Hawkes presents are mythical; they sound the note of approach of the novel and establish the fact that we deal more with myth in this book than with reality. Here we have (as is soon evident from his monologue) the most earthbound of men aspiring to a knowledge of the workings of the heavens; this pursuit of the mysteries may well be synecdoche for the yearning of the Sheriff's people, for humanity chasing the stars. The futility and barrenness in the image conjured by the horoscope imply a waste land, a place of no fertility. There is a curious resemblance, most especially tonal, between the horoscope and the lament for the dead fertility god, Tammuz:

> The wailing is for the plants; the first lament
> is 'they grow not.'
> The wailing is for the barley; the ears grow not.
> For the habitations and flocks it is; they produce not.[7]

—and we might do well to consider the tone-establishing power of such a mythically referential passage. The characters behave not only as individuals acting out their needs, but as participants in a ritual drama.

There is a parodistic tone to the opening of the novel. The Sheriff puts down his book, marks his place, and begins to talk about prevention—prevention, primarily, of sexual activity, almost as if he had been appointed to see that no spark of vitality were left in the world. He glorifies his job—the act of prevention—and echoes all pulp-Western and video lawmen: "But a man gets used to a pair of handcuffs on his hip. . . . And there's not one shirt I own but that it's got badge holes through the pocket. Some men don't commit crimes, but they're ready to. I've had two ranchers come to me in the middle of the night with a horse between them, and they trusted me to know whose horse it was" (7-8). Thus we have a soap-opera Solomon telling us the doctrine of original sin; this is a land of the born-guilty.

The Sheriff is called by two small girls to see a strange man—Mulge Lampson—who sits by the banks of a nearby river. The Sheriff lurks in the bushes and watches this strange figure "just squatting in the desert" (12). He says of this latter-day Christian Hermit "here's a man, I thought, is snarled with this river. He'll have more trouble with it yet, I figured" (13). The half-clothed Lampson sits and stares at the water, and the Sheriff, after foreshadowing his end ("trouble" with the river) and suggesting the air of differentness about him, goes back to his office, disappointed that there has been no patent malefaction. It is at this point that the action of the novel begins.

The Beetle Leg

Our first narrative encounter is with Luke Lampson, a wagon-driver and occasional seed-scatterer (fertilizing crops runs in this "sacred" family), who rides home from work past the tar-paper buildings and arid ground of the waste land. Luke comes home to Ma, his brother's widow, who works and wails all day in a room decorated with animal *memento mori*, "a pair of antlers, patches of hair and dried skin stuck to the yellow bone chip of skull" (20). It is significant that the mourning household's reminder of death is the remnant of a dead animal; for implicit, as a result, is the idea that all the human lives of the novel are related to the lives of animals and are seen analogically as animal lives.

Ma's pastime is complaint for Mulge's death and for the passage of the years. Her only pleasure lies in imitation of the mythical American pioneer woman: "Ma never sat to any meal. She kept her back to the world and her face toward the red range, toward the cartons of matches, the row of pans and long-handled forks. Sometimes she pushed the lid off the skillet and stole a bite on a long blackened prong or a sip from a wooden spoon" (21). Hardened, devoted to serving the male, eternally cooking in a hellish environment of matches, heat, a "red range," Ma is as much an earth mother in this novel as Stella Snow is in *The Cannibal*. The men she serves are only two: the dead Mulge, whom she worships—"'Don't you say anything against Mulge. I won't have it!'" (23)—as the earth mother reveres the water god; and Luke, who, at the outset, is more figure than character, a virtually speechless and emotionless "old-time cowboy" who seems as parodistic of the myth of the American West as do Ma and the Sheriff.

Outside Luke's house, we are shown, wait the Red Devils, "a pack of dogs" (23). We are told little of them except how, on their motorcycles and in their leather jackets, they wait for something important, wait silently, these "several creatures" who ominously "watched as hunters by a pond in the marsh from which a single old bird, flapping and beating across the flat water, is unable to rise" (24). Because they are described in terms of bestial behavior, the reader has every right to expect something strange and terrible of them.

After dinner Luke walks from the house, past the hiding Red Devils, to the highway, where "a thin lizard leaped from the ridge and away down the brown clay rut." He ponders the man buried in the mountain and wonders "if his body ever shifted in the sand, he thought of it when seeding. 'Someday he'll worm himself right out to the open air,' the cowboy said. 'Mighty like he's crawling around in there right now'" (24). The folk-hero of this blighted land is seen in animal terms. Moreover, Mulge's imminence seems as much a threat as a promise.

On the highway, near a sign warning of poisoned water, Luke encounters Camper and his wife, Lou. They are vacationers who stop when Camper's son is bitten by a snake. Camper, who wears "cat-eye glasses," once worked on the dam that has entombed Mulge and has now returned as if on a religious pilgrimage. He has come past "'warning signs posted every fifty feet. It's a hell of a thing when you can't take a leak without kicking up a pack of rattlers'" (26). If the land is the paradisiacal home the god-in-the-water once made fertile, or if it is an Eden of sorts, the snakes and Red Devil motorcycle riders take on an extra significance: the paradise is under siege, or in some sort of jeopardy; fertility is gone; Eden is about to be disrupted.

The reader is told again how the land is becoming a place of horror, in terms of this novel's ever-present beasts: "Luke had seen them stricken before: Ma was not immune to rattlers on the water trail and even the Mandan [Ma's Indian kitchen-helper] was struck one blow from a startled head. The snakes were driven further and further from the bluff and new highway, and gathered wherever a few rocks or sticks could hide them deeper in the fields. . . . But still their bodies might dart from a forkful of hay or dash from under pail or wheel to strike" (27).

Luke administers first aid to Camper's son and Camper, the pilgrim, asks after the height of water in the dam, telling how "'I hate to be shoving off. . . . I know there's fishing'" (28), as if he were a quester on the mythical journey to fish for the god in the waters.

Luke continues to the town of Mistletoe—mistletoe, symbol of the natural cycle which the god-in-the-water signifies.[8] It is in Mistletoe that Luke asks after Bohn, the crippled former rodeo hero—the land's maimed king?—who is perhaps what the Old West has, in this waste land, become.

The narrative then returns to the Sheriff, who has some of the Red Devil motorcycle pack in jail. He talks of watering them, as if they were animals, and then looks at them. "Awkwardly spread eagle in the cell, the black driving mittens of one flung upon the seamless snout of another, tangled, sleeping, perhaps ready to spring with wild rubber limbs high and low against the bars. In captivity, sometime during the night, they had heaped themselves in the middle of the painted floor." The Sheriff warns his deputy not to place his arm near their cell: " 'you'll get it bit off' " (35). Premonitions about this doglike gang of contemporary Devils mount.

The Sheriff sends his deputy, Wade, for his dog. Here animal-image becomes symbol, and we see Old West and beast coincidentally:

> In a stoop Wade pulled the pointer through the doorway. It brought with it the smell of rain, the smell of paws, forelegs and chest soaked in storm and caked with the mud of a downpour; it twisted its head, drops beating against its eyes, and shook, would have spattered the walls, between Wade's knees. All day it shied and staggered under the sun. But by nightfall it was able to force moisture, to yelp at the shell-like roll of a cloudburst in its ears, to walk as if leaving puddles across the floor, to smell as if the rain had actually come down and driven it bleating and thin into a rivulet filling ditch. . . . All four of the animal's paws were rigid, hind legs clamped straight up and down, front paws crossed over its bleeding snout. (43–44)

The dog is as sick as the land: suffering under the sun, waiting for the relief of water. The Sheriff notes this sickness and turns— *"Trim no trees or vines. . . . For they will surely die"*—away from this animal objectification of the waste land's disease; he prefers his horoscope. He notes that "It is a lawless country" (46). In the beast-ridden land all myth is dead or impotent— except in horoscopal writings and except in the mind of the

Sheriff who, by exaggerating crime, makes part of the Old (dead) West's myth, the most accessible part, seem to continue.

The story returns in a typically Hawkesian warp of time to Camper and his wife, driving in their car and searching for the Mistletoe which Camper once knew. They are attacked by a snake: "They ran over it. Flat and elongated, driven upon in sleep, it wheeled, rattling from fangs to tail, chased them, caught up with the car, slithered beneath it, raced ahead into the light and reared. The snake tottered, seemed to bounce when it became blind, and, as Camper touched the brake, lunged so that it appeared to have shoulders, smashed its flat pear skull against the solid, curved glass of one headlamp, piercing, thrusting to put out the light" (50–51). The virtually human malevolence of the snake increases the tension of forewarnings of evil already encountered. There is wickedness afoot (or on its belly) and Hawkes's animal metaphor portrays it. The generally loathsome beast has human characteristics; and so it not only disturbs us as any snake might, it doubly alarms us because it shows a human antagonism and doggedness in its effort to extinguish the light.

The couple takes refuge in a rundown hotel near Mistletoe. Camper, the pilgrim repeats the mythical note: " 'The best fishing in the world is right here, Lou' " (52). She watches him, her fury growing, as he ignores her unhappiness in the night of the waste land, and prattles about fishing; then she calls him a dirty dog and he leaves. Lou is left alone and is suddenly "unable to move as she stared into a watchful, silent figure pressed close" to her window: "The creature continued to watch. It was made of leather. Straps, black buckles and breathing hose filled out a face as small as hers, stripped of hair and bound tightly in alligator skin. It was constructed as a baseball, bound about a small core of rubber. The driving goggles poked up from the shiny cork top and a pair of smoked glasses fastened in the leather gave it malevolent and overflowing eyes. There was a snapped flap on one side that hid an orifice drilled for earphones. Its snout was pressed against the screen, pushing a small bulge into the room" (53).

This creature is one of Hawkes's exquisite creations—for it is no animal at all, nor is it human. It is a congeries of insect and

The Beetle Leg

reptile associations created in terms of leather and rubber that are suggestive of bugs and other crawling things. But the parts of the beast are not specifically derived from specific beasts. It is a signal to childhood recollections of strange things staring into bedrooms at night from the pages of spooking stories, a signal to our revulsion from glistening creatures with snouts and overflowing eyes: it is an animal image that taps us, one to which we bring fears that the image leeches from us. Although the animal is specifically described, it is unnamed; it is "it," a depersonalized, unnamable, and therefore unknowable creature. It is essentially nightmare and, as such, is most appropriate to this strange milieu in which Hawkes has placed his reader—a land of entombed heroes, mad sheriffs, dying multiple myths, red devils, and snakes.

Lou flees from her room and encounters Bohn and Thegna. Bohn, though thirty, is a relic of the land: his fingers are chopped from tractor-accidents, his legs are crippled from rodeos, he walks on sticks. When he leaves the kitchen at the sight of Lou, an outsider, he starts at the sight of "the metal relic buried in the middle of her chest. . . . At that time it was the only cross in Mistletoe" (56). And we are alerted, again, to the possibility that the myths of Eden and of Christ, and that of the god who rises from the waters of the maimed land, are somehow operative on events in the waste land.

Lou complains to Thegna about her husband. " 'He ran straight to it all right. Like a buried bone.' " (The maimed cowboy's name is *Bohn,* and, like *Lampson,* calls attention to the character's function in the ritual drama.) Thegna, the cook, a server of men as is Ma, only laughs and invites Lou to play cards with a woman named Fatima. And, like Eliot's Madame Sosostris, a reminder of the magic summoned through use of the Tarot deck, Lou, a Christian pilgrim unwilling, and Thegna, a creature of the waste land, sit down to play.

The narrative moves back again to Ma, as she ponders her buried Mulge, entombed in the moist earth at the foot of the dam: "It moved. The needles, cylinder and ink lines blurring on the heat smeared in the light shade of evening, tended by the old watchman in the power house, detected by a creeping, downstream motion in the dam, leaned against by the weight of water, it was pushing southward on a calendar of branding, brushfires and centuries to come, toward the gulf. Visitors hung their mouths and would not believe, and yet the hill eased down the rotting shade a beetle's leg each several anniversaries" (67–68).

Although "beetle leg," or "beetle's leg" seem to be used in this novel for terms of short measurement—the slow motion of Mulge's corpse—there is this secondary meaning: a wooden pestle or bat for striking or pounding. It may be of some value to note that the pestle can signify the powers of the medicine man who is Fisher King, and can be seen as related to the spear of questing warriors, which is their symbol of power, their fertility sign. Such a reading of *beetle* might suggest that mythic importance exists even in the title of the book, but there is no evidence for such a specific conclusion to be firmly made.

Ma recalls how Thegna, part of the spirit of the land, cooked enormous quantities of food when the landslide buried Mulge and how, then, "with line, basket and rusty hook, she made her way to the tidewater and darkness under one wooden bridge in the country, fixed her gear and sat down to fish for eels" (70). The motif of fishing for the god occurs again: Ma reads a recipe— "Cut 1 lb. fish fresh as it buys to four pieces" (72). It may be important that the sought-for yet threatening Mulge is here associated with eels. They are evocative of the deadly serpents that abound in the book. And Mulge *is* "entangled with . . . a hundred feet of hose," which might also be evocative of serpents.

The narrative turns to Thegna, that spirit who is somehow not only affiliated with the land, but with its tragedy: "She had not been away since the Great Slide" (72). Thegna's great love is Harry Bohn, the cripple, "and she had never loved him as she now loved Bohn in the shadow of the dam and as long as it stood to hold back the changing waters" (73). By now it is patent that the dam cannot be seen merely as structure, that it must be viewed as systematically related to each character in the book as each is related to the land.

Through his use of animals, Hawkes further suggests the possibility of a mythic system that binds characters and land in

The Beetle Leg

a web of fertility motifs and Christian filaments. Thus Luke, always asking for Bohn, is what is left of the mythical West; the wailing woman (Ma) is attached to the dead god; Thegna is in love with crippled remnants. The land is of disease and animal-informed tragedy, a mad land of mad images. For example, as Ma reminisces of her marriage to Mulge, a thrumming animal imagery comes to life: "Blister beetles sat on the grass terrets or suddenly still, fell dryly to the ground" (84); she says to Mulge's mother, " 'Hattie. You ain't going to be doggish' " (87); there is a long colloquy on dogs' worms (87–88); and when the Sheriff tries to keep the wedding party out of town (because it might cause lawlessness: he is again a preventer of sexuality), he says, " 'I don't care if the whole pack aims to rut' " (90).

Luke then meets Camper at a bar. They talk of fishing, and Camper tries to bargain with Luke for Luke's boots, as if the high-heeled boots of the mythical cowboy are talismanic to this pilgrim in search of paradisaical memory. While they speak, a Red Devil drives his motorcycle to the edge of the dam and "looked over his shoulder toward the trailing dogs." Where dogs run in a Hawkes novel, evil is rampant. The devil "sat like a bird still flying, in dead motion the wind still seemed to flatten his driving clothes. . . . Now and then a short claw tugged at the strap around the neck . . . and he twitched . . . and lifted his nose toward the freshly scented path. Behind him the scampering dogs with rough fur and winded ribs, jaws clamped on hanging tongues in the over-country race, drew near with forced cries and shaggy heads, bewildered in the sudden opportunity to run. With each crafty burst of the engine, the barks, a sound hoarse and long unheard, started anew" (104). Somehow the Red Devils are part of the disease scourging the land; the plagued dogs running through the novel signify that fact to us. Where dogs go, the Red Devils go; and, as noted earlier, the red devils are often described (in the prison scene, for example) as dogs. Another waste land animal image—T. S. Eliot's—comes to mind:

> 'That corpse you planted last year in your garden,
> 'Has it begun to sprout? Will it bloom this year?

'Or has the sudden frost disturbed its bed?
'Oh keep the Dog far hence, that's friend to men,
'Or with his nails he'll dig it up again!'[9]

Although "the Dog" refers to the Dog Star, which is dominant when the Nile overflows to fertilize Egyptian crops (and, in ancient times, hurl the carved talisman of the water-god's head upon the land in a gesture of resurrection), the danger of "the Dog" referred to by Eliot still speaks to that portrayed by Hawkes. For it is the fear of fertility that Eliot's Waste Landers express—hence the threat embodied in Mulge. That element of fear is also carried across the dying West by Hawkes's running dogs; and always with the dogs are the animal-like Devils, whose presence, for the reader, grows from chapter to chapter.

It is in the last fifty-two pages of *The Beetle Leg* that the heart of the novel lies. In this portion the animal imagery is brilliantly achieved, and the mythic elements, layer upon layer of them, come together.

Camper, the Finn—a resident of the hotel at which Camper stays—Lampson, and Harry Bohn are on a fishing expedition. Hawkes reveals more about Harry Bohn: "By miracle born of a dead mother and thereafter in his youth—he looked quickly over his shoulder lest he be caught thinking of it—drawn to the expressionless genitals of animals . . . doted upon the stomach kept distended with effort, and lest they be torn to pieces, slept with his hands drawn in from the edges of the bed. . . . Then Bohn burst with feebleness and fought, with laughter and pains of senility, a past in which life moved deep within the woman's body though her hands were cold" (108).

Afflicted with bladder trouble (like the Sheriff's dog), a physical ruin, thirty years old and antique, born of a corpse, Bohn is the nadir of sex and fertility, a young man in the Old West who is simultaneously as physically dated and dry of deed as the West is dry of the realities that once may have been behind its myths.

The Beetle Leg

He is a parody of birth, a spirit of death, an anti-Adam. This much is learned about Bohn, ironically, when he goes fishing—an action that may represent efforts, in the waste land framework of symbol and connotation, to resurrect the power of fertility and restore paradise.

The men in the fishing party hear "the faint jumping of the fish or cry of the wolf"; Camper "licked his mouth for a taste of the imaginary spawn of game and feared through the night the footfall of the hunted" (109). As if this imagery is preparation for strange events (with Hawkes, it usually is), the narrative turns toward Ma, who plucks her divining rod from its hiding place and, like Mother Earth searching for Tammuz, climbs to the dam and quests for Mulge.

Animal imagery is used in the description of her quest: "Old herself, distracted, now and then her mind snapped back to his mother who visibly had spoken, tottered, folded wings and died. On one side swelled the artificial sea over cabin, gulch, and bedstead, washing against the dam and nests of barometric instruments hidden in cut rocks by the engineers. Below her the rows of boxed fowl stretched from dry bank to bank and the birds, now crying and frightened in the night, dropped feathers through chicken wire and filled the river bed with a crowded, sleepless scuffling" (116).

Like the wailing women, Ma pines and cries for Mulge, then gives up her quest and returns home. It is fitting to the water-god mythos that Ma seeks Mulge in the water with a divining rod, for the search for water that makes the waste land fertile is futile unless the Fisher King is able to mediate with the god and unless the god is well. Ma's quest is futile.

And then the narrative jumps to Cap Leech, the medicine man. When Cap Leech was a practicing physician, "he attended the birth of Harry Bohn. The mother, dead but a moment, gave up the still live child in an operation which . . . was more abortive than life saving and, when the doctor drew back, lapsed into her first faintly rigorous position. *The son, fished none too soon from the dark hollow, swayed coldly to and fro between his fingers.* Leech left his scalpel stuck midway down the unbleeding thigh, buried the wailing forceps in his shiny bag, stepped outdoors with the infant and disappeared, thereafter, through all of his career, barred from the most fruitful of emergencies [italics added]" (121).

It is hardly surprising, in view of Hawkes's grim writing and in view of the milieu of this book, that the hero of the Old West is born of a corpse and becomes a cripple, senile, and unsexual, and that the Fisher King who delivers the West's own version of a god (a rodeo hero) gives up delivering (disavows emergences, "emergencies") and becomes an "old obstetrical wizard who now brought forth no young" (123). The image, given in terms of a wriggling fish, is important for the waste land level of myth; and, considering these same figures—the impotent old king, the medicine man or Fisher King who has lost his powers, the weeping woman, and the others—the birth of Harry Bohn may, as well, comment on the Christian level of myth: we may see how man has been brought under the most horrible (not glorious) of conditions into a dying world by a God who then surrendered His powers and wandered the earth. God has turned wanderer in redemption for having created the earth and its "first man" as foully as He did.

As the Red Devils ride faster and faster across the countryside, Leech watches the Sheriff load with guns and ammunition a truck that already contains a cow, in preparation for pursuit of the devils. Leech follows the truck in his medicine man's wagon, while Bohn, Luke, Camper, and the Finn leap from the side of the road and climb aboard—why and how they are there, and no longer fishing, is not explained. What is significant about their action is that they crowd the cow against the walls of the truck and hold on to her neck. Bohn watches her "hold her bush up uselessly for love or rain" (128)—the two qualities this waste land so desperately needs. The cow, for Hawkes—as is evident in *Second Skin*—is almost always a figure of gentleness, mercy, and innocence. And, when Bohn commands Camper to sacrifice the cow, hurl it from the truck for the sake of greater speed on the trip to violence, we are struck with the waste land people's abandonment of innocence. Cap Leech sees the cow fly from the truck: "The calf lay on her side in the air, about to crash, pink spots spun on the red hide and a gentle whistling loomed over the wagon. She disappeared. Then Leech looked down and there on her back in the road she sprawled with milk rolled jaws, albino eyes in wrinkled pads, and a clean crack splitting the amorphous skull that struck; nothing more ugly than the placid mask—its mouth roared wide enough to eat meat—of a shocked cow twisting upwards in the moonlight" (129).

If Leech is the Fisher King, the bringer-of-life to this waste land's denizens, he sees, certainly, an enactment of the evil he has delivered. The gentle cow is for a moment carnivorous-seeming; nature is perverted.

Then back again to Luke: he is fishing once more, or, perhaps, he is seen fishing before he joins the Sheriff's party. Caught in a rainstorm, he feels that he will never be dry: "Some vast spider lay on its back with a shellful of warm fluid, sleeping through the rain of an afternoon" (131). He notes that "Across the western body of water not a fire burned" (130). The overwhelming rainstorm (its effects exemplified through the bizarre spider image) and the absence of fire in the face of water is a reversal of the first 130 pages of the novel. Suddenly, all is water, the omen and result of the water-god's birth, the source of fertility for the waste land. We are told, then, that everything that has prevailed now has a chance to be changed. Moreover, in the context of so much biblical imagery, there is the promise of a cleansing Flood.

Luke does not find life. The animal imagery in the following passage is impressive, as is the irony of what Luke does fish up when we expect him to fish up life.

> The white line tugged the bending pole and he began to draw it in, a long cord from the whale's belly. . . . He lifted the huckleberry pole and there, biting the hook, swung the heavy body of a baby that had been dropped, searched for, and lost in the flood. The eyes slept on either side of the fish line and a point of the barb protruded near the nose stopped with silt. It

turned slowly around and around on the end of the wet string that cut in half its forehead. . . . The white stomach hung full with all it had swallowed.

God's naked child lay under Luke's fingers on the spread poncho, as on his knees and up to his thighs in the river, he loosed the hook, forcing his hand to touch the half-made face. His hook cracked through the membrane of the palate; he touched cold scales on the neck. (132)

References to a whale's belly, and to the setting off of an infant alone in the stream, recall the Jonah and Moses episodes of the Bible. Certainly the whale was, to Old Testament Hebrews, a holy fish; and, as certainly, it is thought by some contemporary readers of the Bible, the finding of Moses in the Nile is analogous to the fishing-up of the god-in-the-waters.

More important, however, is the fact that Luke fishes up death, even in the flood of rain that would, for the waste land, be life-giving. There is a finality about this moment in the novel: there is no hope. Following the waste land motif, it is obvious that there would be no hope. If the old king who dies with the coming of autumn, the barren period, is resurrected with the rising waters in the form of a new king, fertility returns to the land. The old king, Mulge, does not rise up as the new king; no new life comes. The new king, the child, is dead. There is only death, and the waste land does not flower. The power and import of this moment in the book is carried in the image of the child which is rendered, in turn, through references to fishing and "scales" as an animal image. The image embodies the greatest mammal and a small fishlike creature. In Hawkes's world, ontogeny does not recapitulate phylogeny; instead, the passage of the baby through evolutionary stages is perverted, the human level is not achieved, and death is spawned.

Luke looks at Bohn's disfigured mouth and "thought of that slim and vertical mouth as carrying a hook, barbs lodged in the roof years before." It is almost as if, through animal imagery, Hawkes is creating Bohn not only as objectification of the waste land's plight, but as emblem too of the condition of the king who, resurrected, might save the land. At the same time, Bohn laughs

The Beetle Leg

harshly and tells Finn, "'You ain't going to be buried, Finn, you hear? You're going to drown'" (134). Life-giving water suddenly takes on an ominous quality, just as it did when the dam was made, and in order to control their environment the people of the waste land flooded a valley containing hundreds of homes and, incidentally, drowned a baby. The action of promoting fertility was murderous. The attempt to control the elements defeated the resurrection of the god by killing the child who was to be the new god. In effect, the waste landers commited suicide.

Close on Bohn's warning, Cap Leech, Luke, and Camper venture out on the water in a rowboat. Camper, in this fearful scene, is still convinced that he is merely going fishing. But Luke is still searching for the corpse of Mulge, rising from the waters. And Cap Leech goes because, when he sees Leech, Luke calls him "Pa" (135) as if to affirm that both levels of myth are now one and that the Fisher King is God the Father. To the accompaniment of animal images—"the small boat was like the hollowed body of a bird. Its keel was a breastbone hung over with dry calking" (135)—the three, like three magi, set out, Bohn on the shore calling, "'Watch out, Lampson . . . watch out for him!'" (139) as if, because of the condition in which Leech set him on earth, Bohn knows the damage Leech can cause.

The boat—"the capsized shell of an insect" (139)—moves out, and the three soon come upon clear water where they can see down to a house that was flooded when the dam was built. It is the past which Leech and Luke can see, a vision of Eden that has been lost or that is in the process of being lost forever. Leech thinks, "the first man had died in Eden, they pronounced him dead. And now, with brightening eye, he found himself sitting in the middle of the washed-out garden's open hearth" (140). He turns to Luke and, almost in admission of his sins of Godliness, calls Luke "'Boy'" (141).

Leech, on returning to Luke's house, sees an old cock in the barn—"with one stroke, a cupping of the wan hand, he could withdraw the rooster's coiled meld while it died vertically on the wall. He was the dismantler of everything that flew or walked or burrowed at the base of a tree—he could not stand peacefully in the barnyard accepting his eviction by the chicken" (152)—and his thoughts of it reveal him, finally, as the god who made the waste land, the Fisher King who cannot draw forth the god-in-the-waters. He—doctor, medicine man—is a destroyer. God murders.

And then comes the Old West showdown—Red Devils (now also seen as parodies of stereotypical American Indians) against the defending townsfolk. The townsfolk are inhabitants of the waste land, the land forgotten by God and then visited by Him (but still not, as seen from the incident of the cock, to be cured by him); they are the inhabitants of the Old West that is imitation of its own myth. Their land is Paradise Lost and The New World, America.

Just before the crusaders depart in their "mechanical mule" that feels "hoof by hoof for the running scent," Lou pleads with Camper to " 'Take me out of here' " (154). Lou is the only person in Mistletoe who wears a cross, and she can no longer abide what the waste land is or what it is about to become.

The pursuit is given in animal terms: "Haunch up, falling haunch, they nuzzled the beating bush, silent again as the suckless engine geegawed cautiously into the hollow: that intense silence of set jaw and frown, waiting to pick up the scratching of a bird's ear. Strain, and they perspired, three abreast on the front seat, lips tasting the far-off fur" (155–56). And in animal terms is given the confrontation of the Red Devils by the waste landers: "From the parapet of the truck a tinkling cloud of shot landed among the vandal herd . . . one motorcycle, as its rider fled, turned to flame under the little seat, reared, contorted into a snake embrace, and fell writhing in fire." The snake image is reminiscent of that drawn by Hawkes when Camper was attacked by snakes on his journey into the waste land. And the animality of the Red Devils is further suggested by their falling, waving, "jointless arms" (157).

Luke stares at the barrels of his shotgun and slowly brings them toward his face. Saying, " 'This is for one. And this is for another' " as he loads the gun—he perhaps refers to the two dead gods, or the two lost emblems of paradise: the farm under water,

The Beetle Leg

and Mistletoe lost in a cloud of scapegoat murder—Luke squeezes off the triggers and feels, at the last, the "double dinosaurian footfall" (158) of the twin bores. Luke dies in sad imitation of Oedipus, tearing out one, then the other, eye. He is this parodistic tragedy's hero who finally sees what the gods (or God) drove him to.

The devils may be invading devils surging into a paradise. But it is more likely that they are some manifestation of what plagues the paradise. As the waste landers purge Mistletoe of the devils, they also exact revenge on these scapegoats for the failure of the myths that might, had they been enacted, have sustained the waste landers. Finally, the people of the waste land are killing themselves, just as Luke commits suicide and just as the building of the dam was, in terms of hoped-for salvation through the water-god, an act of suicide. These people are murdering a part of life because all of life is intolerable.

The penultimate passage of the novel is Hawkes's ironic knotting of the strands of Old West myth that have run through the book. He dispels the myth for once and for all:

> And suddenly, from the isolated battering truck, shrill and buoyant . . . there came that cool baying of the rising head, the call to kill, louder and singsong, faintly human after the flight of Devils, the nasal elated sounds of the cowboy's western bark.
> Yip, yip, yip, (158)

The dogs that pursued the devils earlier in the book, and that were always associated with them, are now seen to be an extension of the people of Mistletoe themselves. And the call of a wild dog, that stereotypical accompaniment to all cowboy myth, is now seen to be the savage call of the cowboy himself—"faintly human."

Thus, paradise is violated in the name of its defense. The worshipper of the Creator of Eden, Luke, has surrendered hope of salvation. We are treated to the notion that we are witnesses here to the cleansing of heaven, but this purging is far different from Milton's: it is characterized by savagery and the failure of the theological system, not its triumph and majesty.

The final passage of the book, called "CAP LEECH," follows logically upon the failure of Christian belief described above. Cap—God, the Creator, the Fisher King, bearer of life—has also given up. He starts his journeys once more, as penitent Wandering Jew—or as Satan on his search for the new Paradise of man: "*One town further then: last seen by a river peering upward into his lumpy jaws. Take me there*" (159).

Thus, all myth seems perverted, all systems seem to have failed: God is Satan, Eden is heaven become hell, hope is vanished, man—made in God's image—sings the final animal notes of this symphony of joylessness: "Yip, yip, yip."

The Beetle Leg is a rendition of the failure of three myths, each operative on the other, each existing comfortably, on Hawkes's pages, at least, with the other. Fertility rituals and Christian belief, as well as what is perhaps a peculiarly American mythology, that of the cowboy, are each shown to be powerless in the face of man and before the moods of God or the gods.

Certainly, Hawkes pursued the idea of fertility and its absence in *Charivari*. But he did so, as was seen with regard to the style of *The Cannibal*, without the concentration or density of imagery that characterizes the latter novel. There can be no question that animal imagery plays a major narrative- and mood-establishing role in all of the novels examined thus far; but there can be no question either that, of them all, *The Beetle Leg* has the densest imagery, the densest animal imagery, and the densest animal imagery which advances the themes of sterility and hopelessness.

While the animal imagery cavorts through all the novels, it tends to decrease as the human-animal, animal-human metaphor increases in concentration. This is not to say that background imagery is thin or lacking in *The Beetle Leg*; it is present and its presence is felt. But the book does not depend on it so much for its effect in the way that *Charivari* did. For, early in *The Beetle Leg*, the Red Devils *are* dogs, do travel in a pack, are closely

The Beetle Leg

associated with deadly snakes; the waste landers *are* intimately involved with water and fish—and there is little need for reinforcement of these facts.

Hawkes's writing grows more poetic with this novel. In none of his works thus far has he employed traditional straightforward narrative techniques. From the outset, he has used interior monologue, a diversity of plot-lines, and a thorough disregard for unities of time, place, and person. He often presents his prose fiction almost as juxtaposed fragments of speech and movement, at least thus far; he presents a *mélange* of people, places, and things—much as does, say, Eliot, in his *Waste Land, Prufrock,* or *Gerontion.* With *The Beetle Leg,* the impulse to many dimensions of thought and action, to more and more metaphor, to small parts resulting only in a climatic whole, but not, in any significant sense, in an illumination of themselves—such impulses are the strongest thus far seen. If such are the impulses to poetic writing, then Hawkes may be thought of as a poetic novelist.

Along with his growing mastery of poetic structure, Hawkes's mastery of the lyrical note has grown as well. While there is little song or grace of line in *Charivari,* there is much in *The Beetle Leg:* the violent euphony of "Haunch up, falling haunch, they nuzzled the beating bush, silent again as the suckless engine geegawed cautiously into the hollow" (155–56); or the graceful analogy of wagon to boat in this passage: "The boards on which they sat, scraped of fodder, might have burst aflame if the sun were caught briefly in the eye of a watch glass. They traveled in three lifeless dories with dead oarlocks and rotted sails; they sang stiffly, managed to hold the reins. They backtracked, chewed the sand and made their way over weary, salty miles to see one woman their own age brought to bed" (82).

There is, too, a lyricism of terror in this novel. Hawkes increasingly injects it into his savage animal images, making men beasts or beasts men. He no longer needs to ram with force the awfulness of that which he metaphorically makes beast; he now can render beastliness with the sound and rhythms of his words as well as with their sense: "He crawled jerkily across the gumwood floor, stethoscope pressed upon the shell of a beetle sweeping hurriedly its wire legs" (122–23).

If we can conclude that the animal images are effective, the lyricism achieved, the ideas engaging, we must also conclude that the characters of *The Beetle Leg* almost do not exist at all as people. As components of a treatment of myth, they are superior to those in *Charivari*, a novel that offers much detail about characters but little rendition of them. Here, for certain, ideas are enfleshed; in the first novel they were not. But, still, the enfleshment does not extend too far. Luke is taciturn, and we believe that there is a Luke; Ma bemoans the past, her losses, and we believe that she does so. But we do not know much more about them.

There is an ideational quality to this multi-myth novel that dominates the humanity of Hawkes's characters. Characters are subservient to narrative moments; they do what the point or the intellectual abstraction of each moment dictates they should in order to bring the abstraction of that moment home to the reader. They are not developed as people; they do not progress in their development while we observe them; they act as if to prove the truth of an equation.

In other words, the characters are present as people, but as two-dimensional people. When so much animal metaphor is employed, one might well expect a quality of beast-fable to take over, and that is what happens. We see the characters in much the same way as Snopes, the child, observes his father in Faulkner's "Barn Burning": "he could see his father against the stars but without face or depth—a shape black, flat, and bloodless as though cut from tin in the iron folds of the frockcoat which had not been made for him, the voice harsh like tin and without heat like tin."[10] The father here is monstrous—and so are Hawkes's cowboys and his American West. All myths are peopled by the black, flat, and bloodless monsters of our deepest imaginings, Hawkes seems to say. And one can see perhaps that *The Beetle Leg*, if not populated with "real people," is swarming with what we—readers, dwellers in our mythologies' dreams—create. Our myths reflect us. *The Beetle Leg* reflects our distorted creations, hence ourselves: *we* are its characters.

4 The Goose on the Grave

In *The Owl*, one of the two short novels in *The Goose on the Grave*, the reader is hurled into the Italianate Sasso Fetore, drainage-seeping land dominated mercilessly by Il Gufo, the owl, who is supreme in the area as its hangman. He heads an order that seems akin to that of Catholic monks but which has only one purpose: to punish by death. There are no young men for the women of Sasso Fetore to marry, and so the land is populated with hopeful young women, growing older, and their distressed old parents who despair of their children's matrimony. Only Il Gufo, the narrator, is eligible—along with his male prisoner, for whom the marriage-hungry parents plead so that, his life saved, he may marry a local daughter—and Il Gufo scorns matrimony. And so Sasso Fetore is dying; there is no question that their number will dwindle to nothing. Hawkes quickly shows that, in terms of either Christian worship or the ethics of Christianity, the land is dying too. In this grim world of relative inactivity and absolute cold-heartedness on Il Gufo's part we witness the death of an innocent. That is all that takes place in *The Owl*.

Much the same is true of *The Goose on the Grave*, the second novel in the book. An apparent innocent, Adeppi, is deprived of his mother by priests, who steal her away. Given over from a drunk homosexual to a most heterosexual peasant woman, to the priests who stole his mother, to the cold earth and the memory of the dead, the child is degraded in what is apparently the Italy of the Second World War's end. He loses his innocence and, himself, becomes accessory to murder.

Little by way of plot or character delineation is given. There is much atmosphere, much generation of a sense of place, though that place is unidentifiable whether called Italy or not. Both very surrealistic novellas read as if Hawkes, dissatisfied with his novelistic reactions to war and rapacity in *The Cannibal*, with inhumanity and dying countrysides in *Charivari* and *The Beetle Leg*, resorted to two fragmentary and dislocated fables in order to spit out the butt-ends of his early concerns.

Surely both novels contain what we have, by now, come to expect from Hawkes: a sense of cold examination and scornful scrutiny, a narrative focus that does not reveal the consistent viewpoint encountered in more traditional novelists, a warping of time, and an abundance of animal imagery. *The Owl* and *The Goose on the Grave* may, in fact, strike the reader as the logical results of Hawkes's progressively greater use of animal images in the background and in central metaphors as tools for the telling of his tales.

The Owl

Hawkes thrusts the reader into the dark world of the owl who rejects pleas from the fathers of Sasso Fetore that "the prisoner," sentenced to death, be set free so that he may marry one of the community's daughters. As he expresses his disapproval of the idea the owl stands alongside a statue of Mary; to him, she is not the Virgin, only "the tall lady at my side."[1] He says of the statue, "though I was named Il Gufo, the owl, I was as tall as she" (1). It is the relationship of Il Gufo and "the tall lady," and the relationship of the people of Sasso Fetore and the prisoner, locked in the hangman's high and darkened fortress, that create the tensions which involve us in this book—for as long, at least, as those relationships are focused upon by the aloof hangman-narrator.

Il Gufo's disdain for Mary, in an Italian land, looms large. His power over those who once worshipped only Mary is tantamount to making the land of Mariology a dystopia, a place where evil has perfect reign and where mercy is lost. Il Gufo's ability to withhold marriage in the land given to celebrating the eternal

The Goose on the Grave

Mother strengthens our perception that a dividing line between the religion of love and the order of killing is drawn by Hawkes from the outset. Il Gufo is the narrator, and, as was the case in *The Cannibal*, the horror of evil is made doubly enormous because the narrator, himself an actor of evil, narrates evil events with calmness and even admiration. But Hawkes does not show a conflict between two impulses or doctrines; he shows, rather, merely how things are: briefly, the nature of pulsating experience in and of itself—not in opposition to other impulses or conditions so much as in juxtaposition with them.

Il Gufo tells of his barren land, its corpses of soldiers, its ruins. He relates much of his country in terms of animals, referring to "white skeletons of horses" and "the rook's nests that littered the golden vertical cuts of the cliff" (3). He tells much of himself, as well, and in so doing creates one of Hawkes's most elaborate and extended animal metaphors: a narrator of beastly events in a beast-infested land who speaks in a rhetoric larded with animal figures and who is himself an owl.

Il Gufo tells us of his post, based on "a long firm line of rule" (3), thus creating the impression that the rule of the hangman is as long as that of the Church, that there is nothing new here, only a deathly, somehow holy, tradition:

> By a decree dating to the Council of Bishops and Gaolers, the heart of the hangman's escutcheon burst and became an owl: with wisdom, horns and field-rodent half-destroyed, hardly visible under the talons. The bird, the scholar with his hunger clamped exactingly to the rudimental prey, peered from his shield. The hangmen, as they came down the inviolable line, sat or hooked the demanding winged beasts upon their necks and shoulders, lordly claws digging into lordly men. . . .
> . . . he kept a mute, tenacious, arbitrary peace. . . . His eyes, and the trembling in short armour feathers, the beak that when sated remained locked, were for the cold law and sermon. . . . To some he brought this surety of judgment and the vision, challenging, of the broken neck. I am speaking of myself, Il Gufo. (3–4)

The tradition is cold and merciless. So is Il Gufo—the vision of a broken neck is "challenging"—as he speaks of it. It is as if the carnivorousness of the tradition is seated on a foundation of considerable dimension and honor, as if the "cold law" were born of shields, escutcheons, and chivalry as was the opposite kind of law of, say, the Magna Charta born of the medieval need for political order.

In speaking of his tradition, Il Gufo makes much of the "pet" or, at least captive, owl that accompanies him in his work. That animal is merciless too. As is evident now and as will be more evident later, the animal-owl is objectification of the hangman-owl; they are alteregos, one reflects the qualities of the other. Thus, Il Gufo attributes the judgmental qualities of a hangman to the animal-owl and, in his statement "I am speaking of myself," the feral instincts of the animal-owl to himself. One creature is metaphor for the other; each reveals the other in the course of the novel. And both sum up the anti-Christian elements that make Sasso Fetore a place of violence, un-fertility, and death. It is not unreasonable to wonder how much further Hawkes can go in his use of animals as reflection of people and of people as reflection of animals. It is startling and satisfying that, in his latter novels, he does go further, and to good effect.

The unmarried women of Sasso Fetore are called "mistresses of bridal chests filled with seven years' accumulation of lace and white bodices," victims, despite the long line of hangmen, of a seven-year plague, perhaps. Further, "the girls were not merely virginal, those unseen propagated a sense of timelessness of denial, of death hung rocking around and around on the broken-spoked wheel atop a pole" (5). This image of a perverted May Pole, indicative of an imperfect cycle or pattern, is discussed by Il Gufo more revealingly later on in the book. For now it suffices that the wheel atop its pole strikes a thematic chord: the "timelessness of denial" that is a motif of the world of the hangman.

Signor Barabo (reminiscent, perhaps, of Barabas) wants his daughter, Antonina, to be married. Barabo, called by the hangman a "thin fox" (8), daily surveys the landscape for signs of hope for marriage, believing that each day he sees a dead fox signifies a further postponement of matrimony. Significantly, Il

The Goose on the Grave

Gufo, surveying his land from high in his fortress (or roost), sends his servant Pucento to cut the tails from dead foxes, for no apparent reason; Il Gufo, then, participates in a ceremony of non-marriage and further indicts himself as part of the unfertile plague on the land.

Barabo, a fox who hopes for foxlessness, or for the marriage that foxes seem to militate against, carries aphrodisiacs and charms to further the possibilities for marriage. He appears to be a walking contradiction, a summary of the locked impulse in life that is the hangman's domain. Hawkes renders this fact more graphic, and in animal terms, when he describes Barabo, whose "heart, consciousness, and ambition ended in an appendage that housed the kidney and overhung his groin like a tapir's snout—blind sack he lightly rubbed while discoursing and guardedly measuring the passers-by. . . . Outside he was a peasant, inside a fish whose concealed pouches could inflate to considerable size until he groaned in his own monstrous dimensions" (9). Barabo's disease, his burden, is ironical in that its urinogenital nature appears to be proof positive of the hopelessness of his wishes for sexuality and of Sasso Fetore in general.

Unsurprisingly, at this point of the novel, nothing has happened. The owl imperiously watches from his roost (listening to the hoot of what he calls the "parochial" owl) the land he controls. He notes the condition of that land, exposes the ruined wheel (the cycle of life and death in Sasso Fetore is obviously a ruined wheel, a cycle gone imperfect as death has come to dominate life) for what it is—a water wheel that is no longer fed by water. As shown in *The Beetle Leg*, where there is no water there is death. And, in addition, Il Gufo remarks the proximity of Sasso Fetore's forests, "barbed and stripped to order" (12), to the "Donna" or Madonna—the old order next to the brutally controlled new.

There is a surfeit of background imagery in the hangman's exposition: "the death of a prized boar"; a donkey; dead ravens and cats; "wolves at the dugs"; the hangman's donkey with bells tinkling "unnaturally at the tips of his long white ears." Il Gufo speaks about the town prefect, whose work takes him through piles of dung, animal corpses, and water closets and into "foundations hunting for ripened curd" (12). This is the ruler of great power who, in this land's pecking order, is reduced to the level of garbage feeder and jackal, serving a ruler whose job is to kill.

Just as the hangman has his owl, so the prefect (perhaps the temporal ruler if the hangman is a perversely religious leader, supplanter of the Madonna) has his metaphorical birds—four geese. Hunting small animals and insects, picking over garbage in a "tense hungry step," "the four of them, Sasso Fetore's flock, never emitted the shrill crabbing sounds of their species but appeared on the steep slippery cobblestones in silence, checking themselves, and it was with precision, quickly, that they pecked forward the snowy Netherlandish throats like serpents" (12–13).

The religious leader and his metaphoric bird do their hunting by killing or controlling impulses to life. The lay leader and his ominously silent, snakelike, metaphorical birds rut through offal and peck on the sewage-washed stones of Sasso Fetore. In creating the antipodal systems of man and bird, Hawkes goes far toward creating animal-human combinations that might rightly belong in a bestiary of traditionally correct nature. That is, he appears to be using animals as almost allegorical figures instead of simply as reflectors of human qualities.

Il Gufo's narrative—and one might, at this point, ask "Of what?"—returns us to the Madonna. Standing in evening at the base of the statue, Il Gufo looks up toward the cliff-city and thinks of garrets "filled with ransacked portraits of dignitaries and half-eaten goose" (16). He thinks of wives who, in the unsexual, unvital city, warm their wedding bands only by holding them in their armpits at night in bed. And he concludes that "politically, historically, Sasso Fetore was an eternal Sabbath" (17).

As if to prove that God is at rest, is away, Il Gufo—with a chilling lack of concern—strikes a flame at the base of the white statue of the Madonna and muses upon her:

> Surely the Donna made the scaffold majestic. Week after week of Sabbaths attested to this, when the regimen set down for the citizens was not perfectly autonomous and in the blue night some worshipped object was accountable to the spirit, or the

spirit for a moment was awed in some simple fashion. . . . The character and the code, right upon right, crashed into the pale heart when the culprit hanged, her prayers for him so soft as hardly to be heard. She saved none—salvation was not her purpose—yet, like the virgins, stood off with low head and waited for movement from him bound on the gibbet. Her statue was placed before the cave near the forest and owl's tree. (17)

Analytically, unemotionally, the hangman notes the Madonna's lack of efficacy. She is, as can be seen from her proximity to the scaffold, for much the same purpose: not salvation but the generation of awe. Consequently, the scaffold is the stronger mover of the spirit because it works better. As for the statue, it meets "the spirit of black and white in the peasant" (17) and satisfies the need for understanding and communion with controlling powers, while the scaffold gets on with the arcane but essential job to be done. Located in the domain of the owl, the statue is impuissant so far as the owl, and most of the peasants, are concerned.

The hangman speaks of setting the prisoner's death for the day after Pentecost. He proudly "set in motion the proceedings that drew ledgers from their vaults and inkpots to the oak table, pushing the rafters, the spokes, the axle cold and thick with bear grease, touching these ancient parts in the law's carriage house" (20). Again the wheel-figure appears: the cycle of life and death creaks in Sasso Fetore, or is halted; it moves with efficiency only when Il Gufo decides that it is time to take a life. The reader concludes that, if there is really a god for Sasso Fetore, it is the predatory beast called the owl. Hawkes makes a bizarre people's god an owl—hunter, coldly-staring killer. He has pushed animal metaphor to its extreme.

When Il Gufo hints that we are to see his mysterious prisoner, we encounter much animal background imagery again: water runs "from under the bristling swine"; a "foreign crow" watches for refuse; the owl spits and picks at his feathers; rooks cower in their nests; children run, their feet sounding "like a monkey clapping his hands"; "the sound of dogs leaping with torches in their jaws"; far-off women who "beat their loaves upon an oxen's haunch"; the ganders of the village march between the prefect and his prisoner (22–27).

Then a symbolic encounter takes place between the hangman and the statue of the Madonna: "The Donna stood before the cave, an idol whose nights were spent with a few small deer and speechless animals. The donkey turned a sharp foot, the lumbering saddle creaked, and even this far I saw the defamation, the Donna's face smeared with blood. I galloped. As I passed her I raised my boot and, ramming her chest, dislodged her so that she fell and rolled upon the crackle of the clearing. . . . the owl . . . beat his wings (37).

An all-powerful representative of what is virtually an inverted religious order—dedicated to death instead of grace—sees the Madonna as "an idol" ignored by all but animals. The animals are gentle deer—medieval Christ symbols—and "speechless animals": metaphoric creatures again, who reflect on the "idol" to show that it also is too gentle to survive (as was Christ) and speechless, incomunicative through works or results—useless. Il Gufo topples the statue, and his owl, his constant metaphor, beats his wings.

If God is not dead in Sasso Fetore, certainly representation and worship of Him are. Death's viceroy is in the saddle, and this supremacy is made clear as the reader progresses toward the prisoner through a rhetorical wall made of animal images. The wall serves not only to create a kind of narrative tension—we want to see the prisoner, for his nature tends to define that of his captor—but to hammer home the bestiality of Sasso Fetore and its animal religiosity.

Il Gufo dines with his powerful council of twelve men. There are thirteen fish at the dinner: "The fish was the fare of all the verdicts delivered and with its complicity of bone and deathly metallic flesh, it had the character of a set jaw and seal ring" (40). This food "of no sweetness, small pleasure" (41) brings to mind the holiness of fish so frequently alluded to and employed by Hawkes in *The Beetle Leg*. This is the dinner at which it is announced that the prisoner will die on the next day; this is the Pentecostal dinner. The irony of a "holy" fish eaten for Pentecost by thirteen men is unmistakable. This parody of the Last Supper has the earmarks of a black mass.[2]

Hawkes pays much attention to the ritualistic, religiously perverted eating of a "holy" supper. Then, Barabo having fruitlessly pleaded that the prisoner be pardoned (to marry his daughter), the owl inspects his prisoner. He wears a uniform, carries maps and printed pleas for mercy in the event of capture, and is ill; we know little more than that. Il Gufo sees him "sacrificing his last days to conversations with insects, growing a beard and fasting without recognizing hunger" (54). He makes his prisoner, thus, more of an animal than a man. He steps to examine him more closely: "That one human might inspect another, I peered at him and was aware of the declarations and betrothals within him. But, as he raised and bent his arms, I saw only the white tips of his elbows protruding from the sleeves in the coat. . . . He was ragged! I would not remember him for long. . . . And then I shouted at him: 'What is your name, *immediatemente*' Your name. . . .' He did not answer, and we left him in the darkness" (55).

Il Gufo does not see the prisoner as one human being might see another. He sees the piteousness of the prisoner's condition in a pejorative way: the prisoner is a ragged, unmemorable creature —not a living man who will be hanged. Il Gufo is not a human being; he is a beast. His behavior with the prisoner should be compared to that with his owl, a moment later, in his apartments. The owl is ruffled and restive: "But I wet and smoothed the feathers under the triangle of his beak with my tongue and he regained himself, once more folded into his nocturnal shape, and only the eyes did not relent. I gave him a large rat and slept near him the night" (56). Nathanael West's influence on Hawkes is evident here, as seen in the passage from *The Day of the Locust* in the early pages of the Introduction.

Before the execution of the prisoner, a festival takes place in the town. It is as metaphorical a festival as one could expect to encounter, though in the context of Hawkes's writings it comes as little of a surprise. Pucento, Il Gufo's servant, leads a trained dog to the center of the town square. Keeping a leash taut between them, Pucento and the dog dance: "First the two completed a square, then a circle, then the dog twisted and arched its back.... The dog stopped. As bidden, its front paws came to rest lightly upon Pucento's back on each side of the neck. Thus they remained rigidly, heads damp, white, lifted into the sun" (65).

Here the animalistic and absolutely unfertile history and future of Sasso Fetore is revealed, and here is the nature of Il Gufo's reign. Dog and man become equal partners in their dance: "he and the dog maneuvered together and the one obeyed the other" (63). And not only are they equals; man and dog are mates. The dog comes to rest (as "bidden," as he was trained to do) in the mating position at Pucento's back; this barren transfusion, done in mime, makes man an unnatural dog, a dehumanized creature with no biological future.

It is from death in this land that the prisoner seeks to escape. He flees his cell and climbs to the highest ledge of Il Gufo's fortress. Il Gufo, below, sees him: "The prisoner was covered with great feathers, pin feathers and flat feathers.... The wings hung down as arms and even below the hands, swaying, and were fastened across his shoulders. He crouched heavily, but his waxen feathers, his flying skein billowed angrily in the wind. His head stuck over with red wax turned loftily" (69). In a matter-of-fact tone Il Gufo describes how the prisoner flees: "I saw him lastly fly defiantly through the smoke of Monco's deserted fire and into the red sun that sank and drew him down over the edge of the earth" (71).

So we have another man rendered beast. In an environment of predatory birds, it is appropriate that the prisoner, the owl's prey, becomes a bird himself. But the fleeing bird also becomes predator. For evidence of his landing is revealed to the town through its murdered ganders: the ferocious watchmen of the area are found with their necks wrung. The man fleeing from a bird-murderer becomes, himself, a bird and murderer. And the fact should not be overlooked that there is something like Icarus in the prisoner's ascent and decline: man's hopeful, romantic spirit—the spirit of artificer, art, escape from the mundane—brought back to earth and to murder.[3] In Sasso Fetore there is no hope.

The prisoner is found, his wings are burned. Hawkes again turns to understated writing to perpetrate a sense of horror: "Some days later—the prisoner was still suspended on the hooks—the skin was drawn away from his belly in one piece and stretched across a drum that was beaten through the streets while they stopped work and listened" (81).

Pentecost is past. The dinner eaten by the owl and his unholy henchmen was that meal traditionally held to celebrate the descent of Christ's spirit to man. If symbolic importance is attached to the prisoner's flight and descent in the context of this Pentecostal period, he may be seen as someone Christlike in the world of Sasso Fetore. He may be seen attempting to escape his fate of descending to the people of the city. He may be seen, when he does descend, coming to his death at the hands of that which man's spirit has permitted to replace the Church. If he is Christlike, the prisoner's descent is at the least ironic, for Pentecost is past and spring is present. Spring comes, here with death instead of rebirth, and Il Gufo offers a bestial hymn to it: "The millet grew ripe and blood apples were left in the hangman's piazza. A stone of bread was left also. Those in the cafe waited and made no move to kill the lizards that came from their caves in the fireplace . . . the rooks flattened themselves in their nests on the cliffs. The fox came into the streets but was not noticed . . . the monarchial owl stared about the proximity of the execution. The prefect buried the ganders" (82).

In the hymn are the fox, symbol of no fertility in the offing, and a stone of bread, blood apples—proximations of the wine and wafer that normally celebrate Christ's transubstantiation but which here serve as notice of His death in spring.

Then the prisoner is killed. The trap door in the "tall lady," Sasso Fetore's replacement for the Madonna, opens and the prisoner is dead. At the moment of death Il Gufo proclaims: "And then there was the air damp and cold and the owl exerting himself into flight, beating through the top branches now, shutting his eyes and crashing through the twigs to the dripping hole in the trunk, settling himself and sitting inside the bark for summers and winters, and he stayed thus, peering out of the warmth, the tenure of silent feathers in a cold tree" (89).

"Tenure of silent feathers in a cold tree" is evocative of lines in T. S. Eliot's *Gerontion:* "an old man in a dry month," or "Thoughts of a dry brain in a dry season."[4] It is not only the rhythm, or the adjective-noun, adjective-noun progression, that evokes Eliot; it is the creation of a mood of barrenness, hopelessness, and religious failure that corresponds between Hawkes and Eliot. For Il Gufo's statement is the end of a hymn of sterility sung to the tune of civilization's decline at its own unmerciful hand. Not only have the hangman and his metaphorical owl supplanted religion in Sasso Fetore; they have taken on its form and mode for purposes of murder and power wielded for its own, traditional, sake. Sasso Fetore is, indeed, a dystopia, and this disjointed and difficult novel of juxtaposed horrors and sacrilege, done largely in animal terms, is a bitter and anti-utopian tract.

The Goose on the Grave

If an overriding sense of death and futility marks *The Owl,* it is more apparent in *The Goose on the Grave,* a novel of disorder and victimization.

The novel opens with three priests on white donkeys riding silently down to an Italian city. Their approach is heralded with animal imagery: "Under the sign of the winged cock chopped in relief from the door arch, butting its broken stone-tip out of antiquity, the dismounted priests made their own sign" (95). And then there is the "hindward spectacle of meeting dogs," which witness the unspeaking seizure of the mother of Adeppi, the little boy who is "one of Italy's covey of fragile doves." Wordlessly the priests take Adeppi's mother back through the mountains—to a fate not discovered until the novel has almost run its course—and silently Adeppi, alone, wakes and runs out to the town's

The Goose on the Grave

marketplace where he sees the wartime vista: "Ovens and operating benches merged beyond lake-blue plaster walls" (96). Hawkes emphasizes this merger throughout the novel, as if history or Hawkes's vision of horrid repetitions were creating the injured and maimed with the routine, simplicity, and productiveness with which bread is baked. One must think of modern Europe emerging from its noble antiquity—or a past *envisioned* as noble—to become a Europe of murderings and people burned in gas ovens: systematic, measured murder. The novel is a recipe for the West's decline.

This is the milieu in which the orphaned Adeppi (his father is never mentioned), a child known among bakers and injured veterans as a songbird, meets the wounded Nino and Edouard, who is a homosexual hand-me-down from the fringes of European aristocracy. As they speak, as Adeppi sings, as the sound of starving guinea hens drifts through the mingled smell of iodine and hot crusts, there are periodic references in the third-person narrative to the three priests who hide from view and spy on the child and Nino. Because of the constant animal reference, and because of the silent priests, known by us already as inscrutable and powerful, there is an air of menace that wafts through these early pages and that establishes a tone of inexplicable troubledness for the rest of the book.

It is worth noting how quickly Hawkes establishes Adeppi as one of Italy's "fragile doves"; in seven pages, Nino borrows Edouard's guitar, swings Adeppi to his shoulders, and parades before verandas, strumming the guitar while Adeppi sings: "He swayed from the shoulder as a mad bird on a perch" (103). Hawkes again presents a bird-metaphor—a far different bird from Il Gufo, the owl. This is a captured lyricist, a rather stupid and unaware waif who unemotionally and automatically sings on the shoulders of the injured—one of history's awful loaves—and, therefore, on the current of history itself. He is a songbird on the winds of a most terrible time.

Soon after Adeppi is hoisted to Nino's shoulders, he is completely caged. Hawkes narrates this section in the present tense, whereas the early part of the novel has been in the past tense.

It is as if Hawkes seeks to emphasize the immediacy of this capturing, to show clearly that the child's state is one of concern to us. Adeppi sings in a hot small room, surrounded by Edouard and his guitar, Nino, and five women. He has changed—grown "fat, smaller, isolated in a glaze of medieval lyricism, sweating and working at the song." He is a caged bird as he "forces himself to voice those ecstatic melodies to which so many countesses have met and sinned, so many wolfhounds bayed" (104).

Then Nino's wound is healed, and he is to return to battle. Nino leaves the town, Adeppi accompanies him, walking past the stealing priests, past cats crossing a bridge, past a guinea hen darting among piles of manure, past Nino's paramour, "clutching the old guinea hen to her breasts." Nino asks Adeppi to photograph his mistress and, as Adeppi clutches the camera, she hauls her skirt above her waist in order to give Nino sensual remembrance, and the skirt hangs "like parted wings on the dusty air" (112). The animalism here is incontestable.

Adeppi walks away through the silent portion of the nameless city; Nino follows him and encounters the town's Madonna. Although the statue is small, it is burdened with heavy painted cloaks and sashes and is portrayed as still pregnant. Like the Madonna of *The Owl*, she is powerless: covered as she is, and still undelivered of the Christ Child, she represents the inability of the bestial inhabitants of this novel to realize the Holy Mystery, to transcend the animal mundanity of their world.

With Nino gone, Adeppi returns to his other protector, Edouard, who is defined, promptly, in terms of animals. He calls himself, in a crowded cafe, "'Edouard, the cat. . . . I have a tail' " (115). He drinks beneath a portrait of Siamese cats, amid the smells of sardines he has given to every fellow-drinker, and "the smell of cat hairs on the wood" (116). And then there is this hint of death in the strange land: "The vermouth smelled of cold skin" (117). It is a shocking sentence, equating pleasant drink with the flesh of corpses, quietly merging the idea of consumption of flesh with social pleasure. In a milieu such as this, with homosexual encounters alternately pleasing and disturbing Edouard, Adeppi is made, again, to sing in his captivity. A trained bird passed from one owner to another, in an atmosphere of carnivorousness, Adeppi begins to learn survival.

The narrative shifts to Edouard. Having defined him in terms of cats, it now illustrates him in terms of horses. Hawkes shows how important the riding and control of horses has been to Edouard, and how "he introduced himself as a horse trainer, he took his walks where the best of the breed paraded, and grew to know this all-curried and handsomely saddled world of pleasure. . . . The horse was his aristocrat" (123), but he is currently in a decline: "Now there was only the horse fly . . . how the horse flies had shamed him there, finding him so readily, settling upon him with such familiarity" (124). Edouard, who saw Europe as a world of fine horses, and whose pretensions were delineated by horses—who may be for this novel an index of aristocratic decline—is now thoroughly rejected by horses: "Long had he been driven back to the country of flies like blue ticks, thrown back perhaps only hours before the Grand Steeplechase, as neatly as if he had been tossed off into a muddy ditch. He brought with him a pair of opera glasses for the field. . . . The old world took the bit in her teeth and stood still like an ass. He was accustomed now to the toilet in the street and waited for the buzzing to approach, grow loud, and become a sudden irritant feasting with mouth full between his neck and collar" (124–25).

If he is index of the royalty of his world, Edouard may represent to the reader a people that once rode and which is now ridden, a people who have declined from mastery of the horse to agony caused by the parasites of the horse. It is difficult to avoid such socially oriented conclusions when faced with a sentence such as "the old world took the bit in her teeth and stood still like an ass." The idea of a horse's taking the bit in his teeth and racing away is abruptly reversed, as if to say that the old world raced toward progress and then halted; such would be the case if the oblique commentary were about either European war. The final calumny is that the old world, as horse, becomes the lowly ass; nobility is lost as motion is lost, and the failure to act nobly has resulted in thorough loss of station—for Edouard and the world he represents.

HAWKES: A Guide to His Fictions

In a moment of passionate embrace, when Edouard is with a homosexual lover, he recalls a portrait of harem nudes "packed together white and featureless like eels" (128). However, where as it has been relatively clear in what direction Hawkes has manipulated animal metaphors and background imagery in earlier novels, the narrative drift of this short work is quite opaque. Hardly have we seen something of Adeppi's plight and of his new master, Edouard, than we are shifted to Nino, near a "bird-breast blue" ocean (129).

Nino is in a speeding train, sitting opposite a small priest who stares harshly at him, and who summarizes the apparent condition of the land (and of the novel) by saying, suddenly: " 'Secrets. And I suspect no saint to guard your nights' " (130). As if in confession, Nino shouts Adeppi's name, and the padre immediately leaves the compartment and the train, which is now in the station. Although the narration of action seems disjointed at this point, there is a continuity of symbolic concern. The priest, as he passes beneath the soldier's window, lifts his hand covertly, shielding his gesture with a wide sleeve, to make the sign of the cross. Then he continues to the station hut, kicking the dust with his black-pointed boots—the same boots that kicked the ground when Adeppi's mother was stolen. The hiding of the sign of the cross is suggestive of the hidden condition of the Madonna, swaddled in painted clothes. And the "little black-pointed boots" (131) are *leitmotiv* of the menace that was introduced on the first page of the book.

We return to Adeppi, who stands on a bridge and observes a troop of eels that doze beneath. Later, outside the bakery walls, he "listened for the emerging of mice" (133). He observes, then, from Edouard's room, the attempted conscription by force of old Jacopo, a homosexual partner to Edouard—an attempt accompanied by fleas, a whining street dog, and reference to an aqueduct where "a wolf or dog had rubbed his quarters against the Roman watercourse and blurred . . . its inscription." He hears "the sound of rats walking the tunnel on their long way to Rome" (137). Civilization's noble past has gone to the dogs, literally and figuratively.

The Goose on the Grave

And then, walking with Jacopo, who has been released by the conscripting soldiers, Adeppi passes through "the country of solitary animal pens and refuse," past a "cowed pig with a basket in its teeth" (138), to watch the trains pass on the tracks outside the city. As they watch, "two harpies flap uneasily to a haymound" (142). One may be reminded of the train that, in *The Cannibal*, rode through Germany and time toward war, death, and disorder. And one may recall as well "Harpier cries, 'tis time, 'tis time" in *Macbeth* (IV.i.3) in which the reference to harpies is in the context of the witches' animalist chant—a prelude to dissension and disorder in the peaceable kingdom.

The narrative suddenly changes focus, to a Contessa, at her estate, where she ruminates upon Italy's past which she has helped to make. In a small building behind her villa live Arsella, her mother, and Pipistrello; with them is their cow, of whom we learn: "Her horns were hollow. She had turned gray wading across the fields and now lay with back caved as if under blocks of stone, two delicate forelegs doubled beneath her breast in the straw. Several small chests, covered with dung, were stacked around her. Her whole face was swelled about the tongue which grew large, as did her haunches, while she guarded the stucco and statuary of a milkless past." "Arsella herself had the bare corroded legs of the cow. . . . Year in and out the flannelette skirt was open to the winds that caught her above the knees, a skirt which in its weave had become part of the countryside along with the legs that rubbed against the animal in its dirt" (144).

So Hawkes presents here two testimonies to the past, a dumb cow and a cowlike woman (who virtually share the same weak legs) living in a tumbledown house, itself belonging to the past, owned by a woman who lives in the past. The peasant woman's husband, Pipistrello, is blind: "at his wheel, he listened for the shape of the pottery that he turned." In *The Owl* the wheel of time was shattered and moved only when the chief murderer bade it move; here the wheel is turned by a blind man: the conditions of the Italy in which the novel is set—the place of civilization's former heights—are those set loose by the blind. The potter's mother-in-law sits behind him, imitating the noise of the wheel and cursing. "These two, the eyes of Italy, sat to the cow's rear on the other side of the wall . . . waiting for the news of the Contessa's death" (144). The "eyes of Italy" are blind and senile, and these references point to Hawkes's summary of the nature of all of Europe: disabled, unseeing, avaricious, slightly mad, animal, and awaiting the death throes of the age.

Arsella wears a rosary at her waist and her mother wears a hair shirt: "Long ago it had been stitched unevenly up the front and little punishment remained in it. . . . In winter it broke the wind" (145). The disintegration of religious power is again affirmed, and that power is seen as vestigial. Such affirmation, however, does not weaken the menacing nature of Dolce, the priest on the train, or the other priests who, despite vestigial Madonna, rosary, or hair shirt, creep silently to and fro in the book, just under the surface, coming occasionally into view to remind us that they are the silent ones, the stealers of Adeppi's mother. The power exerted by the priests has not been religious; religion itself may here be entirely vestigial in that its "official" practitioners exercise an apparently wholly mundane power. As in *The Owl*, inversion of spiritual concerns is suggested, just as are inversions of all temporal order.

So, too, is all narrative order reversed. For Adeppi is suddenly on the Contessa's villa, inquiring of Arsella's mother why she wears a hair shirt. His movement suggests that he searches for family or any portion of it—and that he fails, always, to achieve it. As Adeppi inquires, and as the woman recoils in horror at his presence, "outside a whelp began to bay, a political signal for inbred dogs and hungry factions" (146).

The howling dogs here are not unlike the dogs of *The Beetle Leg* or of *The Cannibal*, since they signal carnivorousness in a country, a political and spiritual disquiet. But, while Hawkes has heretofore either created dog-metaphors through an accumulation of metaphoric references (a poetic catalog), or concentrated canine metaphor that leaves no question as to object and analog, he here simply *tells* us the nature of the dogs. There is no tension of disturbing details gradually accumulating, no shock experienced at the power of the metaphor (as there was in *The Canni-*

The Goose on the Grave

bal). Instead, the comparison becomes unsurprising simile, a fit figure in the rhetorical context of this section of the novel, but a rather disappointing use of animal imagery when compared with the extended metaphor of Il Gufo-as-owl or, even, Adeppi-as-songbird.

Adeppi, who has fled Arsella's house to sleep on the ground, dreams of Nino. The dream is rife with animal images: "Behind him [Nino] a wolf, with pups still dragging at the dugs, laps the rain"; as he walks, "The black stones ring lightly, as a goat walking its quick pace" (147). Nino, again wounded, limps back to the city where he and Adeppi met. The piazza is gone, the town deserted, the street names puzzling. Calling his love for Edouard —and not Adeppi—he puts his pistol to his head and shoots. The dream is of homelessness, which is a reflection of Adeppi's condition, and it is, furthermore, an evocation of Adeppi's plight or curse—he is always being deserted, he is alone.

And so Adeppi is left with Arsella, who finds him, at dawn, sleeping between the front legs of the cow—dumb relic, milkless as the rosary is fruitless. It is significant that Arsella finds him in this fashion: "He lay on the first morning, sore and innocent of the manner in which he as the child and the cow as the Bible's mistaken sheep mocked the nativity of the crèche, asleep on the thin and sacred straw which Arsella herself had pitched to the animal" (148). In a setting in which the Madonna has not delivered herself of Christ (in a land, therefore, to which Christ has not come), and in a setting without vigorous religion or its attendant ethics, Adeppi's arrival "on the first morning," as if newly born to the world, as was Christ, seems tantamount to the land's Nativity.

Upon finding Adeppi, Arsella stays in her room, keeping him with her until it is dusk and time for him to do his minimal chores. The two are described as roosting in the upper story (151), where she lies with her eyes closed and where Adeppi dutifully strokes her naked skin—again, he is in servitude.

Then Arsella steals away from the house with Adeppi, hauling a bag of religious relics. They pass an old man who, squatting before them, clutches a dead goose to his chest: "The goose's body—it was enemy to rodents and the pups of wolves—smeared blood from the old man's foreflank to his collar bone" (153). The old man, himself described in animal terms, has destroyed the goose that traditionally dances on graves to drive off carrion eaters (157). It is not surprising, in a world where corpses are turned out like loaves of bread, to find that the last sanctity or dignity is withheld from the dead. Violation proceeds from murder into the grave.

The sack is hauled to Brother Bolo, another mysterious priest, whose sanctuary is a small hut in which, in place of guidance or protection, a small child (another orphan) receives wine, lapping it from fingers dipped into a saucer. The action is catlike, as was so much of Edouard's, and Hawkes reminds us of the atmosphere in which Edouard moved. Like the continuity of religious emblems, like the priests themselves, like the presence of death, there is another reminder—a hint of animal imagery that, in this novel, replaces any unity of narrative.

Arsella offers to sell to the priest a religious relic, one stolen, perhaps, from the Contessa. They dicker about the price of the relic and monastic huts—repositories in the Middle Ages of worship and learning—are seen as little more than pawnshops.

The narrative moves again, focusing on thematic concerns and extended metaphors, not on a logical progression of action. And so Hawkes shows us Brother Dolce, the priest on the train. He is at confession, in the course of which he remembers once seeing Astrella's mother "with the same eye that caught the birds at that moment hurrying to roost" (159). And his thoughts are full of such animal references: the church he stopped at had "a cross which lay high like the skeleton of a nest fled by the rooks" (161); "the dogs would not drink when he approached, and he went dry if the animals had been at the pond before him" (163).

Dolce then begins to pray: "In confession he crouched biting at his master's heels" (163). As part of the metaphor of dogs as signs of corruption Dolce prays with no humility at all, and what he recalls is certainly not humble: "In the novitiate we were cruel" (165). He remembers having given to Astrella's mother, who begged for chastisement, a hair shirt made of rat pelts. His cruelty, not comfort, and his unremitting hubris—"Christ had a sharp face. Dolce know every line of it" (158)—are testimony to the political and spiritual decadence that subsume these pages. It is obvious that, in this strange land, the powers of the mysterious priests are part of the degeneration of religion.

The narrative returns to Adeppi who, before an open window, strokes Astrella. Simultaneously, "Children run to pat the donkey's haunch"; now Astrella is no longer merged only with the useless cow, but with the ass as well. She, the peasant, like the aristocrats Edouard admired, have joined in their common destiny: they have all become asses. Of Astrella we learn further that sometimes "without a word she shifted under his hand and then he climbed down [to the 'stall below'] and at the window watched for a raven or some other winged boy-fowl to tumble across . . . the sky" (171). Astrella's room is "the stall above," and she is wholly beast, Adeppi is still a bird.

It is summer, and Adeppi has been with Astrella for months. On hot afternoons he slips from her room to the garden nearby to watch insects battle: " 'Look how they crawl, Astrella!' he tried to say, eyes fixed on their efforts which were only to keep themselves marching in the sun. He spent hours on this terrace watching the bugs move in circles that would not keep their order as an old garden sank to decay" (174). In the context of the novel this animal image can easily be recognized as analog for the events of the whole book: the dying land, at war with the fixedness of ant-armies, moves purposelessly in a pattern dictated by the decay of social and spiritual power.

Then it is night, one "for the hounds to run." Adeppi listens to them: "No mastiffs, these, but the inbred packs whose prey, when run to ground, came to no harm. He felt them circling the villa, giving chase to the great rat tails distended rigidly from the bones of the quarters, damp and never winding. . . . Atop the aqueduct they did not lose their footing, scaled like flesh-eating sheep the walls of a monastery. . . . The hound was out" (175-76).

The running dogs, similar to those of *The Cannibal* and *The Beetle Leg*, suddenly out in unusual number, signal the novel's movement to conclusion. These are the dogs of war, disorder, and violence; when they are out even the sheep become carnivorous. Listening to them, Adeppi, the lamb or songbird, once creature of gentleness, takes up a mandolin, walks into the garden, and, seeing the ants winding through the terraces, crushes them with his fists. "Again he took the mandolin in his arms" (177), but it is no longer an innocent song that he will sing.

Adeppi has festered too long with the corruption of Nino, Edouard, and Astrella. It is not unsurprising when he moves from a metaphorical animal murder to the killing of another human being.

After he has "yawned like a small animal of prey contented a few hours after being whelped" (181)—no longer only the child found in a crèche, Christlike in his innocence—he encounters Astrella's blind husband in the fields at morning. The old man asks to be led up a steep hill—reminiscent of Oedipus, Gloucester —and Adeppi complies. He sees, on the top of the hill, workmen laboring to move a huge boulder. As the boulder rocks and trembles, then begins to roll toward them, Adeppi says nothing. The old man, hearing the whistle of the approaching stone, asks Adeppi which way to run. And Adeppi says nothing, permitting the blind man to be swept from the hill and crushed. Crawling insect is equal to man, no less; man is no more than insect; Adeppi has killed without compunction. The old man, unlike Oedipus, never does "see"; unlike Gloucester, he does not provoke vision in others: this land is chaos, there is no redemption. And Adeppi apparently agrees that man's fate is doom; he aids in the disruption of the Sisyphean cycle, which is tantamount to signaling apocalypse.

Adeppi is then caught, as if in punishment, by a soldier in his home-city to which he has fled. The soldier beats the boy (for what reason we do not know) over a dung heap "between the church covered like a lighthouse with the white of rooks and the shop hiding its row after row of incomplete coffins" (189). The scene described above, with its intimations of befouled church and impending death, is suitable to the novel's world. In this

The Goose on the Grave

strange place, near a donkey which seems to be that of the priest Dolce, Adeppi is saved from being beaten to death and is led away as his mother was.

Hawkes then interjects a section ironically called "Palms," in which the three priests, as at the novel's beginning, are riding away from the city with Adeppi's mother a captive. "The trio wear black smocks upon which are painted rough white stripes, bones, false ribs" (197). Everything religious in this setting is covered over and false. As the priests travel, "gray dogs come out from their dens, from under haystacks, from white abbey and villages, to sniff silently their train" (198). The presence of the dogs makes death seem inevitable.

And it is. The woman is dragged to a nunnery of a perverted kind: "Spread eagle in each tall window is a black angel" (198). In a book where bird images play so large a part, even the angels (strangely, awfully, black) are spread *eagle,* evocative of hunting and ferocity. Adeppi's mother is thrown headlong into the coals of a huge fire. No words have been spoken, no reason given for the live cremation. The action here is as unmerciful, as absurd, as the religious elements thus far displayed by Hawkes have led us to expect.

For three days Dolce prays for Adeppi while Adeppi watches a spider descending its web. Like the spider, which ultimately dangles without movement, Adeppi is himself dangling between humanity and an arachnid emotionlessness—between people and bestiality. Adeppi's silence, his lack of remorse for the murder he has committed—his thorough lack of any human communication at all—make the callous and cold priest seem almost human. Then Edouard appears: "The front of his nightcoat was blotched and one of the flies remained with him, spreading its blue wings to his death. . . . The veins had burst under his eyes, there was a disused sling hanging from his neck, the cold fingers could be seen feeling his heart" (202). And at this sight—civilization crumbled, a kind of love dying—Adeppi is driven to the side of the priest.

Adeppi is next seen standing before Dolce who, with a crowd

in a fetid bog, swings a censer above a corpse in the clay. The crowd watches the body, but Adeppi notices a carrion crow flying above. And then the body moves, dragging its fingers over a helmet in the mud, and Adeppi flees.[5] The corpse flings its head up as Adeppi runs, and we are told that "The earth was cold" (206).

This passage seems to be our final opportunity to solve much of the novel's enigma, and because it denotes so little, it becomes the most perplexing event in the narrative. If we assume that Adeppi runs toward the corpse, toward the "miracle" that is taking place, he may be running to his last hope—a resurrection of all that which has been lost, both for him and the world. It is, then, fitting with the tone of the novel that the earth, "cold," does not receive him. It has been argued, as well, that it is the mother's corpse toward which Adeppi runs.[6] It may seem strange that a body presumably consumed on the coals of a vast fire is now whole and in a bog. But Hawkes's lack of concern with any logic of physical condition or action makes it entirely possible that a burned corpse may rise.

More significant than the penultimate passage discussed above is the final one in which Nino's corpse lies high in the mountains, not in the city where Adeppi's dream had him: "Under his hands, behind the face, deep inside the dark sac of the brain, he dreamed of them [sentries and sea gulls] and it persisted, a continuous dream, warm and without waiting and despite the presence across the valley of the enemy" (207). This passage —reminding us, perhaps, of Mulge Lampson of *The Beetle Leg*— comments on the penultimate one, as if to deny the possibility of miracle—as if to suggest that there is no sudden change from death, since the condition of man is a kind of death and since the dream of preying birds and warmakers is continuous, always in man. It is that which remains after death of the body is recognized—man's essence: the urge of the carrion feeder and of the creator of carrion. What is Christlike in man dies before the dream. This is civilization's heritage and essence.

The Goose on the Grave

Hawkes's use of animal figures in these two novels is undiminished. His unflagging application of the dog image has been commented on, and his assertion of the bird (rooks, crows, owls) is obvious. He continues to use the cow and horse, also, and they will figure far more prominently in novels to come—the horse in *The Lime Twig* and the cow in *Second Skin*. Concentrated animal metaphors—the owl, the cow, and geese—are as impressive and as communicative as in novels already considered. But the animal background imagery differs in these two novels from those latterly considered in that it is more full than in any novel since *Charivari*.

One reason for this dispersal of animal figures, this tendency toward loosely-strung catalogs of images, may be the similarity of these two novels and *Charivari:* the concern with atmosphere, with milieux of confusion, that typifies all three. They are alike in narrative focus (or its lack), which is at times confusing. The reader is shunted back and forth, from character to character, from scene to scene, until he loses the thread and is lost. What is not lost, and this is true again of all three novels, is the sense of a land infested with crawling and baying creatures in which nothing is as it should be.

As has been stated earlier, the generation of these two novels seems to be a sense that religious failure, sexual failure, the death of charity, have not been exhaustively treated. These two short novels, using animal metaphors copiously, and a wealth of background imagery, seem to be efforts to cover areas of novelistic terrain that were not previously treated fully. The concerns, abstracted and dehumanized, are now for a time abandoned by Hawkes—at least as primary concerns.

The human failings to which Hawkes has paid such singular attention are still with his novels, but they are integrated henceforth into the interaction of his very idiosyncratic characters with their bizarre environments. It is as if with *The Lime Twig* Hawkes stopped writing of concerns and started writing about people whose nature was delineated by those concerns. The concerns are no longer treated as characters in themselves.

With animal imagery still very much dominating his increasingly lyrical and flexible prose, Hawkes now forsakes atmospheric and thematic consideration for the scrutiny of people who live in a particular world, not a generalized world of smells and swine. He focuses particularly and creates universal resonances, instead of focusing widely, capturing the universe and, in a strange corner of it, one creature arbitrarily called "character."

5 The Lime Twig

The Lime Twig is perhaps the most studied of Hawkes's novels. Its appearance seems to cause a sigh of relief among students of Hawkes, perhaps because of the increasing "realism" Hawkes implants in what is both a suspense novel and a novel about racing, as well as an intense and bizarre character study.

Robert Edenbaum offers this summary of the events of the novel:

> The Lime Twig is one of the most studied of completely ordinary lower-middle class Londoner who is lured into a scheme to steal an aged racehorse, Rock Castle, and run him as a ringer in the classic Golden Bowl at Aldington. Michael is introduced to the scheme by his lodger, William Hencher, who acts as go-between for an unearthly archetypal gangster known only as Larry, and Larry's gang. Since Michael's function, unknown to him, is to be a respectable front for Larry, the gangster lures Margaret, Michael's equally ordinary wife, to Aldington and holds her prisoner as a guarantor of her husband's behavior. The lure for Margaret is Michael; that for Michael once the plot is under way is the sexually flamboyant Sybilline Laval. But the overriding lure in The Lime Twig, the central image of sexual potency and phallic thrust, is the horse of Michael Banks' imagination which materializes as Rock Castle.[1]

One character overlooked by Edenbaum is Sidney Slyter, who never appears in person, but who is represented by fragments from a racing column called "Sidney Slyter Says." Hawkes comments on Slyter in this fashion:

As soon as he read the manuscript of *The Lime Twig*, James Laughlin, the publisher of New Directions, . . . suggested that this novel might be more accessible if it had some kind of gloss or reader's guide. I believe that he even suggested the idea of a newspaper sportswriter as an appropriate kind of "chorus" to comment on the action of the novel. I don't know how I arrived at the sportswriter's name (I may have been trying to echo comically the common English term "blighter"), but at any rate that's how Sidney Slyter came into being, with his snake-like character embodied in the ugly sibilance of his name which was also related, of course, to Sybilline, the dark temptress in the novel.[2]

Hawkes, in his interest in this character, betrays what his novel betrays: an increasing interest in character in general—people behaving as people, not thematic embodiments alone. As Guerard says, adding to this notion of Hawkes's concern with characters and verisimilitude, "the predicted movement toward realism has occurred . . . in the sense that the later novels are much more orderly and more even in pace, and distinctly less difficult to read."[3] So apparent is this movement toward realism that Leslie Fiedler comments: "If *The Lime Twig* reminds us of *Brighton Rock*, which in turns reminds us of a movie by Hitchcock, it is of *Brighton Rock* recalled in a delirium or by a drowning man—*Brighton Rock* rewritten by Djuna Barnes. Hawkes, however, shares the effeteness of Djuna Barnes's vision of evil no more than he does the piety of Greene's vision of sin. His view avoids the esthetic and the theological alike, since it deals with the mysteries neither of the world of art nor of spirit—but only with the unmitigable mystery of the world of common experience."[4]

But, lest we forget that Hawkes is a very complex and mystifying novelist—lest we think that, at last, we have come down to the rewritten moving picture plots that so many contemporary novels seem to be—there is this reminder from W. M. Frohock:

> Playing hide-and-seek with perspective is a key device in *The Lime Twig*. . . . After the prologue in which the protagonist tells his story—about living there with his old mother and the

bombing plane shot down in his backyard—we switch to the story about racehorses and crooks and switch also from first to third person narration. The narrator of the first part remains a participant for a while, and for a while also the point of view is still his; but this has to stop, of course, when he unguardedly enters the horse's stall and is kicked to death. His erstwhile partner in crime, Banks, moves into the center, but only to be replaced by his wife—and so on. Since the relation of the prologue with the rest is not specified, and one can only guess at what Hawkes has in mind, it is hard to say what the point of such shifting about really is, and whether it adds or detracts so far as the phantasmic nightmare of the main story is concerned.[5]

Hawkes is still confusing, surrealistic, "experimental." And so is *The Lime Twig*.

As Michael Hencher describes his life with his mother in the London of World War II—a life of itinerancy, poverty, and meanness—he does so with heavy reliance on beast figures. There are "small premises still rank with the smells of dead dog or cat," a room-dividing screen of "horsehair brown" (6), "the gilded cherubim big as horses that fly off the top of the Dreary Station itself" (7). Then there is the child noticed by Hencher as he and his mother are turned out of lodging after lodging; as a "flying goose darkened the mornings in that alley off Pinky Road" (8), Hencher sees the child and his dog: "The boy would waggle the animal's fat head, hide its slow shocked eyes in his hands, flop it upright and listen to its heart. His fingers were always feeling the black gums . . . or quickly freeing and pulling open the eyes so that he, the thin boy, could stare into them. . . . Loving his close scrutiny of the nicks in its ears . . . pictures he could find on its purple tongue, pearls he could discover between the claws. Love is a long close scrutiny like that. I loved mother in the same way" (9).

After the extended animal metaphors of *The Owl*, in which people and animals were analogically juxtaposed, such a simple simile may seem quite limited for Hawkes. But, because the elaborate description of the dog is so striking, the simile is nonetheless effective: Hencher's mother is yet another Hawkesian figure who is like an animal, and who is loved as a beast is loved. And the simile becomes more extended than the reader may suspect.

As Hencher describes the effect of the war on London, the fear of fire and bombs, he mentions that Michael and Margaret Banks—as yet not introduced in the novel—"were only children then, as small and crouching as the boy with the French sailor's hat and the dog" (10). The simile then can perhaps extend in some fashion to the Bankses. And Margaret and Michael may also be analogous not only to the crouching and frightened child but to the dog—victims of the war and its effects.

Hencher's mother is killed by fire started during a bombing. Hencher takes to night walks—"I expected to see the boy dancing with his dog" (18)—and, on one of his strolls, witnesses the crash of *Reggie's Rose*, a returning British bomber. The plane does not ignite, and Hencher approaches it, leans against the engine cowling, "and it was like touching your red cheek to a stranded whale's fluke" (21). He climbs into the cockpit, breathes oxygen from the pilot's apparatus, works the flying controls, then places the pilot's flying helmet on his head. He wonders how he looks "with my bloody coronet in place at last" (23). Shortly thereafter he has moved in with the Bankses—who now occupy the house in which his mother died years before, during the war.

Before allowing the narrative to move us across some twenty years or so, we ought to consider Hencher with his coronet— Hencher who is somehow a kind of ruler who has inherited his authority from the dead pilot of a ruined dealer of death. In commenting on Hencher, Hawkes says: "since Michael and Margaret were mere children during the war, incapable of even recalling the bombing of London, the problem became one of dramatizing the past, of relating wartime England to postwar England, of providing a kind of historical consciousness for characters who had none of their own. Hencher served this function. He became the carrier of Michael and Margaret's past as well as of their future; I thought of him as the seedbed of their pathetic lives."[6]

The Lime Twig

So Hencher is ruler because he is of the generation that has contributed to the formation of an England in which the events of this novel are possible; he is ruler because he will influence the particular fates of Michael and Margaret in the general climate to which he has, through his generation, contributed. Michael and Margaret are analogous to the puppy mentioned above in that they are in the childlike hands of someone who has extreme power over their destinies. They are like the puppy's master in that they once were in his situation—that of crouching in rubble while the bombs fell. And if they are to be wholly analogous to the dog, they are loved through the rather perverse scrutiny that the child exerted on his pet and that Hencher exerted on his mother.

Thus Hencher wonders what he can do—twenty years later—for his landlords, examining Michael's talc and hair brush, sitting on Margaret's wooden stool, and preparing breakfast for them. He recalls how, after urging the couple to picnic some time ago, he stood before the bathroom mirror and, with Margaret's lipstick, "drew a red circle with it round each of my eyes. They came home laughing and brought a postal card of an old pocked cannon for me" (27). Hencher's scrutiny, bordering now on the intimate—he has already lain in his landlord's bed—is made ironic with the presentation of the postcard, emblem of what he has wrought and what he will wreak.

Hencher decides what he can do for his landlords. Staring at an empty goldfish bowl and listening to "a little bird trying to sing," he says, "I can get along without you, Mother" (28). And indeed he can; he has a new pet, or pets, a new power to exert in a new way in order to demonstrate the perversity of his pet-collector's love. Like a minor character in a drama, just before the major characters come onstage, Hencher foreshadows their dilemma.

Michael and Margaret are first seen at dawn of a typical weekday, with Margaret preparing for her habitual fortnightly shopping trip and Michael evading her presence by slipping from room to room. The relationship between the Bankses can be summed up by Margaret's devotional shopping for him, and by "most Wednesdays—let her stay, let her walk out—Michael does not care, does not hold his breath, never listens for the soft voice that calls good-by" (30).

This morning is untypical in that Michael sneaks a long drink from a cached bottle and actually thinks of what Margaret's thoughts may be like. He recalls her fear upon entering the apartment and finding an abandoned cat, and then he ponders her nightmare and his dream:

> Knowing how much she feared his dreams: knowing that her own worst dream was one day to find him gone . . . that his own worst dream, and best, was of a horse which was itself the flesh of all violent dreams; knowing . . . that the horse was in their sitting room . . . seeing the room empty . . . and, in the middle of the floor, the tall upright shape of the horse draped from head to tail in an enormous sheet that falls over the eyes and hangs down stiffly from the silver jaw; knowing the horse on sight and listening while it raises one shadowed hoof on the end of a silver thread of foreleg and drives down the hoof to splinter in a single crash . . . knowing his own impurity and Hencher's guile; and knowing that Margaret's hand has nothing in the palm but a short life span. (33–34)

Here the cherubim big as horses become actual horse and Michael's dream. The massive power of the horse, its mysterious importance to Michael, is told in a dreamlike scene; the horse will, indeed, become part of the dream of everyone in the novel: of Michael, Margaret, Hencher, Larry, and Sybilline. The horse will gradually become the central symbol of the book which, in *The Lime Twig*, is the hinted-at dream-life of each most unreal character.

Michael is next seen as he and Hencher journey to a destination which is, as yet, unknown; it soon is revealed as the stable of the horse, Rock Castle, ownership of which—at low price, too—seems to Michael to be the consummation of his dreams. The pair move past "a small skylight drawn over with the shadow of a fat gull" (34–35), a "crabbed address," "flesh-colored masts," (36) and a long monolog by Hencher on the ancestry of Rock Castle, in which twenty horses are named. As Michael listens he "once again . . . saw the silver jaw, the enormous sheet, the upright body of the horse that was crashing in the floor" (39). Hencher feeds his dream, its repetition, with an elaborate description of how Rock Castle, put out to pasture on account of age, will surprise the racing world with his power and endurance.

Amidst "white hair strands" (44) of fog and the scampering of rats, Hencher and Michael wait on a quay for the *Artemis* to dock with Michael's horse. And then, from the ship, the horse appears: "the black space, the echo of bilge and, without movement, snort or pawing of hoof, the single white marble shape of the horse, whose neck . . . was the fluted and tapering neck of some serpent, while the head was an elongated white skull with nostrils, eye sockets, uplifted gracefully in the barge's hold" (49). This is more than Michael's dream; the horse, a metaphor of dreams in its own right, is also the metaphorical snake that glides in and out of Hawkes's novels, signaling danger and decline; he is the present reminder of future death.

If the ominous passage above is insufficient notice of terror in the offing, this reference to Michael's vision of the horse should suffice: Its "silver coat gleamed with the colorless fluid of some ghostly libation and . . . [its] decorous drained head smelled of a violence that was his own" (50). In that concluding phrase, "a violence that was his own," something may be seen of the projection of Michael's dreams, of his lust for fulfillment through the horse. But more should be seen than that, and more than the menace in the "ancient head" encircled by a huge fly. For the horse is not alive; if he is Michael's dream, a realization of it and metaphor for it, he is still dead as far as Michael is concerned: the horse is of "silver," the ears are "unfeeling . . . unlikely to twitch," the head is "drained." When the horse comes to life for Michael, when Hencher's dream of giving comes to life, there will be horrible shock for the dreamers whose artifact of wish turns upon them as Faustian wishes must.

The horse is loaded into a van and transported to where he

will be kept until the Golden Bowl is run. En route, while Hencher rejoices that the horse is Michael's at last, Michael "was tasting lime" (54) and growing uneasy with the smell of the horse from the back of the truck. Each time the van turned a corner, "he felt the horse—his horse—thump against one metal side or the other. Each time the faint sound and feel of the thumping made him sick" (55). This may be a warning of the malevolence that is to be unleashed and of Michael's inability to deal with it.

And then the narrative returns to Margaret, who is less important here, since the horse—this novel's central animal figure—is with Michael. She speaks to herself in such a way as to emphasize her loneliness for the absent Michael and unwittingly prepares us for the action that will result in her abduction. Hawkes presents a logic of character motivation and arranges the narrative here so that his characters will react to plot stimuli in such a way that their actions are more understandable and accessible than in any previous work.

Hawkes returns to Hencher again, and a figure named Larry who, awaiting receipt of the horse, asserts a brutal power over Hencher (58). In an effort to extricate the horse from the van and move him into a stable, Hencher "squeezes himself against the white and silver flesh." As soon as he physically touches the animal, he glances down at a helper outside the truck "and slides suddenly into the dark of the van" (60), as if simply touching the power that the horse is means death. That, here, is what it does mean: "The ramp bounces . . . the chassis, cab and high black sides all sway forward once at the moment they absorb that first unnatural motion of horse lunging at trapped man. Shakes, rattles, and the first loud sound of the hoof striking . . . to metal fades. But not the commotion, the blind forward swaying on the van . . . the noise, the directionless pitching of the van—those rear hoofs never cease their dancing. The horse strikes a moment longer, but there is no metallic ringing, no sharp sound, and only the ramp drags a little more and the long torch falls from the cab" (60–61).

The dream, or the vehicle of many dreams, has turned live and lethal. Of this death, Hawkes says: "My own feeling is that

The Lime Twig

Hencher's innocence, like Michael and Margaret's, can only suffer destruction by ruthless victimizers in a time of impoverishment. . . . Paradoxically . . . even the victimizers have 'their dreams of shocking purity,' to quote Albert Guerard."[7]

Margaret, almost a week later, has had no word from Michael. She is reminiscent of Emily Van (of *Charivari*) in her impracticality and childlishness when, at this point, she first begins to miss her husband. Keeping herself busy, she feeds the cat, and the cat's meal does much to gather together the strands of predatory suggestion that have pervaded these early pages: "It ate quickly, choked on every mouthful, the head jerked up and down. . . . Her back to the window, kneeling, Margaret watched the animal eat. And the cat, creature that claws tweed, sits high in the hallway, remains incorrigible upon the death of its mistress . . . now sucked and gagged on the fish as if drawing a peculiar sweetness from the end of a thin bone" (63). The description of the cat—creature that is unchanged "upon the death of its mistress"—foreshadows Margaret's end. It suggests, as well, the kind of greedy feeding upon the unreal that the dreamers of the novel indulge in. And it establishes the motif of the gulping predator that Larry, the silent and powerful gangster, will prove himself to be.

Then Margaret is sent for by Michael. Her train is met by Larry, "an impassive escort who, by chance, could touch a woman's breast in public easily, with propriety, offending no one" (74). Already the lethal tension that Larry generates is gripping Margaret. And, as if that tension, even attraction, were dangerous, we are told that she sees, at the station platform's edge, "a field sunk like iron . . . a shape that might have been a murdered horse or sheep"; she smells "the faint odor of manure" (75). Larry then leaves, and Dora, a moll, escorts Margaret past coffins being unloaded from the train and into the presence of Sybilline and her child, Monica, before Margaret is taken to a cheap hotel overlooking the racecourse with its "oval of roses in which men were murdered" (77). Death is unquestionably proximate, and trusting, insipid Margaret is unaware.

Although the novel is thus far easier to follow in narrative and is grounded in a "real" world peopled by "real," if strange, characters, much information is still withheld. We do not know why Larry is unquestioningly obeyed by his men and adored by his women, nor do we understand the source of his power; we cannot yet see what has become of Michael, or why he has sent for his wife; although death and misery are forecast, we cannot know why or how they will come about. But the tension of the novel is, thus far, sustained—and perhaps it is the withholding of information that helps to sustain that tension. We *want* to know why events move as they do, and the dark hints that surround each event whet our appetites and draw us further. This kind of narrative tension is analogous to the power of the description of Hencher's death: there was no vivid imagery of hooves striking flesh or of blood spurting—only the shaking of a darkened van in a dark night and the sounds of hoof meeting steel; because suggestion permitted participation in the action, or its observation, we became involved. The desire created in us to supply details and find answers, to participate in their formation, is one of the triumphs of *The Lime Twig*.

Still, there is more to be known about the mysterious Larry, and the next section of the book reveals him further. He washes the muscles of his neck and arms but leaves his fingernails black; his elegance cannot belie the kind of black work he does. He wears a vest of linked steel beneath his shirt; he waters plants and loads his pistol in immediate sequence, and, after shining his own shoes, he has the aptly named Sparrow, a gangland sycophant, kneel, spit on the shoes, and shine them again. He is a mixture of the toff, or English swell, and the street-king wielding basic power unattractively.

When Larry is with Dora and Margaret—she is tied up now, and dressed only in a white and shapeless gown (for unknown reasons)—he is described by Hawkes as "Larry who was an angel if any angel ever had eyes like his or flesh like his" (83).

It remains to be seen what kind of dark angel Larry is, and why Margaret is bound and held, and why she is told that she cannot see her husband, who is mysteriously "engaged" (84). Again, the narrative moves forward by disclosures; Hawkes provides enough information as hints so that the terrors that exist simultaneously with the actions witnessed can be inferred or guessed.

Back with Michael now, we see him accosted in the racecourse lavatory and threatened by three men who warn him that, if he betrays Larry (and, since we don't know what Michael is supposed to do, we cannot know what he must not do: the tension increases), he will be murdered with pellet bombs: lethal droppings, or pellets, from deadly, bestial men. The men deliver one other message, repeated twice: "'Sybilline's in the Pavilion'" (96). At this point, we are as ignorant as Michael as to why this information is important.

But he goes to find out, and sees a glamorous, exotic woman with red hair "like the orange of an African bird" (98). She exposes her tongue to him, and moves in such a way that he can see there are holes cut in the tips of her brassiere; she caresses herself suggestively. She is a temptress, a Circe, a succubus-like voluptuary, and she leads him away with her as, before, she led her child.

While Sybilline tempts Michael, and while Margaret is imprisoned with Dora, two of Larry's cohorts ravage the Bankses' house—stripping linen from beds, then smashing the beds, then sawing the beds into lumber to be carted away—until the house is a shell and there is no evidence whatsoever that Michael and Margaret Banks were ever there. If we see Larry as a dark angel, we see now the absoluteness of his power: he can make people vanish, he can keep them in what seems more and more to be an unknown hell. As the van-full of the Bankses' possessions, the touchstones of their life, is dumped into a quagmire, frogs croak, and the coincidental suprahuman and bestial characteristics of Larry and his gang are brought home.

In a hellish scene, Cowles, the gangster who witnessed Hencher's death, is inexplicably murdered by Sparrow and Larry in a steam bath. Michael, who has entered with him, gets weaker and weaker, less and less able to assert his will; his reaction to the steam renders him similar to the horse, as he saw it with "drained head"—"all the fluids of his body [came] . . . to the surface"

(113)—and he is somehow being engulfed by his dream. He hears Cowles shout and thrash as Larry and Sparrow methodically stalk him; when he finds Cowles' body, the throat cut, he does so by becoming bestial—by crawling on all fours in the murk of the steam room (116). In this moist and murderous scene, Michael has undergone a sea-change; whatever was the soul or core of him, its public manifestation at least, is now lost.

Michael is next seen at a loud and drunken party attended by Larry and his gang—and by Sybilline. As he drinks and dances with her—as he comes into proximity with her flesh as Hencher did with the horse—"he remembered not the Baths, the Damps, poor wretched Cowles, nor the rooms in Dreary Station, but a love note he had written at the age of twelve when the city was on fire. And remembering it he looked at Sybilline and saw in her eyes the eyes of an animal that has seen a lantern swinging on a blackened hill" (121). Michael is forgetting to worry about the absence of his wife, after whom he no longer inquires. He has forgotten the murder he witnessed and his rooms that Larry has caused to disappear. He can recall only his effort to express love at a time when Hencher's generation was softening the texture of the world. The dragon seeds planted then are flowering now. And he is becoming, thoroughly, prey to the animal that is Sybilline.

The narrative then moves to Margaret, bound to a brass bed, nearly naked, hungry, and terrified. Thick, the tough who is guarding her, becomes aroused by her near-nudity, by her helplessness, and begins to beat her as she almost regales herself with the fact that "she was a child anything could be done to" (126). As Thick swings his truncheon at her, it comes down "hard and solid as a length of cold fat stripped from a pig," makes "a sound like a dead bird falling to empty field" (129). After much savage beating, Larry, drunk and disheveled, enters. Margaret sees his bullet-proof vest "like fish scales." And she sees in his face "the angel's whiteness, except for a broken place at the corner of his mouth" (136). Larry, the dark angel and beast at once, begins to cut her until, bleeding, dying, she is raped in coma as "sunlight roused the day's first warbling of the heavy oven tit" (137).

Margaret, whose dream was submission, has had that dream fulfilled—indirectly through the deeds the horse set in motion.

At the same time that Larry begins his slashing, begins to rouse his perverse lust, Michael is in bed with Sybilline. Moiling together in bed, roughly making love, they enact the myth of Circe. Each time Sybilline loses a pearl, she asks Michael to retrieve it; he dives, snuffling, into the sheets, and her, and they couple. She loses a pearl four times, casts pearls four times before the swine that Michael has become. It may be remembered that Michael, rendered doglike by Hencher, is now turned into the dog with pearls "between his claws" (6) that Hencher noted in bombed-out London. Through his libidinousness, he is unmanned and crazed, and he rejoins the party to fulfill his sexual fantasies further with a widow and his next-door neighbor who, inexplicably, appears at the party as if only to be taken by him. According to Edenbaum, "Larry manipulates the dream of a Hencher or a Banks for his own ends, as the devil would. The twig he limes for Michael is . . . the primal one, for Larry speaks with the Devil's voice."[8] Larry, then, is responsible for this party, for what happens to Michael—for all the fulfillments of all dreams. The horse is his creature, and its powers of wish fulfillment are endowed by him. Its ability to kill through surfeit of granted wishes is Larry's.

Later, alone and exhausted, Michael watches dawn come up. The hour is immediately after Margaret's death: "The mate of the oven tit had found a branch outside his window and he heard its damp scratching and its talk. Even two oven tits may be snared and separated in such a dawn. He listened, turned his head under the shadows, and reflected that the little bird was fagged . . . himself fagged and tasteless as the bird on the sick bough" (159). The metaphor for Michael and Margaret is appropriate, and in more than its execution. The unification of Margaret's end, as Michael sees that end's witness without knowing it, with what will be his end is careful foreshadowing, submerged prediction. Hawkes not only dislocates time in this novel, he takes pains to show that the dislocation is that of the characters and the book's narrative voice. Here is how the chronological jigsaw fits together, he tells us by reiterating the image of the tit; while Margaret was raped, so, in effect, was Michael. By putting the pieces together again, by showing us that our notions of time are not threatened, he refrains from threatening us. His book does not comment on *our* world, only that of the characters. Hawkes's concern for historical veracity with Hencher and, in *The Cannibal*, with Stella Snow—historical continuants, "realistic" links between times —is that of a student of people in their place and time, not that of a cold abstractionist.

On the day of the Golden Bowl,[9] the horse's tongue is tied down, its mouth "filled with a green scum." Coincidentally, "a plaster held Banks' lips together at a corner of the mouth and impaired his speech" (164). The similarity of the condition of Michael and the horse suggest that more is shared between them than a gag.

As the horses begin to run, Michael thinks of Margaret and races toward the course, climbing fences, trampling flowers, thinking that "he must put a stop to it" (169). The "it" that must be stopped is not identified; but it does not seem extravagant to suggest that the "it" is the power of Larry, symbolized in the powerful horse, the ability to end men and women by offering them their desired ends. Michael rushes to the green: "He was running in final stride, the greatest spread of legs, redness coming across the eyes, the pace so fast that it ceases to be motion, but at its peak becomes the long downhill deathless gliding of a dream until the arms are out, the head thrown back, and the runner is falling as he was falling and waving his arm at Rock Castle's onrushing silver shape, at Rock Castle who was about to run him down and fall" (171).

Michael does end "it," racing as Rock Castle races, and gliding like a dream. At this point all three—"it," the horse, and Michael's dream—are united in the collision that looks like "an explosion's smoke" (171), reminiscent of the bombing which, sociologically, began these terrible events. Michael and his dream, and Larry's powerful magic, merge. The meeting means, as it has meant before for Hencher and Margaret, death.

The Lime Twig

The novel ends with policemen discovering Hencher's body and then driving "through vacant city streets to uncover the particulars of this crime" (175). The reader has witnessed the "particulars" and is aware just how undiscoverable they are—how inaccessible the calculated passion and merciless exercise of power are to the deductive logic of the policeman. A final irony— the policemen meticulously make note of a dead wasp caught in a green splinter near Hencher's body (174)—serves to emphasize the otherworldly chain of events that was set in motion by a predatory innocent who lived with his old mother in coldwater flats while the Second World War raged.

Earlier in this chapter reference was made to Hencher's description of Rock Castle: "And what's his age? Why it's the evolution of his bloody name, that's what it is. Just the evolution of a name—Apprentice out of Lithograph by Cobbler, Emperor's Hand by Apprentice out of Hand Maiden by Lord of the Land, Draftsman by Emperor's Hand out of Shallow Draft by Amulet, Castle Churl by Draftsman out of Likely Castle by Cold Masonry, Rock Castle by Castle Churl out of Words on Rock by Plebeian— and what's his name if not the very evolution of his life" (38).

Clearly, the horse is the product of wishes and desires, orders and craftsmanship. He is a shaping; he is a work of fiction, an artifact of language, a dream brought to life. Hawkes speaks not only of Larry's commands, Michael's wishes, and Hawkes's own fictive craft: he refers ("Words on Rock") to Graham Greene's craft in *Brighton Rock*. As Ida in that novel says, " 'It's like those sticks of rock: bite it all the way down, you'll still read Brighton. That's human nature.' "[10] The Editor's Note in the Viking Press edition of Greene's novel explains that "Brighton Rock is a form of stick candy as characteristic of English seaside resorts as saltwater taffy is of the American. The word *Brighton* appears on the ends of the stick at no matter what point it is broken off." Ida's reference to the candy suggests that the melodramatic actions of

Greene's characters are more than skin-deep—that their melodrama is the drama of their souls—and Hawkes's use of "Words on Rock" suggests analogies between his novel and Greene's.

The Lime Twig and Brighton Rock are both set in Brighton during the holidays. Each is involved with horse racing, betting, and mobs bent on influencing the course of events. Each has murder as a central event. In Brighton Rock, Ida, a force of life, a figure of the earth-mother, seeks to avenge the death of a witness to mob murder before the Second World War. The Lime Twig seems to be a reply to Greene's novel, or a continuation of events set in motion at the time in which Greene's book is set; Hencher carries the action from the time of Brighton Rock to the time in which Hawkes's novel is set; The Lime Twig ends as the detection in which Ida engaged is set in motion once more—but without her moral (and destructive) emotional fervor. Both novels, in differing degrees, deal with errant detection—Ida's misguided search for (and presumed discovery of) the facts of Hale's death, and the English constabulary's futile search for "the particulars of this crime" (175). In both cases the reader knows that the truth of these matters will not (advertently) be learned. The quest for truth is offered by both Greene and Hawkes in variations of the tale of detection. The sifting through the facts of existence for clues to knowing a truth about that existence and its mysteries is a perfect form for the epistemological novel, and that is what Greene wrote in Brighton Rock and what Hawkes in The Lime Twig responds to. Hawkes has spoken of his "need to parody the novel form, in this case to parody the soporific plot of the thriller." He adds that Hencher's death seems "an appropriate violation of fictional expectation or fiction 'rules.'"[11] It is worth noting that other serious novelists have seized upon the form in similar ways: Anthony Burgess uses the espionage variation in Tremor of Intent, Nicholas Mosley in Assassins. Thomas Pynchon has written a detection novel involving Americans, V, and Norman Mailer, taking his clue from Dreiser's American Tragedy and Wright's Native Son (as well as Crime and Punishment, of course), has produced the quintessential American crime story in his An American Dream.

The Lime Twig

Aside from similarities of form, setting, and even events, Hawkes presents more specific similarities to *Brighton Rock*. The loyal, avaricious Dallow and the less loyal Spicer bear resemblances to Hencher— who is as loyal as Dallow, as weak as Spicer, and who is killed by the evil he partakes of just as Spicer is. Dallow's fealty and Sparrow's, in *The Lime Twig*, are not dissimilar. Ida's maternal attractions for Hale are not dissimilar to the pull Hencher's mother exerts upon him.

Further and closer resemblances exist between Rose of *Brighton Rock* and Margaret of *The Lime Twig*. Margaret is weak and, separated from her husband by mysterious affairs to which he attends, cloyingly loyal: "A wife would always ride through the night if she were bidden. Would ride through rainstorm, villages like Wimble, through woodland all night long. All of it for Michael's sake" (70). Pinkie's sense of Rose sounds like Hawkes's description of Margaret: "He could already see the patience of the poor and the long-married working up under her skin like a second personality, a modest and shameless figure behind a transparency" (*BR*, 251). Rose reiterates her total surrender to Pinkie in the note she leaves in his pocket: "I love you, Pinkie, I don't care what you do. I love you forever. You've been good to me. Wherever you go, I'll go too" (*BR*, 273). And just as Margaret assents to her torture at Larry's hands in *The Lime Twig*, Rose, as Pinkie pinches her wrist "until his nails nearly met," says "'if you like doing that . . . go on'" (*BR*, 70).[12]

Larry, Satanic in appearance and vicious in action, bears certain resemblances to Pinkie. Like Pinkie, his hands are dirty: he is of the streets, despite his size and handsome dress. Larry's bravado—"'and I told the Inspector he was making a horrible botch of it. I said it would never do'" (147)—sounds like Pinkie's boastings to his mob. Both are melodramatic criminals in their flamboyance and in the people with whom they surround themselves. Each is partially defined by his relationships with women— Larry in his attractiveness to them, Pinkie in his fear of them. Both are melodramatically described—Larry in his fondness for a vest of linked steel, his affection for the crippled Sparrow who polishes his shoes, his delight in torture, and Pinkie, whose thoughts range from the hyperbolic "It was worth murdering a world" (*BR*, 130) to his pulling the wings and legs from a live insect (*BR*, 134). While Larry exerts hellish powers, Pinkie, burning with his own virtriol, plunges down a slope into hell. Neither—despite Greene's constant linking of Pinkie to his crippling past and environment—is a "realistic" character: each, like the villains of crime tales, carries a seemingly unnatural charge of evil, thus enabling the novels in which they appear to deal not only with them as people, but with the evil they trail after them. Each provides an opportunity for his creator to investigate unnatural doings in the natural world. Both Larry and Pinkie are aggressive, militaristic, in love with the milieu of their men, their mob—their army. Hawkes's distaste for Larry's militarism informs his treatment of Larry and Sparrow, the subaltern. Hawkes has written a moving short story about Sparrow as a military man who comes home on leave. Here he is masterful, loving, beloved, and strong; his perceptiveness is extensive. As is true of the world of *The Lime Twig*'s Sparrow, his thoughts are not far from the war, and he returns to the world of war when his leave is over, leaving his family (who live in a fleet's washed-up wreckage, for they are war's victims too) for the "world from which he had come," the army, the forces of destruction Hawkes also returns to again and again.[13]

Hawkes's investigation takes him further from the real world than does Greene's. Conceivably, the ending of *The Lime Twig*, with its emphasis on the ineffability of the events it contains, is a response to Greene's more conventional use of the detection form. Whereas Greene suggests that *some* investigation into the mysteries of murder and suicide, cruelty and victimization, are possible, Hawkes seems to say that nothing can be known. Like the war during which the events of *The Lime Twig* were set in motion, catastrophe falls upon man, and despite attempts at clue-collecting or historiography or psychological investigation, all that remains after the holocaust is emptiness and an unknown corpse: man, his own victim.

The Lime Twig

It is evident that in *The Lime Twig* Hawkes has reduced the amount of animal imagery below that of any preceding novel, but this is not to say that his animal figures play a lesser part in his fiction. Continuing the trend toward extensive and pervasive animal metaphors, as seen in *The Goose on the Grave* and *The Owl*, Hawkes has spread the figure of the horse through *The Lime Twig* as a subsuming force. But he has very clearly reduced the amount of animal background imagery that so dominated the pages of his early works.

That imagery is now firmly condensed, and the all-important horse unifies the actions of Michael, Margaret, Hencher, and Larry. The straggling, often redundant background imagery of the early novels is virtually unnecessary here, although it does appear sporadically at times of crisis.

If the animal imagery is woven tighter, so too is the prose style. The syntax is less elaborate than before; the declarative sentences have become shorter and clearer; the diction has moved from a reliance on the names of creatures, plants, and foreign expressions to a reliance on the significance of action. And action has come to be more significant for Hawkes, as less information *about* the action is given and more of that action's nature is revealed. Action becomes metaphor for character, and that action is effected in terms of animals. But characters are no longer described, move by move, word by word, *as* animals; their relationships and motivations are instead shown to be animalistic in subtle fashion through concentrated, underlying animal metaphor.

Finally, Hawkes's prose has become increasingly lyrical. This passage, for example—"Or perhaps you yourself were once the lonely lodger. Perhaps you crossed the bridges with the night crowds, listened to the tooting of the river boats and the sounds of shops closing on the far side. Perhaps the moon was behind the cathedral. You walked in the cathedral's shadow while the moon kept shining on three girls ahead. And you followed the moonlit girls" (4)—reveals a growing grace of style. Its alliteration and assonance, its use of specificity (*three* girls) in a context of generalized hypothesis, its aural and visual directness couched in the vagueness of wondering—all point to the grace and persuasiveness that Hawkes reveals in his next novel, *Second Skin*, in which his affinity for animals is translated into a character's actual insemination of them.

6 Second Skin

Second Skin is probably the most frequently read and frequently taught of Hawkes's novels. It has been the subject of many articles, the source of numerous arguments, and possibly it is his most complimented work. Hawkes himself considers it his first "affirmative" fiction—this despite Michael's death in *The Lime Twig*, which heroically proclaims life over illusion and the individual over his darkest desires. One can safely argue that, in terms of imagery finely wrought, relationships made compelling among compelling characters, and the masterful use of first-person narrative, the book has few equals in our modern literature.

Hawkes tells us this about *Second Skin:*

> I wanted to use some of the fictional methods that I have become increasingly aware of—mainly the first-person narrator—so I used a first-person narrator who is a fifty-nine-year-old ex-naval man, who comes out of a world of suicide—his father committed suicide, his wife committed suicide. Finally the drama in the novel, the conflict in the novel, is the narrator's effort to prevent his daughter's suicide—he is not successful, she dies. However, he himself undergoes all kinds of tribulations and violations and by the end of the novel, I think we do have, in effect, a survivor.[1]

From the first page of the book—"I will tell you in a few words who I am: lover of the hummingbird that darts to the flower beyond the rotted sill"[2]—to the middle of the novel, where Skipper, the protagonist, is an officer aboard the U.S.S. *Starfish* (138), to the end—"the hummingbird sucked their tiny drams of honey at my still window" (206)—Hawkes uses animal figures extensively. As both background imagery and central metaphor, animals enforce the shape of events that Hawkes sets in motion. The title itself, in fact, relies on lizards and iguanas, those creatures that shed their skins and take on second skins for new seasons in their lives.

The novel is the logical conclusion for the rhetorical, imagistic, and thematic trends noted previously—and this is most especially true of the animal figures in the book. It is as animal and through animals that the protagonist makes, and is shown to make, his escape from the morbid kinds of worlds Hawkes has portrayed in his previous works.

The novel begins with Skipper reminiscing on his life and, by doing so, identifying the novel's characters: Skipper's father (who is not important until the concluding portion of the book) who shoots himself in his bathroom; Gertrude, Skipper's alcoholic and nymphomaniac wife, who kills herself; Cassandra, Skipper's daughter, who plunges to her death from a light tower in Maine; Pixie, Cassandra's daughter, who survives; Fernandez, Cassandra's homosexual husband, who kills himself; Miranda, a widow, who is the last stronghold of the society Skipper flees, and who fails to hold him; Sonny, Skipper's Negro mess boy, friend and father to Skipper's child by Kate, to whose unidentified and distant island Skipper escapes. The mad family history, survival of the desperate daughter's daughter, and flight to negritude, remind one of Faulkner's *The Sound and the Fury*.

Although early identification by the narrator of himself and other characters is a traditional method for beginning a novel, there is nothing merely traditional about what Hawkes does here. Mentioning at the end of the first chapter how his mother reacted to his father's death, Skipper adds, almost as an afterthought, that she "deafened hereslf one muggy night . . . by filling both lovely ears with the melted wax from one of our dining room candles" (9). The horror of this statement is calm, it is oxymoronic—the juxtaposition of *lovely* with the searing act—and (a parody of the murder Hamlet's mother committed on his father) it leads to the final statement of the introductory chapter, "on now to the erratic flight of the hummingbird—on to the high lights of my naked history," which suggests that Hawkes's carefully

Second Skin

wrought images of terror and delight will work simultaneously throughout the length of this story of a middle-aged man's flight to life.

The novel opens in a western city, during World War II. Although he departs from custom in setting a book in America for only the second time, Hawkes does not depart from his preoccupation with war. Skipper is with Cassandra and Pixie as they await their bus to the east, and Skipper is noting in Cassandra the "seeds of death" that his dead wife, his dead father, and mother have planted through him. Like Jutta's daughter in *The Cannibal* and Adeppi in *The Goose on the Grave*, Cassandra is alone and victimized—as was the child with his dog in *The Lime Twig*, as were Margaret and Michael Banks. Amidst the swaying bell-bottoms and shouts and crowded confusions of a seaport cafe, Skipper sees his daughter's purse, which he knows to be empty: "No stockings, no handkerchief, no lipstick or keys; no love, no mother, no Fernandez" (12). Through her pathos, Cassandra, the victim, renders more threatening the world from which Skipper will ultimately flee.

Torn with love for his daughter, Skipper tries to make her smile and succeeds this far: "I was flooded with the sound of the whisper and sight of a tiny golden snake wriggling up the delicate cleft of her throat—still no smile, never a smile—and curling in a circle to pulse, to die, in the shallow white nest of her temple." He drops her hand and feels his Good Conduct Ribbon, "like a dazzling insect" (13).

Cassandra asks Skipper to do her one favor, and he, remorseful about her fate and her unhappiness, agrees at once. She takes him to a tattoo parlor—"only a rat's hole"—where the proprietor wears the "peacock colors of his self-inflicted art" (15). His tattooed hand begins to "swim like a trained seal in the slime of a drawer" (16) as he prepares to comply with Casandra's orders: tattoo the name *Fernandez*—he has deserted Cassandra—in bright green, over Skipper's heart.

Skipper submits to being branded with his daughter's grief, to carrying her blight on his heart, and his own description of his reaction to the pain of tattooing is a triumph of Hawkes's use of animal figures to create a sense of horror: "The scream—yes, I confess it, scream—that was clamped between my teeth was a strenuous black bat struggling . . . fast as the stinging of artificial bees, this exquisite torture—I with my eyes squeezed tight, my lips squeezed tight—felt that at any moment it must thrust the slimy black tip of its archaic skeletal wing out into view. . . . But I was holding on. I longed to disgorge the bat, to sob. . . . But I was holding on. . . . There were tiny fat glistening tears in the corners of my eyes. But they never fell. Never from the eyes of this heavy bald-headed once-handsome man. Victim. Courageous victim" (19).

Skipper looks in the mirror to see the shape of his pain and remarks *Fernandez*, "this green lizard that lay exposed and crawling on my breast" (20). It is this burden of guilt, made reptilian skin—and, so, capable of being shed—that Skipper will exchange for his second skin. In bearing a brand of guilt, Skipper reminds us of Hester Prynne and her brand of guilt, and we may again remember how American this book is. As in *The Beetle Leg*, Hawkes, when he deals with America, does so fundamentally, in terms of its myths. The movement of this book is toward that American Dream, the New Eden America's colonists sought in New England—and which Skipper will create in his wandering island of the mind.

Having left Sonny, Skipper's black companion, behind, father, daughter, and granddaughter board the bus and travel eastward. On the bus, Skipper's thoughts are of the tragic loneliness of his daughter, of the death she suggests she will meet when she tells him that all of her loves have been blind dates and that "'this is my last blind date'" (31). When sad ends and misery are suggested, in Hawkes's works, an animal imagery usually reinforces their effect. Thus Pixie, when she boards the bus, cries—"insect going berserk in his glass, little fists socking the window" (27–28); Skipper senses that outside the bus are "the flat shoe leather bodies of dead prairie rodents" (31); the horn of the bus is an "inane orchestrated warning to weak-kneed straying cows"; Pixie, now asleep, has bad dreams and makes "little pig sounds" (32); and, when the bus has a flat tire and the passengers must get off, Skipper notes the debris of the desert, "tiny cellular spines, dead beetles, the discarded translucent tissue of wandering snakes, the offal of embryonic lizards and fields of dead dry locusts" (35). Here we are back in the terrain of *The Beetle Leg*.

Then there is a new threat; Skipper senses danger to the travelers stranded by their defective bus and, instead of sleeping as they do, becomes "the solitary sentry with quick eyes for every shadow and a mass of moonlit veins scurrying across my naked scalp like worms" (38).

The danger finally does materialize, in the form of three soldiers AWOL from a nearby infantry post. But they are more than simply soldiers, as the Red Devils in *The Beetle Leg* were more than nomadic motorcycle riders. Hawkes created the almost supernatural quality of the gauntleted and helmeted Red Devils through constantly comparing them to dogs, to insects, and to unnatural and unidentifiable beasts; the same may be said of Hawkes's treatment of the three soldiers who, rifles at the ready, "invade" the enclave of travelers: they are closer to beasts than to men. First, the soldiers peer over a sand dune at the group, and their "heads sank down until the men were only turtle shells" (40).

Then they charge, arriving to take up skirmishing positions: "Web belts and straps, brass buckles, cactus-green fatigue uniforms—name tags ripped off the pockets—paratrooper boots dark brown with oil; they lay there like three deadly lizards waiting to strike, and all of their vicious, yet somehow timorous, white eyes began blinking at once." The soldier who leads the other two—"all little tight tendons and daggers and hand grenades and flashing bright points and lizard eyes" (40)—tells them to dig holes in the sand and "'Now get rid of your eggs . . . bury them'" (41). The extension of the lizard analogy—for lizards bury their eggs in sand in order to hatch them—may be more than artistic neatness, a desire on Hawkes's part to continue a metaphor as far as possible: "egg" is the term often used by American military men for bombs or hand grenades. If these men are burying their explosive eggs, they are planting virtual dragon's teeth; they are sowing death and disorder. Military men, in this anlogy, are reptilian; and Skipper, himself a military man, wears the insignia of the reptile on his chest—"this green lizard that lay exposed and crawling on my breast" (20). Skipper himself has already told Cassandra: " 'I grew up very familiar with the seeds of death; I had a special taste for them always' " (12). So, in time of general war, Skipper's particularity—his close association with the seeds of death, one of whom may be his own Cassandra—is extended by metaphor to a generation. His nation is reptilian, and it plants the seeds or "eggs" of death. It is from his world and himself as well that Skipper must escape; it is, in a sense, his world's skin, as well as his own, that Skipper must ultimately shed.

The soldiers then strip their uniforms off and bury them, too. They stand "white and thin and half-starved and glistening like watery sardines hacked from a tin" (42). They line up and, one by one, kiss Cassandra once—as if they were meeting her on the "blind date" she has alluded to earlier. The last soldier to kiss her evokes response in her, to Skipper's horror, and she kisses him back, whispering, " 'Give me your gun . . . please show me how to work your gun' " (43), as if to presage her death by suicide and to suggest the close tie in this novel between love and death: human sexuality is murderous—in America, at least.

The soldiers flee, stealing clothing from the passengers, and the bus eventually is repaired and on its way to the East, where Skipper is to perform his final shore patrol duties and find Fernandez. At this point the narrative jumps to Skipper on the island to which he has fled and on which he recounts the events leading to his flight.

The island is unidentified, but is obviously a pardise for Skipper. He speaks of Catalina Kate, the mistress with whom "I have only to drop my trousers to awaken paradise itself . . . with the sympathetic sound of Catalina Kate's soft laughter" (46). That the island is a place of rebirth for Skipper is shown through his reference to snakes—presumably snakes that have shed their skins: "But the wind, this bundle of invisible snakes, roars across

Second Skin

our wandering island—it *is* a wandering island, unlocated in space and quite out of time—and seems to heap the shoulders with an armlike weight, to coil about my naked legs and pulse and cool and caress the flesh with an unpredictable weight and consistency, tension, of its own. These snakes that fly in the wind are as large around as tree trunks; but pliant, as everlastingly pliant, as the serpents that crowd my dreams. . . . Cassandra is gone but I am wrapped in wind, walk always—from the hips, from the hips—through the thick entangled currents of this serpentine wind" (46).

While snakes have always been dangerous in Hawkes's novels and have always accompanied evil with their appearance, here they are beneficent; the soft sensuality Skipper ascribes to them is the first gentle note in this novel, the first animal reference that is not companion to acts of unpleasantness. In a context of reptilian horror, the passage quoted above becomes singular and emphatic. When we plunge back into Skipper's wartime world, our confrontations with the malignant reptiles so common to Hawkes's novels will be doubly distressing and affective because of the contrast this passage provides.

Skipper remarks that his near-nudity is most comfortable for his work, which is, extraordinarily enough, artificial insemination of cows: "In my flapping tennis shoes and naval cap and long puffy sun-bleached trousers, and accompanied by my assistant, Sonny, I am much esteemed as the man who inseminates the cows. . . . And I am brown from walking to the cows in the sun, so brown that the green name tattooed on my breast has all but disappeared. . . . The mere lowing of a herd, you see, has become my triumph" (47).

His skin shed, Skipper now spends his days planting the seeds of life, not death. His days are spent with the gentleness of cattle, the joy of procreation—and not only of cows, for Catalina Kate has announced that she is pregnant by either Sonny or Skipper. To some degree, then, the uncomplicated Kate—"this mauve puff of powder who still retains her aboriginal sweaty armpits and lice eggs in the pores of her bare dusty feet"—is cowlike. It may be safe to reason that the uncomplicated offspring of the cows will serve as pattern for the child Kate will bear: there will be no suicide, no self-torture, no emotional complications, no seeds of death cast off. There is in this birth a merging of friends (Sonny and Skipper), a sharing of responsibility for the life of the child, and, therefore, no solitary guilt for Skipper to bear over his heart as the tattoo of Fernandez' name has been borne. It is this birth, Skipper says, that will "complete my history . . . my hymn to the invisible changing serpents of the wind, complete this the confession of my triumph, this my diary of an artificial inseminator" (49). Clearly, the island is as magical as Prospero's, and Skipper has undergone a sea-change. His change, though, depends upon mechanical, artificial "white magic" in dealing with nature; it depends upon shared responsibility for the creation of life— upon the possibility that he may *not* be responsible for creating life. Skipper, as Prospero, has language for his magic. And we must note that artifice, art, flourishes, as does human association, away from America—in the imaginary landscapes Hawkes's characters seem always to shelter in.[3]

While awaiting the birth, the reader must further endure the horrors shared by Cassandra and Skipper, this time in a house on the Maine coast where Skipper and his daughter are inexplicably staying. One reason for the stay there might be the "recent and terrifying secret knowledge about Fernandez" to which Skipper refers. Certainly the house will reveal unhappiness, or so one may assume from this typical Hawkesian imagery spoken by Skipper: "Every morning from my bedroom window I watched a single hungry bird hang itself on the wet rising wind and . . . submit itself endlessly to the first raw gloom of day in the hopes of spying from on high some flash of food in the dirty undulating trough of a wave. And every morning I stood blowing on my fingers and watching the torn and ragged bird until it flapped away on the ragged wings of its discouragement . . . smiling to think that here even the birds were mere prowlers in the mist and wind, mere vagrants in the empty black dots of that low sky" (51).

The animal imagery in this section of the book is thickly applied. The house, rented from a widow, has a wasps' nest under the eaves and a settee filled with mice (51); dogs are

Second Skin

chained behind the house; the closet contains three sea-chests made of "bone and brass and dried-out cracked turkey skin"; the bath tub has lion claws; a black brassiere left in the bathroom dangles "as large and stark as an albatross"—clothes are always doffed in this novel, standing between the wearer and his experience of the world (Skipper finally tells his "naked" history) (52); the house is "worm-eaten"; the gulls outside groan (53); when Skipper goes out to face the freezing weather (so much in contrast to that of his paradise) he sees the ragged bird of his daily observations hovering over the lighthouse—"black missing tooth for a door"—where Cassandra will die.[4] He thinks to himself that "time, the white monster, had already gripped the edge of this island in two bright claws, had already begun to haul itself out of an ugly sea" (57). Skipper will have to create an island outside time, one of art, to which he can escape.

It is in this atmosphere that Skipper first encounters Miranda, who says, "you look like a damn seal. People shoot seals around here" (59), and then she disappears.

Miranda—beautiful, similar in her overt sexuality to Sybilline of *The Lime Twig*, and so named as to remind us again of *The Tempest*—leaves a greeting for Skipper in the kitchen: the nipples for Pixie's bottle have been sliced with a knife so as to be unusable (it is nearly a work of voodoo, a gesture of hatred toward life, sexuality, and self). If Skipper's goal is the island on which he will create and nurture life, Miranda's island, her house, and her personal aura suggest the desire to stop life: death is the sea change she seeks. She plays a recording of the *Horst Wessel lied*, uses heroin, drinks too much bourbon, and reminisces about her husband, killed by a land mine in Europe. She is the spirit of death that is the age's, the world's.

And she entraps Cassandra. When she drinks, Cassandra drinks. When Miranda knits with black yarn, Cassandra sits at her feet, the yarn about her wrists, linking herself to Miranda with what Skipper calls "their shapeless squid" (70).

Miranda then accompanies Cassandra on a "blind date" with two local fishermen. Cassandra sleeps with her escort while Skipper tries to find her but is halted by Miranda. She tries to seduce him in her car, offering him her buttocks in scorn. (In love, he will later—protected by artifice—accept the hindquarters of a cow.) By the time he has left the car, having rejected her, Cassandra is home asleep, the passion of her "last blind date" expended and death imminent.

The narrative next moves back to Skipper's island, where he is taking Kate into a swamp in which, her child now ready to be born, she wishes to give birth in a state of nature and of amphibians like Skipper. He leads the way and does not notice a huge iguana until Kate slips, falls, and is seized by the beast, which fastens to her back with its claws and will not let go. Thus begins Skipper's final wrestling with reptilian skin: "His head reached her shoulders, his tail dropped over her buttocks, and he might have been twenty or thirty pounds of sprawling bright green putty. . . . Thick and limp and weak, except for the oversized claws which were grips of steel. Kate was looking at me and smiling and the iguana was looking at me, and I heard the noise of locust or cricket or giant swamp fly strangling behind a nearby bush" (105–106).

Skipper stands over Kate and tries to pry the beast from her back, from his breeding-ground for the seeds of life: "I got him with the first grab. Held him. Waited. And with my feet buried deep in the sand, my legs spread wide and locked, my rump in the air, tattered shirt stuck to my skin like a plaster, nostrils stoppered up with the scum of the swamp, heart thumping, I made myself hold on to him—in either hand I gripped one of the forelegs—and fought . . . not to tear away my hands and run. . . . Feeling of being glued to the iguana, of skin growing fast to reptilian skin" (107). But Skipper is not strong enough for the task. He cannot move the iguana and so must wait, with Kate, until the beast grows hungry and moves away of its own volition—which it does.

Although the threat of the "first skin" is dispelled, it might seem that, because of Skipper's inability to tear the reptile from Kate, war, evil, guilt, and death have won a victory—that the "first skin" may attach itself again. Such seems not to be the case, though, if we keep in mind the hole in which the reptilian soldiers

Second Skin

buried their eggs, and juxtapose it with this passage: "I took her hand. I covered her back with the remnants of my own dissolving shirt and I reached down into the enormous egg-shaped hole in the sand and helped Kate to feel with her soft young fingers what I could feel with mine: the warmth of the recent flesh and the little humped hieroglyphic in the warm sand" (109). The early hole of death, that in which the seeds of death were buried, is matched by this hole of life. And Skipper's shirt finally covers Kate's back in place of the lizard-skin that was there. Skipper's escape is a triumph.

The story returns to Skipper and Fernandez as they drive to the inn in which Fernandez and Cassandra will honeymoon. The time is only shortly before the beginning of the bus trip East. Time is then moved further back to Skipper on the *Starfish* when, in mutiny, the crew sweeps him along in its violence and one of the rebelling seamen forces his pederastic will on Skipper. Skipper's memory of the *Starfish* suggests, in Malcolm Lowry's *Under the Volcano* (a "peacetime" book haunted by war), the incident on board the *Samaritan,* which branded the Consul with a guilt he was to bear all his life. The memory of his victimization through violence gnaws at him when Miranda turns her buttocks to him, and the pain of that memory is comforted when, standing behind the cows he is to inseminate, he recalls "the fullness of my own hips, sensitive also to the time of cows" (48). He has redeemed his oppression in a world of violence by imitating the stance of that violence in an act of giving and creation.

Hawkes then moves to Skipper as he discovers the body of Fernandez, while he is on shore patrol before his sojourn with Cassandra and Miranda on the cold island antipodal to the one he comes to rest on. Fernandez has been killed in a fight with homosexual lovers and he is literally beaten to a pulp, the fingers of his left hand chopped off, a string from his guitar wound around his neck. Fernandez is another of many deaths and mysteries that Skipper must recount to Cassandra—for which, in her eyes, he must account.

As if in association, the narrative moves far back in time to the death of Skipper's father, who locked himself in the bathroom and, while Skipper sawed desperately on his cello in an effort to coax his father out, shot himself. The events are linked by the strangling music, the choking guitar string.

Juxtaposed with that shot, that planting of death in Skipper's line, is this description—back on the wandering island again—of Skipper's insemination of a cow: "and at the very moment that the loaded pipette might have disappeared inside, might have slipped from sight forever, I leaned forward and gave a little puff into the tube . . . and pulled back quickly, slapped her rump, tossed the flexible spent pipette in the direction of the satchel and grinned as the whole tree burst into the melodious racket of the dense tribe of blackbirds cheering for our accomplished cow" (171). The explosion of seed, of applause for accomplishment at procreation, at the lending by man of ease and certainty to the processes of beasts—these stand in opposition to the explosion of cordite that heralded the end of Skipper's father; these latter events are the beginnings of things, and the beginnings—the opportunities to start again—are the design of Skipper's second skin.

Animal imagery abounds in the latter portion of the novel, in which the narrative moves us back again to Miranda's island, and to the end that Cassandra has said she will meet. The dogs are mentioned again, as are cows, mollusks, and chicken feathers. There is a smell of dead fish, and field mice cower in crab grass (174–78). Cassandra and Skipper are taken to sea on a fishing boat by the sailor with whom Cassandra has slept. Again Skipper is on the sea in a boat, and is again victimized. When they are far from shore, Skipper is knocked unconscious by a crewman while something happens to his daughter. He is in ignorance, and so is the reader. The narrative tension with which Hawkes proved himself so capable in *The Lime Twig* begins to grow. This is especially true when Cassandra revives the injured Skipper, unbuttons his shirt, and shows her paramour the mark of death, Skipper's burden carried for his daughter's sake, tattooed to his chest. Although we do not know what transpired while Skipper was unconscious, we may infer that it is related to the tatoo the way most events in Cassandra's life are—through violence and the scent of death.

Second Skin

On an afternoon in May, Cassandra's lover comes for her in a black hotrod, and they drive off. Skipper borrows Miranda's car—she accompanies him—and they drive in frantic pursuit of Cassandra. As they draw nearer to the sea, there is more unpleasant odor—kelp, "armies of mussels and clams" (194), the smell of salt—which is usually a sign in a Hawkes novel of imminent death.

Then Skipper is afoot, running through sand to reach Cassandra in the lighthouse. Although we suspect what Cassandra's fate will be, Skipper's effort to reach her is still compelling. Hawkes involves us in the nightmare of Skipper's world: "What heavy steps I took in the sand, how deep those footprints that trailed behind me as I took my slow-motion way down that desolate beach toward the lighthouse. Slow-motion, yes, and a slogging and painful trot. . . . And crab grass, pools of slime." Skipper races toward a lighthouse called Dog's Head light amid "the brittle feet of the luminous crab" (196). Every animal figure used here adds to the unhuman atmosphere in which Skipper runs—only to be too late. As he reaches the top of the tower, after an exhausting climb, Cassandra hurtles to the ground, leaving him "an old bird in an empty nest" (198).

The immediate reason for Cassandra's death is not given until —the time is June, a month after the suicide—Miranda casually points to a wrapped jar at Skipper's place on the breakfast table: a two-month-old embryo, the child that would have been Cassandra's. We may surmise that Cassandra's suicide was a self-punishment for bearing another seed of death, for Skipper buries the embryo in a local graveyard (as the soldiers buried their eggs and as Skipper will bury his guilts), takes Pixie to a distant cousin's home, finds Sonny,[5] and leaves for his wandering island —as if to escape this final planting of death, as if to expiate all the plantings by creating life—in safety, in art, in a guarantee of no further responsibility.[6]

Much that was said of *The Lime Twig* can be said of *Second Skin*. The novel depends upon copious use of animal imagery—

especially in metaphors—for its strange effects. The use of reptiles and eggs as extended metaphors is obvious. The manner in which the cows are used is not obvious, for there is no easily spotted object for which cattle in this novel may be analog. Although Kate seems to be cow-like, she alone would seem insufficient justification for the constant reference to cattle in *Second Skin*. We would be justified in wondering whether the cows are metaphors at all, whether they may not exist in the novel as characters, part of the protagonist's environment—and yet as more than simple imagery. We may wonder whether the cows are the opposite of everything that Skipper has encountered on his lifelong journey to the island—lean and maddened Fernandez, tortured Cassandra, and insane Miranda. We may wonder whether the cows are the island, its spirit, the placid and accepting state of life in which even such a horror as the iguana with its threat of "the first skin" will go away if one is sufficiently patient.

As was true in *The Lime Twig*, there is considerable animal imagery, but not nearly so much as in *The Cannibal* or *The Beetle Leg*. While Hawkes uses it sparingly—to set a scene, emphasize a dramatic moment—it does not cover the pages; animal metaphors are large, almost as if at the expense of background imagery, and the extended metaphors attract the reader's eye and intellect.

Hawkes uses sentence fragments and jagged rhythms in this work to create a sense of staccato perception; "moonlight. Black shadows. Soft silk of the dirt road around the island, and larches, uncut brambles at the side of the road and a dead net hanging down from a luminous branch . . . every few hundred feet a water rat leapt from some hollow log or half-buried conduit, dashed under our wheels" (191).

The reader sees what Skipper sees as he sees it; his process of discovery is also the reader's. Hawkes's poetic prose reaches heights in *Second Skin*. The rhythm of the passage below is as sustained and driving as is no passage in *Charivari;* the juxtaposition of Brahms with suicide renders the death more awful through use of such a romantic particularity; the image created is one of exquisite pathos which is heightened by rhythm and

Second Skin

particularity, but which never descends to the bathetic. The objective tone of the all-seeing prose narrator, which Hawkes began to develop in *The Cannibal,* is still evident:

> And my arm fell and the bow dragged, sawed, swayed to and fro—hair on gut, fat fingertips on gut—and the cello and I rolled from side to side together.
> So I played for him, played Brahms while my father must have been loading the pistol. . . . I played with no thought of him, really, but he must have gagged a little to himself in there, choked like a man coughing up blood for the first time as he tried to decide how best to use the nickel-plated weapon. . . . I suppose the first sounds of the cello must have destroyed the spell of the faucet. So I played on, phantom accomplice to his brutal act, and all the while hoping, I think, for success and pleased with the song. (160)

If it is mastery to achieve characters who easily grip and move the reader, and a sense of suggested cause-and-effect among absorbing events, then Hawkes, in *Second Skin,* has displayed his mastery as a novelist. The interrupted and disturbing interplay between different times is still present. It works to good end: we can feel the fragmentation of Skipper's world, feel his imagination pull that world together again. But the fragmentation seems more manageable than it did in, for instance, *The Beetle Leg,* because it is the narrator on whose actions we focus and through whose eyes we see events. Watching things as he watches them—in bursts of recollection and shifts of attention—adds to the credibility of that character: he is believable to us, and we follow where he leads, accepting that to which he leads us.

Second Skin is a triumph of structure and language and the manipulation of those animal figures whose primitive ancestors came to light with the appearance of those forty-year-old jackdaws of *Charivari.* Moreover, it is a triumph *for* language. In the face of Cassandra's inward fall and Miranda's brutal madness, the novel appears to proclaim the setting down by man of what has befallen him. Fernandez, the homosexual guitar player, is apparently an impotent Orpheus. Skipper's art and way with life's creatures is also impotent—in his case, before his father's urge to death, since his cello-playing cannot lure his father to life. The book would appear not to be about art's triumph; it is, rather, about the victory of the desire or need to create an orderly structure (in Skipper's case, his island): it celebrates Prospero's trade without guaranteeing that his magic (Skipper's sung language) will always work. What is crucial, though, and optimistic, is the mere fact that Skipper's magic and salvation is a contrapuntally structured *narrative*, about the loss of which to history, psychoanalysis, and fiction Lionel Trilling has brilliantly complained.[7] Hawkes affirms the need to tell what led to what or what might have *caused* what. *Second Skin* ends with a man who controls his sense in the face of enormous Job-like defeats. It is a triumph for those who believe that narrative order (that of Henry James or Flannery O'Connor or Djuna Barnes or Sigmund Freud) leads to sanity and delight.

But we must not exaggerate the nature of this triumph. The title, *Second Skin*, and the constant stripping-away of clothes, suggest that Skipper moves toward his authentic self, away from the guilt imposed on who he really is. But who he "really" is never becomes determined in the novel; his triumphant final self is as fictive as his early guilt-laden self: his triumph simply is that, at the novel's end, *he* creates who he is—no one else renders him. However, Kate's child will come from either Sonny or Skipper—two men with different-colored skins—and their shared responsibility for Kate's child means that one *or* the other creates new life—black *or* white. The implication is not racial, but rhythmic: it suggests the dynamic of sad-glad, bad-good, death-life, guilt-innocence. The novel's sane and salutary conclusion is temporary, linked as it is to a narrative whose rhythms belong to the basic social unit of tragedy—the family. The narrative has dealt with the heartbeat rhythms of birth and death in Skipper's family; it pauses like the hovering hummingbird on birth, but what it is—a cyclical narrative moving always from fetus to corpse to fetus again—suggests that death might well come next. Skipper knows this. It is part of life, as he is; affirming himself, he affirms all life—even the death which may be the next beat of the novel's rhythm.

7 The Innocent Party

The Innocent Party,[1] Hawkes's eighth major work and sixth book, was written during 1964–65, when Hawkes was awarded a Ford Foundation fellowship to work for a year with the Actor's Workshop in San Francisco, under the direction of Herbert Blau and Jules Irving. The book is composed of four one-act plays.

They are fiction-writer's drama: there is minimal use of the stage as a familiar hunting-ground on which to pursue dramatic action; the language is virtually unaltered from that of the novels; there are few characters. On the other hand, these characters' dialogue is engaging, often frightening, and hypnotic; Hawkes's timing of pause and speech benefits from his novelistic experience with dialogue; the humor, sometimes very broad, is also very effective. And "the innocent party" of the title—the person whose innocence (often dubious-seeming) is about to be encroached upon—is present in every play as an engaging, sometimes maddening, character. In the midst of absurdity—and these are absurdist dramas; Tennessee Williams and Samuel Beckett, Harold Pinter and Edward Albee are not unlikely influences here—Hawkes creates character. He is as obsessed as ever with narrative: the act of telling where some action came from and toward what its dangerous arc goes. Thus, his characters in these plays are concerned with telling where *they* came from, out of what fright and nightmare they have come to test their dreams among frightened people. The pattern of the plays is confession or story-telling or ritual rehearsal or prayer or—as in especially *The Questions*, the last play—psychoanalysis.

Herbert Blau's Preface is not concerned with an analytic introduction to the plays as much as with praising Hawkes and generating momentum for the collection. But he does offer this useful paragraph on the plays and on Hawkes: "In Hawkes's plays, as in his novels, there is an inscape of wonder in a landscape of mutilations. Innocence is on the limb, ripe for perversion. Brute ignorance encroaches. We see deadness descending upon the gift of play. Whether he knows it or not, the new form in which Hawkes is working does double duty for his theme. There is a time-serving brutality in the theater, which confounds playing with acting. In the theater you must play, but *play before your time is up*" (10).

These plays do demonstrate ends to innocence, to kinds of virginity. They show time—as history, memories of death, and disaster—encroaching upon imaginative constructions of dreams and artistic shapings by the characters of their own lives, and thus wreaking misfortune in the lives of characters who, before an onslaught for which they are unprepared, seem virginal. By showing concern and by insisting upon confrontation with the narrative mode, Hawkes looks back to *Second Skin* and, as will become evident, forward to *The Blood Oranges*.

The Innocent Party is set in "an abandoned motel in a subtropical area of the United States"; its dried-out swimming pool is partially filled with debris, and the residents—Beatrix, now barren wife to the impotent Edward; Jane, their daughter, "part tomboy and part Aphrodite-as-young-girl" (14)—are visited by rich, sophisticated, beautiful Phoebe who brings a force of life to this waste land. They want money from Phoebe; Jane wants to escape their sterility; Phoebe wants Jane. There are overtones of incestuous feelings toward Jane on Edward's part—and toward Phoebe on Edward's part, too. Over-all, the feeling is of the waste land of *Charivari* and, because it is an American waste land, that of *The Beetle Leg*.

There is the obsession with money that so many American

The Innocent Party

writers impute to America. Here, in a motel that is the wreckage of the American Dream, Beatrix berates Phoebe (who arrives in a white Cadillac) for enjoying her wealth while the family is impoverished. Referring to a cruise ship on which Phoebe sported, Beatrix cries: " 'Well, I hope it was worthwhile. I hope you found your soul on the *Santa Maria*' " (35). The reference of course is to Columbus' ship, the dream of the New Eden that drove Columbus and other explorers to America. The implication is that the New Eden is in ruin, collapsed. Phoebe says: " 'Can you imagine an ambulance in here? The long white emergency arm of medical science in the Garden of Eden.' " Beatrix replies: " 'It's not paradise. Believe me' " (62), then goes on to say: " 'An abandoned motel on the edge of the universe. It smells of obsolescence and rank decay, it smells of the tears of uncouth strangers and the refuse of their sordid pleasures. It smells of death. Is this any kind of home for me? Is this any kind of home for a growing girl?' " (63).

That the American house is in ruins—a theme out of Tennessee Williams and William Faulkner—is further suggested by the sign that Jane has found on the edge of the property; Beatrix describes it to Phoebe: " 'Laugh, laugh! But it's not my invention. I swear it's not. Listen to the words, you pitiless woman: COLORED ONLY. VACANCY. Is that ignominy, Phoebe? COLORED, COLORED, COLORED ONLY! That's what I call ignominy, Phoebe. Ignominy and disgrace and degradation!' " (73).

Of course it *is* Beatrix' "invention": it is the invention of America—the sale of people for profit which is a founding-stone of the American Dream. Hawkes uses the issue of black enslavement as Faulkner does in *Absalom, Absalom!* and as Melville does in *Benito Cereno:* it is the symbol of the death of the American house and the threat, too, of its punishment. This is for Hawkes the first such direct management of basic American social and historical material; the concern runs throughout these plays. That the curse will continue is suggested by Beatrix' complaint that " 'my daughter has been stealing from the Negroes' " (43). The accusation creates a scapegoat, permitting Beatrix to cry " 'it's not my invention,'" and to dismiss the past, blame it on Jane, who is the virginal figure. What happens to her, in the terms of this play, will determine what happens to America.

As is true of Michael in *The Lime Twig*, Edward is a victim of dreams, and so is Jane. At dawn, every day, Jane comes out to the empty, littered swimming pool:

> Then I listen, and I think I'll hear it trickling, or I think I'll hear drops of it dripping at the edge. And you know what? I think of fish and whales and seaweed and big jellyfish sitting like eggs without shells in little pools of water. . . . Still I think it's filling up—maybe it's already reached the top—and I start walking over to it. . . . I kneel down at the edge and think I'm going to pop out of my bikini. And do you know what I'm looking at?
> *Phoebe:* No, baby.
> *Jane:* Me! For a moment there's water in the pool and leaning over like that I see myself, Aunt Phoebe, my own face. (18)

Jane is her own dream, she is the fruit of the American Dream. And Phoebe, who says of herself, "'old Phoebe's the angel of joy. . . . Remember that!'" (28), promises this about the foundering dream: "'She's a virgin. She doesn't know whether she wants to be a girl or boy. But she'll find out'" (44). The implication is that Phoebe will help her to determine what she—a radio-listener (to limpid music, "Comic Strip of the Air," and other cultural ruins), narcissist, witless doll—shall become.

Edward, too, has his dream. He collects sea shells. Like the others, he approaches the magical Phoebe while she sleeps and speaks to her form, discusses his shells: "'I want to show you my sea shells. I've studied them, scrutinized them, catalogued them. The shells come from the sea, but they're really products of my own mind. You have to think about shells to love them. (*He moves away, rearranges the shells on the table.*) These rare things, these delicate abstractions of human life . . .'" (51). Edward is like J. Alfred Prufrock, happier at home beneath the sea, where there is no communication, than in the world of men. His sea-world is his mind, and he hides there, as Prufrock wished to scuttle along ocean floors. The sense of incest—Faulkner uses it in this way also, to signify the curse turning the family in upon itself, ceasing its reproduction, wiping it out—emerges as Edward further discusses the shells before the recumbent Phoebe, the catalyst in this play for such discussion: " 'And in this shell the mouth (*with emphasis*) is wide and pink-lipped, but orange within. A short canal, a swollen body whorl, an orange mouth—is it a fitting totem for an only daughter, Phoebe? For a young daughter?' " (52).

If Edward has his dream, he has his nightmare, too; the entire family suffers it, but perhaps Beatrix more than the others—for she must deal with it. Begging Phoebe, " 'touch me, Phoebe! Turn me to gold!' " (48), she later tells her the story of the nightmare-curse, as if to ask her to rid them of it: Each morning, Edward goes into the bathroom to shave,

> Then Edward reaches for the faucet, and the first trickle of tepid water must wake it up, because that's the moment the centipede leaps up at us! One minute there's nothing but water trickling down the drain, and the next minute there's the centipede jumping at us, shooting up out of the little rusty drainhole in the bottom of the basin like a monster! That's when I scream! . . . Because the centipede is as long as my hand and as big around as my thumb, a slick wriggling monster like a giant worm with a hundred little thrashing legs and horns on one end and a forked tail at the other, a wet brown worm with yellow spots and enough poison in its forked tail to kill us both! (68)

Clearly, Hawkes's use of animal imagery is undiminished, returning to the nightmare creatures of *Charivari* and *The Beetle Leg*. History, the truth of their lives—and of modern American life—comes wriggling up from where it has been hidden away in the collective subconscious and the individual recessed mind, and it comes as a curse. For after Beatrix collects the monster in a coffee can and flings it " 'as far away as I can into the festering swamp,' " and after Edward " 'shaves in peace' " (68), the centipede returns with the next day's banal ritual shave—" 'day after day it returns' " (69). Hawkes's use of specific sensual detail makes the curse palpable and nauseous; his placement of it in the humdrum daily shaving routine makes it almost a joke; the combination makes it a horror, a cyclical curse (like that of Sisyphus,

Tantalus, and Prometheus) which, because it does not happen to heroes engaged in titanic struggles, serves to further reduce these waste-landers. The return of the creature to the festering swamp, from which the COLORED ONLY sign comes also, suggests that the swamp is the subconscious guilt in the midst of which Americans try to forget it. It will not be forgotten; the past will not be dismissed.

At the end of the play, Jane and Phoebe drink tequila, which Phoebe considers medicinal, and Phoebe tries to seduce Jane. Phoebe croons "'come on, baby, swim to me . . . you baby shark'" (92). Still, as they dance to music from the radio, Jane resists her and Phoebe loses her temper, roars her frustration at Edward and Beatrix: "'You with your grasping hearts, you with your—your pee-pot morality! . . . Taste the ashes of your dead Sunday schools, you two—Jane will destroy you yet, she'll destroy your relentless faces and your frightened eyes. . . . You're nothing but a couple of sea shells that mated by accident long ago in warm water. . . . Nothing but a couple of dead Christians from the faded white time of pee-pot morality. . . . I'm going back for a little trip on the *Santa Maria*. I've got the fare! . . . Watch out, you two. Watch out for the centipede. He bites!'" (94).

Phoebe collapses drunkenly, and Jane claims her: "'She's mine, all mine. I'll take care of her.'" Jane then dances with great vigor and skill, and "at the height of Jane's dance the overpowering sound of water rushing into the swimming pool fills the stage and obliterates the music" (95).

Jane has become Phoebe's creature—in fact, because Phoebe then disappears from the stage, one is tempted to suggest that Jane becomes Phoebe herself. Phoebe is no angel of joy: she is the spirit of vengeance and is its voice. Her speech to "'you two'" is directed to a stage empty of anyone but Jane—and so it is not difficult to believe that the audience or reader replaces the parents as object of Phoebe's diatribe: she offers an apocalyptic warning—which is followed by a flood—of the fate of America; she predicts to "you, too" that because America has tried to ignore its past, it will be unable to cope with its future and will be

The Innocent Party

destroyed by it, by its own children. This is the most public utterance Hawkes has yet made, and he does so, appropriately, in a form that makes use of direct public response. He delivers an apocalyptic prophecy that may put us in mind, again, of *Benito Cereno*—the warning that our blackness, festering (we may think) safely away from us, will nevertheless demand us soon. We may try to keep the dog far hence that's friend to man; but we cannot stop looking in the mirror to shave: we may one day, Hawkes warns us, in the midst of our safest banalities, see ourselves— our most fearful monster—whom our past has created and whom we try to ignore.

The Wax Museum is a small play in which there is one offstage voice and two characters on the stage. Little happens. Bingo, an attendant in a wax museum, encounters Sally Ann, who is waiting for her fiancé, Frank (the voice), who is downstairs in the Chamber of Horrors to which she is afraid to descend. Sally Ann, characterized as "the virgin" (98), is the "innocent party" of this play. By the play's end, she has exchanged clothes with Bingo; Bingo goes out to be with Frank, Sally Ann stays to caress George, a wax model of a Royal Canadian Mounted Policeman. In a sense, the play is a horrific parody of the Renaissance romances in which characters frequently don and doff disguises. In this case, Sally Ann is lured to love the dreamworld of which Bingo has been a prisoner. As she croons and caresses George, she becomes a part of the domain of art. Another Sally Ann may one day come in, be lured into exchanging roles with her, while this Sally Ann goes out toward life. The play hints an endless cycle of comings and goings from art to life to art. In this sense it, too, looks forward to *The Blood Oranges*.

Its preoccupation with virginity—a concern of all of the plays —also anticipates *The Blood Oranges*. At one point Bingo says: " 'You're the last of the virgins—but who wants to be a virgin?' " (112). She then says of Marie Antoinette's face: " 'It looks a little like the face of a virgin.' " And then, after Sally Ann replies that

HAWKES: A Guide to His Fictions

"'I'm not as innocent as you think'" (114), goes on to say: "'Come off it, Sal. I can tell at a glance. You may not have any blood trickling out of your mouth, and your mouth might not be open as if you had swallowed an egg in its shell, and your eyes might not be painted the pale blue color of pain and happiness—but you've got a virgin's face if I ever saw one'" (114–115).

The imagery of Bingo's speech looks forward to Sally Ann's loss of virginity—that moment in which time will intersect with her innocent timelessness. She seeks to escape time, at the end of the play, by hiding in the wax museum. The museum collection is of figures from history, people now dead who have set elements of our life in motion—but people who are artificially preserved and rendered virgin from time. As Sally Ann caresses George and becomes part of the art world in the museum, she prolongs her virginity, her escape from the world of time. Here, history is frozen. It is frozen in a skin that, according to Bingo, is deadly poison: "'It produces fever, a rash as red as strawberries, and blindness. It affects childbearing too. Little newborn babies come out looking like little transparent corkscrews'" (101). This permanent art world is inimical to the world of life's reproduction—it is a world of permanent virginity into which time cannot intrude. This concern will be reiterated by Hawkes in the other two plays in this collection and in *The Blood Oranges*.

The Questions, the final play in *The Innocent Party*, has two characters, "The Man," "The Young Girl"—this play's virgin and "innocent party." It takes place "in a white setting so neutral and shadowed that it might be courtroom, doctor's office, sun parlor, or the pure space of psychic activity" (170). In this "pure space of psychic activity," Hawkes isolates on the stage what is suggested in *Second Skin*'s wandering island and the Illyria of *The Blood Oranges*: the drama between the world and the imagination that is played out wherever the imagination chooses to have its confrontation. This is the setless world of Samuel Beckett: voices in dramatic conflict in the white voids of art.

The Innocent Party

What happens in *The Questions* is this: The Young Girl sits in her wooden armchair and answers questions put to her by The Man, who paces or faces her or turns away. The pattern of what they do together is psychoanalytic—he asks her about her father's dream, she tries to answer his questions; the reader sees that she is also trying *not* to answer his questions, but to fabricate answers or evade the direction of his questioning, and so the psychoanalytic mode becomes confused with cross-examination and trial.

At the outset, we learn that "the dream" is " 'Your father's—nightmare' " which has really come from his wife: " 'Papa didn't tell us the dream, of course. Mama did' " (171). As the girl's parents exchange dreams, so do the people on the stage exchange roles: the man periodically assumes the father's role—and even once takes the part of Adrian, the interloper sometimes suspected of being the mother's lover—while the girl on at least two occasions assumes the mother's role. This "psychic activity" warps time, person, and place, but it does cling to a shred of "story" while insisting that all elements of the tale are relative perceptions leading to uncertain conclusions. There is a fox hunt, and the imagery in which it is rendered is like the animal imagery Hawkes has employed previously, and which serves to unite all his works.

The girl speaks of walking her horse near a creek " 'when a riderless horse crashed through the thicket on the other side, shot me a look of pure murder' " (195). After *The Lime Twig* a hostile horse comes as no surprise; we might wish to recall Lowry's *Under the Volcano* when, as the Consul is falling to his death, his beloved Yvonne is killed by the riderless horse—love's failure animated—which has been tracking her and the Consul throughout the novel. In this play about a deluded family, the apparition out of Lowry is not inappropriate.

Furthermore, the girl—incestuously loved by her father, perhaps loved by Adrian—is tracked down psychically by the men just as the homosexual boy, "the fox," was tracked down in *The Cannibal*. And so, in the latter scenes of the play, in which (freely assuming the roles of others) the man and the woman describe a fox hunt, we see the virgin psychically rent; the metaphoric moment is described by The Man, who now narrates events from the father's point of view: " 'So the clouds grew darker and colder while your father and his rival wallowed in the greasy pit, stripping the white fat from the slender bones and cracking joints. . . . until between them they opened up the animal's little dripping coat and posed grinning together' " (236-37).

Finally, there is this animal image, which harks back to *Second Skin*, the moment when Skipper is being tattoed and holds his scream of pain, like a bat, in his mouth:

> *Girl:* Papa has feelings. He's not a child. But Papa's theory was that some emotions are just hunches and others are little black ugly bats you can crush with your teeth. (189)

But the play's imagery not only unites it with Hawkes's novels; its images unite it with the other plays—as in the case of the photograph which the man suggests. The psychic rape is frozen into art by the camera; Edward, in *The Innocent Party*, froze his dreams with a camera; and in these plays, dreams—the art objects of the mad characters—play an enormous part. The conflict in the plays is as much between time and art's timelessness as between innocence and experience.

These themes are joined as the girl says: " 'Papa had this virginity business on the mind, I guess. He said it was his fervent hope I wouldn't lose my virginity in the hunting saddle or on top of a prickly bale of hay in someone's barn' " (216). She admits that she is not a virgin—her evasion of the questions put to her, her searching for refuge in the art of her dreams, is how she seeks to reclaim her virginity from life. She cries out: " 'I guess you think I'm the kind of girl who loses her virginity in a flash of foolishness on a wire-bound bale of hay. I'm not proud of myself— you know, and I don't believe in this privileged prostitute business, or the sacred whore or the miraculous bride, but Papa and Adrian and Mama and I were a lot better than you seem to think . . . !' " (221). And at the end, she dives back into her dreams:

> Listen—my story was just as good as yours. I mean, they were

The Innocent Party

the same, weren't they. . . . Papa said we were all virgins under the skin, and I guess that includes him too.
(*Pause.*)
But listen—according to Papa the silly virgins always beat the moral barbarians at their own game, so I guess we won. (239)

Of course, there can be no winning: the play is a jousting among kinds of dreams, there is no factual reality—only alternate worlds of art.

The thematic concern with Negroes is part of the concern here with systems of art in which people take shelter. The play is set in Charleston, and its Southern setting makes reference to black enslavement expectable. The girl refers to a hitching iron—"'the little iron nigger with a ring in his fist'" (197)—and tells how "'Papa decided to put a fresh coat of paint on the blackamoor—that's what he called the little black iron nigger boy. . . . Papa always liked to touch up the little black iron nigger boy with the ring in his fist. Papa used a bright and shiny stoveblacking for the skin and boots, and red enamel for the shirt and cap and nostrils, and white enamel for the britches and the whites of the eyes. I always enjoyed seeing Papa doing his art work'" (209–10).

As Richard Wright has said, the Negro here is America's metaphor, and these people of dreams create their metaphor as they create their dreams—as the father tries to create his daughter and as the man, acting out the father's role, creates the father himself: everyone in the play is a manufactured dream, a work of art. The man, calling the girl Hired Hand as her father is said to, speaks for him in this way: "'Hold on there, Hired Hand, what's your rush? You just wait until that fine little blackamoor grows up to manhood and you won't go wrong. Save yourself for that blackamoor, Hired Hand, and you won't regret it. The old master knows what he's talking about'" (216). The "old master" who creates people is himself created by the man who assumes his role and who generates his own narrative of who the father was and how he behaved. The Negro's lord and master is himself dominated, is a creation just as the Negro was. Behind the puppets manipulating puppets is a puppet-master. But, as these two characters call all into doubt, suggest that all is relative, so are they themselves called into doubt: we have no reason to assume that they are any less relativistically drawn than anyone else in the play. And this suspicion quite naturally extends to *their* puppet-master—the playright—who may himself be a puppet in the hands of some artistic force. This suggestion looks forward to the "sylvan sources" of *The Blood Oranges* by whom Cyril, the master-artist, will profess to be artistically controlled.

Although it occurs third in the book, *The Undertaker* is reserved for last consideration here because, while it is clearly part of the over-all effort of the collection, it is distinguished as a reprise of one moment of *Second Skin*—that very touching effort of the young Skipper to woo his father from death by suicide. In his introduction Blau says that Hawkes "described *The Undertaker* as a 'farcical melodrama' based on the father's suicide in *Second Skin*" (12). Although there are wildly exaggerated, "unrealistic" moments, and despite the often pleasurable vigor of the father's hatred for a life which has mistreated him, it is difficult to describe the play as either farcical or melodramatic.

Speaking of the manner in which Hawkes captures the child's-eye view of reality (or fantasy) with regard to the father in *Second Skin*, Albert Guerard refers to Hawkes's commentary on how, for the contemporary writer, "the liberating processes of the imagination may result in his discovery of characters closely resembling the heroes, benevolent guides, destructive demons, or awe-inspiring gods that we find in myths, dreams, fantasies and fairy tales." If *Second Skin* at times represents a child's world, says Guerard, it is a Dickensian one—grotesque, magnified, and brutal. The world of *The Undertaker* is this world also. Hawkes speaks of such worlds, with their

> elemental fears and desires, which are constants in the inner lives of men. Fear of the unknown, fear of sexual destruction at the hands of the father, fear of annihilation at the hands of absolute authority, infantile desire for the security and sublimity of the mother's love—these components of the familiar Oedipal

The Innocent Party

situation as defined by Freud are to be found in significant literature through the ages. Such literature tells us that the adult's life is never completely removed from the life of the child, but that whether we achieve self-fulfillment or suffer spiritual death often depends on our ability or inability to return to forgotten experience and to uncover again the powerful emotional energies of childhood.[2]

It is this search for the "energies of childhood"—to employ them, to overcome them—with which *The Undertaker* concerns itself.

The undertaker and his son, Edward, are the play's only characters. Both are described as being in their mid-forties, and so we know that the play takes place in Edward's memory and imagination, that it is a narrative endeavor—a man rehearsing his trauma for the sake of dealing with it and achieving peace.

Edward is this play's "innocent party," its virgin. His father tells him: " 'There's nothing the matter. You've done nothing. You're innocent.' " He then says " 'But I've planted the seeds of death in you, Edward' " (142), and so we have the same situation as in *Second Skin:* the innocent on whom the historical burden is laid; the virgin who must cope with time's brutal thrusting. As the father suggests, being in history is a curse: " 'Well, we'll see, Edward. We'll see how you bear this silence in later years' " (164).

The father, locked in the bathroom (the play's set), fondles his silver pistol and bullets and talks with—taunts—his son. His son pleads with him to come out, in a parody of Orpheus plays the cello to lure him out, then faces the moment of the killing shot—which is silent, engraved on his mind as a flashing of photographic powder. And we are reminded of the cameras (in these plays and in *The Blood Oranges*) which freeze the dream; we remember too that this dream is nightmare.

Race is the metaphor by which Hawkes suggests that each man's life is his dreamworld, his imaginative construct, his artwork. The father's trade of undertaker suggests the guilt of white America for its history: " 'For twenty years—twenty years, Edward —I've embalmed the corpses of penniless Negroes and financed their purchases of suitable caskets at reasonable rates out of my own pocket. And I enjoyed every minute of it, Edward. . . . Can't you be reasonable, just for once? There's nothing wrong with dead Negroes. Nothing at all' " (140). This overmuch-protestation continues; the father tries to make Edward his metaphor by claiming " 'But you're afraid of the dead Negroes, aren't you, Edward?' "—until the father says " 'I'm going to carry out this business in my own house. Damned if I'm not. And if they rise up out of the cold ground like a mob of raving minstrels and try to stop me, I'll fight them off. Every last one of them. There's gratitude for you' " (141).

At this point the father sounds like a pre-Civil War slave owner, denying his fear yet fearing an insurrection. Hawkes uses the tradition for the creation of his metaphor; he relies upon the audience or reader to grasp the historical reference and apply it to the father: we are to conclude that not only is the father in a way guilty of suppressing black people—in that sense he is metaphoric of all white Americans haunted by their history—but we are also to conclude that the father's fears and dreams, irrespective of his dealings with black people, will rise up to frighten him just as black people rose to claim their freedom. The father is the artist who lays away his constructions of art which he superimposed on human tissue, rendering it lifeless and beautiful; he is the artist whose artwork rebels, becomes independent and, like a rebellious slave, turns upon the master.

Thus we have Prospero surrendering his magic; the artist resigns: " 'It's no dream, Edward. It's merely the act of a cold mind. I'm going to jump off the tandem bicycle, that's all' " (154).

It should be mentioned here that before Edward tries to lure his father to life (back to the world in which we are all artists, all making—undertaking—our dream creations), he tries to distract him by suggesting that he shave (154–56) through some lengthy conversation that centers about opening and closing of the bathroom tap; this moment has resonances later in the play.

The father decides, finally, to do the act of suicide. He says: " 'But I know what I'm talking about—the sound of this shot will kill everything. Everything. Your dream, your mother, my Negroes, my dog—everything. It will all be gone, Edward, all of it.

The Innocent Party

No cheek, beard, toilet water, no signs of the undertaker. Everything will be gone—except you, of course. Nothing could kill you, Edward. Not even me. Do you hear? Do you comprehend what I'm saying, at last?'" (163).

The message his father delivers is clear: his world is his artwork, and with the death of its creator, the world too will vanish —his dream will be done. But Edward is cursed; the seeds of death are in him, and so, ironically, he is cursed with extended life: he must live and, like his father, be an artist, make a world, and suffer it. Unlike Stephen Daedalus, he need not pray to his father, old artificer; his father curses him with the skill of artifice, and the burden of a history that revisits him again and again.

Thus Edward, at the play's end, is in the bathroom in which his father shot himself. He rolls his sleeves up, rinses water on his face, and looks at the shaving brush and mug. It may be recalled here how he tried to distract his father by directing his attention to the humdrum of the daily shave—a continuing chore for the living. It should be recalled, too, how the Edward of *The Innocent Party*, when he addressed himself to his daily shave, was visited by the centipede—the curse of history coming up at him from his buried past.

Here Edward is facing his buried past, and he is acting as undertaker—artist—as well; for when he shaves his living face and looks in the mirror, he is also seeing his dead father, whose dead face he shaves as an undertaker gives a corpse its final shave. He is a victim of the past and a victim of art: he recreates his father and the past in an effort to come to terms with them. Like Skipper, he makes his art to achieve saneness.

Edward addresses the father whose suicide he, artist, has just staged. He tells him "'I still find bits of your angry ending . . . the Indianheads of my childhood, old man.'" He reiterates an image of which Hawkes is very fond when he then says: "'All this time you've been the rusty fishook lodged inside my brain'" (167). And then he no longer rails against his curse—living in time and recreating time's worst moments, being an undertaker. Instead, he fills the shaving mug, drinks from it, says "'Let's get it over with'" (168), and hears his father's final shot roll across the stage, which goes dark. Hawkes concludes with the artist affirming his burden, admitting to—even invoking—the past in a sacramental moment; instead of wine in a chalice, there is water in a shaving mug. He points up the sacred nature of an art which, its own blight upon the artist, can nevertheless lead him, through parody, bitterness, and even madness, to health and a celebration of life—complete with its remorseless ticking of time, its ongoing deaths.

8 The Blood Oranges

The epigraph for Hawkes's most recent novel, *The Blood Oranges*,[1] is taken from Ford Madox Ford's *The Good Soldier*; it is the cry of Dowell, the narrator, for a world in which ideal love might flourish: "Is there then any terrestrial paradise where, amidst the whispering of the olive-leaves, people can be with whom they like and have what they like and take their ease in shadows and in coolness?"[2]

Hawkes creates such a place—the novel is set in "Illyria"—which is the wandering island of Skipper, in *Second Skin*, writ large. Where in the latter novel he created an island paradise, here Hawkes creates an entire coastal land—a "mental landscape" (126), or as he later calls it, a "lyrical landscape" (193). The Mediterranean countryside of *The Blood Oranges* is not a place of imagination in a realistic context, as the island is in *Second Skin*; this novel is *all* imagination, and its setting exists only "in the silken weave of Love's pink panorama" (1). The rest of Dowell's query, which Hawkes did not include in his epigraph—"Or are all men's lives like the lives of us good people . . . broken, tumultuous, agonised, and unromantic lives, periods punctuated by screams, by imbecilities, by deaths, by agonies? Who the devil knows?"[3]—suggests the contrapuntal element of the novel. Timelessness in Illyria is threatened by time and death; joy forever is imminently under the shadow of all-too-human rages and fears. Hawkes says of *The Blood Oranges:* "I began to write this fiction out of the darkest, dark night, thinking that I might not be able to write again. Then suddenly I visualized a fragmented scene of some children carrying a coffin which contained a dead dog, and being followed by four adults, which was the beginning of *The Blood Oranges*. At that moment I was quite aware of *Twelfth Night*, that beautiful whole in which all of our fragmented selves are finally realigned into the ultimate harmony."[4]

In *Twelfth Night* (as in *Much Ado About Nothing* and *As You Like It*) Shakespeare developed prose as a suitable dramatic vehicle for most moods and characters while not altering his usual techniques for moving events on the stage. In *The Blood Oranges*, Hawkes moves beyond his attempts at drama and shows us his superbly developed prose at work on some of the materials of those comedies of Shakespeare's Second Period. Here is the comic spirit, its joyful sense of life, nibbling at the fancies—diseases—that repress life; here is a locale outside the "real" world; here are magical events. These conventions are of course melted and worked by Hawkes: instead of Viola's shipwreck, a khaki-colored bus plunges into a shallow polluted canal; instead of a Malvolio cross-gartered and wearing yellow stockings, a one-armed Malvolio photographs peasant girls in the nude.

The novel opens with the poetry of *Second Skin*, then surpasses it. Cyril, the narrator, calls himself a "sex-singer" (3), celebrant of fleshly love. He describes himself in terms of sexuality, and calls himself a "small white porcelain bull lost in the lower left-hand corner of that vast tapestry" (2) of which he is a part: "I always allowed myself to assume whatever shape was destined to be my own in the silken weave of Love's pink panorama. I always went where the thread wound" (1).

The act of narration, then, is a reference to Cyril's willing participations in a cosmic act or series of acts of art; like Ishmael weaving net on the *Pequod*, Cyril, in this tapestry, is in the hands of higher powers—the "sylvan sources" (142) to which he always defers. Dowell, and the Good Soldier of Ford's book, are in the hands of others—usually women—and are mistreated by love. Dowell, as narrator, is defined by what is done to him by others; his story of a foursome in the coils of love is one in which he learns and orders his life through narration. Cyril orders his world through narration, as we shall see. But we shall also see how his ordering is, at the same time, a seduction-song sung by this

The Blood Oranges

lyrical satyr. But however Cyril may seem to bend events to his own ends, he is being bent by the sylvan sources. Art weaves life to its ends in *The Blood Oranges*. The art of the sylvan sources, attained by fleshly manipulations, seems to be its own end. As Cyril says, "I came to know that the gods fashion us to spread the legs of woman, or throw us together for no reason except that we complete the picture," and "I was there always. I completed the picture" (2).

From a life of willing acquiescence to "the gods," to this strange art form, Cyril has now come to this: he is alone on the Mediterranean coast, except for Catherine, formerly his mistress (now estranged) and his South European maid, Rosella, who speaks "an ugly language that will never be mine" (2), and who cannot understand the language in which he makes advances to her. He has made rules for his behavior—"no touching, nothing overt. Only the spoken tones of joy and desire" (3). He is reduced to artful sounds. He and the maid live in an "abandoned villa which is one of a pair . . . with broken red tiles and fireplaces like abandoned urinals" (2). His world is a virtual waste land, but he is not in despair. Although he asks "why, after more than eighteen years, does the soft medieval fabric of my tapestry now hang in shreds," he also says: "I am patient, I am faithful, perhaps one day I will reach out and close my fingers on Rosella's thigh, perhaps my last mistress may again become my mistress" (3).

Wayne Carver suggests that "my last mistress" evokes the Duke of Ferrara's "Last Duchess"; according to Carver, Cyril, like the Duke, presides over the greatest of evils with a studied self-conscious and all-pervading aestheticism."[5] The last mistress is Catherine, who came to be Cyril's mistress while Cyril's wife, Fiona, pursued Catherine's husband, Hugh. Catherine has had a mental collapse after Hugh's suicide; as the novel opens she is in a perverse sort of convent, presided over by small swarthy people in uniforms. Cyril visits her weekly, to woo her back: his wife, after Hugh's death, has fled with Hugh's and Catherine's children "to impart womanhood to those three little growing girls" (210). Cyril has stayed while Fiona left so that he could "explain Hugh's death to Catherine, to account for her missing children, to convince her that I was not, as she thought, responsible for all her losses, to renew our love" (210-11).

So Cyril, his accustomed life in ruins, is not in despair. He woos Catherine by recounting to her the events we read—how she and her husband and children came to Illyria, how the two couples took up together, how Catherine and Hugh became lovers, how Hugh died. His narration is its own artful weaving: it is argument in the Renaissance sense of rhetoric. He seeks to absolve himself of blame, to win Catherine, to assure himself that his magical world will not dissolve into time. Within the framework of art in which the "sylvan sources" worked him, he uses his art to confirm the supremacy of those sources—now mysteriously absent. He waits for the tapestry's threads to be woven once more. He weaves his own. Part of an enormous artistic argument, he argues, a "sex-singer" narrating to an audience who cannot understand him (Rosella) and to an audience (Catherine) who resists—with decreased vigor, by the novel's end—his admonitions of "Remember?" (55, 187, 229), the chorus to his plaint.

The two parts of Ford's question establish the two attitudes of the novel: Ford asks whether there is an earthly paradise of love, or whether all men's lives are broken by imbecilities and deaths. Cyril's answers establish the form of the book. On the one hand, he answers—insists—affirmatively that there is an earthly paradise of love when he chants confidently that he could ignore an interruption of an idyll among the four characters "because no sex-tableau was ever entirely abortive" (45).

On the other hand, he is trying to win Catherine back, he is seducing her. Thus he recalls to her the sexuality they shared in a magical world of fleshly art, a pagan paradise. By constantly harkening to the past—"Remember?"—he implies process, which is the heart of narration: the past has led to this present which once was called future; this present is predicated upon the fact that Hugh is dead—hence Catherine's collapse, and the necessity for Cyril to pursue her once more. The death ended what was then present and made it past. There is time in Illyria. The very fact of Cyril's wooing disproves his satyr-songs of timelessness. In accumulating, re-accumulating, arranging, and rearranging the facts of their history, Cyril proves his narrative artistry; in trying to prove to Catherine that they should love, he argues that time pursues him. Thus the novel is a dialectic of time, most recent in the long line of masterworks that extends from the *Agamemnon* to "Ode on a Grecian Urn" to *The Sound and the Fury*—man's desperate fight with the fact that he swims in time, and thus must end.

Cyril, the narrator, is a sex-singer—an artist of what is to him the beautiful: the fleshly designs men and women make on the tapestry of love, woven by "sylvan sources." Yet he is not wholly assured that he, artist, *is* fully controlled by supreme forces. Thus, when he thinks Hugh and Fiona are conjoining just as he and Catherine do, he recalls, "so my theory of sexual extension, I thought, was taking root" (147). Later, he speaks of "those who detest my convictions, scoff at my theories" (209). He is a believer, he is a theoretician; but he is not *certain*. And, because he is the narrator in his role as wooer, he knows what he selects to tell. He knows that there are uncertainties behind what he often offers as certainties. Like Zizendorf in *The Cannibal*, he must say one thing and entertain the possibility of its untruth. Like Zizendorf, he builds his argument upon material that includes the disproof of what he wants to believe and wants his auditor to believe. Like Zizendorf, he must depend upon rhetoric to save him from a threatening reality.

Thus, Cyril makes a weekly visit to Catherine in her sanctuary. As he leaves his ruined villa (counterpart of the one, beyond a hedge of cypresses, in which Hugh and Catherine lived) he tells us that "aching candor describes exactly what I felt yesterday, and feel each week . . . my own head, eyes, mouth, chest, felt saturated with aching candor" (6). The rhetoric is to work upon us, upon himself, as well as Catherine. The effort always is to persuade all concerned in the novel that Cyril means precisely what he says. Yet he fears that he does not.

He employs his artistry upon her by blowing the smoke of the thick phallic cigarettes that are so frequently mentioned in the course of the novel, the smoke that smelled of "nitrates, burning paper, animal stains, sex." He blows smoke at her, who will not acknowledge him: "I started to blow smoke rings. . . . For I was an artist at blowing smoke rings" (7).

Catherine, at this point, will not look at him and will not speak: "It was in her power to help me speak for the past, to help me see the future. . . . She still preferred to remain only the inert supine center of my life, the sun that neither sets nor rises" (13).

If he is to win her back, have things as they once were, she must come to him. But to do so, he must deal with time. At this point she—a sun neither setting nor rising—is timeless; she is the essence of the quality he has praised in Illyria. He is trapped in his own rhetoric.

He leaves her sanctuary, and he will return—to find her moving closer and closer to his reality each time he visits. Once she will watch a bird in a cage hung before her; another time she will look at rabbits in a cage; another time she will touch the rabbits; another time she will share with him her pleasure in touching them; eventually she will return to his villa, to lie in a single bed, not touching him. By the novel's end, her proximity will be like that of Rosella—close, yet distant, touched by language if at all, but not by his flesh.

It is important that she return part way to him through the proximity of animals. For animals, as they have always been important in Hawkes's novels, are crucial in *The Blood Oranges*. Thus, when Cyril leaves Catherine's sanctuary, his tires hum "like inflated snakes," and he sees a wall of black stones "that resembled the dark fossilized hearts of long-dead bulls with white hides and golden horns" (14): the use of animal imagery for background suggestiveness, for the sake of engendering an environment of animality, continues. But what comes next is indicative of the growth of Hawkes's imagistic strategies—a growth prefigured in *The Lime Twig* and made clear in *Second Skin*. Cyril sees two birds mating: "Grace and chaos, control and helplessness, mastery and collapse—it was all there, as if the wind was

The Blood Oranges

having its way with the rocks. . . . Obviously the two birds mating on the horizon were for me a sign, an emblem, a mysterious medallion, a good omen. They augured well for the time I had spent with Catherine and for my own future in the electrified field of Love's art" (15).

First, we must again note that the artist of love, the demigod —"too tall, too strong, too blond, too handsome, much too elegant and good natured" (7)—is a creature manipulated by the sylvan sources, one who is anxious for "my own future," who looks for omens, seeks signs; he acknowledges that in Illyria there is future, hence time. Later, and often, he—narrator, selecting what to say, what should be known—will try to overlook the possibilities of time intervening in his world.

We must note, too, that Cyril's description contains the ingredients of art, and of this novel's art, the art that works upon him: grace and chaos, control and helplessness. These elements are the material of the book's dialectic, they are what the narration vibrates between; they are also the novel's "subject-matter": the book *does* what it purports to "be about."

The animal imagery here (and elsewhere, as we shall see) deals with the interaction of time and timelessness, the "real" world and Illyria. More specifically, and more importantly, the bird emblem Cyril sees is highly evocative of a *carpe diem* imagery that subsumes the novel. In Marvell's "To His Coy Mistress," we find this reasoning:

> Now therefore, while the youthful hew
> Sits on thy skin like morning dew,
> And while thy willing Soul transpires
> At every pore with instant Fires,
> Now let us sport us while we may;
> And now, like am'rous birds of prey,
> Rather at once our Time devour,
> Than languish in his slow-chapt pow'r.[6]

The birds Cyril sees *are* "am'rous birds of prey," and he takes them for sign, emblem, medallion, and omen. In his pursuit of Catherine, they are his symbol; he will urge her to seize the day, "help me see the future." The nature of his emblem, though, is contrary to the world he creates for the reader and for Catherine in Illyria. His wooing injects time into timelessness. If he is to have her, he is not to have Illyria. Thus, directly after speaking of this incident, Cyril proclaims that "youth has no monopoly on love." The proclamation seems to be a case of overmuch protesting. Cyril, in denying death through his rhetoric, admits to it in his defensive interjection. The narrator is afraid, and his fear shows— in his claim that "at the height of our season Fiona and Hugh were almost forty" (16), yet were beautiful. The last line of the novel is: "In Illyria there are no seasons" (271). The tension between these two statements is the tension of the book; the fact that the same narrator makes the statements and wishes to believe equally in both, is the definition of his character, the source of the novel's dialectical energy.

It is worth noting how when Fiona and Hugh make love they kiss "so that bone struck bone and teeth lay against teeth" (34); they struggle, maneuver "to eat the other's mouth, to catch the other's jaws between the rows of his own hard teeth." (35). It is also worth noting that, when these am'rous birds of prey kiss, Cyril senses "a special taste of mint tinged with that faint suggestion of decay which I drew every time from the very roots of her perfect teeth" (35). The dialectic is again at work: perfect teeth yield decay; there is rot and time, yet there is not.

Later, coming closer to intimacy with Cyril (brushing into him, eating at the same table)—yet never making love with him, as Catherine never makes love with him after Hugh's death— Rosella prepares ortellans for Cyril, those thrush-like birds that are cooked and eaten whole, heads and all. Here we see Cyril as a bird of prey, devouring others. Delighting in the meal, Cyril once again takes birds, and Rosella's pleasure in obtaining and cooking them for him, as an omen: "Was that whole vast tapestry beyond villa, cypresses, village, crying out for my re-entry into the pink field?" (53).

Whereas earlier Cyril had said that he waited patiently for the torn tapestry of Love to be mended by the sylvan sources, he here betrays an anxiety for that reweaving. As he speaks of "re-entry" into that strange world, he confesses that he is outside it. We may see that he pursues Catherine so as to re-achieve the past, the world of the tapestry, what once was. But his admission that it *was*, his uncertainty as to what will be, his obvious hovering posture—he is a true believer awaiting the return of the blessed state—is an expression of his fear that Illyria might never be again. His narrator's rhetoric seeks to bridge the distance between his certainty and uncertainty, between the impulse to possess Catherine *now* (and, urging the argument of *carpe diem*, admit that he is time's pawn) and the need to return her—and himself—to belief in Illyria. As he woos her, he proclaims time and disclaims it. To win her, he proclaims time; to reclaim his belief, he dismisses time. Yet he feels that he must win her to achieve the Illyria that once was. He is trapped in his own argument: he is a prisoner of his own art.

Another example of his entrapment, and of Hawkes's fine use of irony, is in the possible source of the title. Its examination requires an examination of this novel's most prestigious and publicized foe. In *The New York Review of Books*, Roger Sale, the Spenser authority, in a review entitled "What Went Wrong?" assails Hawkes as a failure. Most of his commentary is based on his disagreement with what he perceives to be Hawkes's cast of mind, and it is best to leave those matters of taste to Sale and those *New York Review* readers who think that a critic's job is to utter such enlightenments as "when horror becomes a pastime it should announce itself or at least know itself."[7] Without lecturing Sale on how to lecture authors on how to think, we can still deal with the substance of his review that bears directly on the art of the novel.

Sale says, referring to Cyril's apparent refusal to mourn Hugh's death: "This deeply *un*receptive narcissism has so little aesthetic greed, furthermore, or even mere desire to write well, that we find, on almost every page, something like 'The sun was setting, sinking to its predestined death.'" The passage to which Sale refers—and which, clearly, he did not understand—is this: "The sun was setting, sinking to its predestined death, and to the four of us [Hugh, Catherine, Fiona, Cyril], or at least to me, that enormous smoldering sun lay on the horizon like a dissolving orange suffused with blood" (37).

This passage might well be considered decorative, therefore unskillful, if we did not see that it is a revelation of Cyril's dilemma and a sign to us that Cyril's language is a shield against time—a kind of prayer: desperate, even moving. We must first see that the conjunction of the vegetable and animal—"dissolving orange suffused with blood"—is a striking juxtaposition of unlike things, as shocking as many images in Jacobean poetry. It suggests an imminence of animality, bleeding, and death; horror is poised over Illyria. Next, we should see that Cyril says what the undecorative speaker would say: "The sun was setting." The language is *not* there so that the writer can avoid saying the obvious in a simple and direct manner. Hawkes first has Cyril say what is clearly the case; he then has Cyril say what is the case in Illyria—that a "death" is predestined, woven by sylvan sources into Love's tapestry. The death of the sun—fearful to a man afraid of mortality as, say, is the case in Shakespeare's Sonnet 73—is not real death; it is part of the controlled and fearless world of Illyria. The sun's death is not real death because Illyria is timeless. Cyril tells us this—but he also tells (reassures) himself. For, as has been shown, he does suspect that things end or that Illyria will be no more. Since the novel is a recounting of events to Catherine, since the events of the novel have already happened by the time Cyril tells them, he knows that things end: he is trying, once more, to say two things at once—that things end, that things do not end. He says both by saying the natural description —"The sun was setting"—and the virtual prayer—"sinking to its predestined death." His statement defines Illyria, then defines his rhetorical plight. He prays, and he describes; he is caught between the world in time and the world of art: exceptional, he is everyman nevertheless. His condition gives us the novel's title—Illyria is a world of no death, a world into which death has intruded: a world made by imagination, a world in which language and imagination fail—and his dilemma defines the sad failure of critical insight in a critic upon whom readers have depended.

As he discusses the origins of the novel, Hawkes talks about

The Blood Oranges

the puzzling title most usefully, reducing its mysteriousness: "One of the marvelous French moments was eating cheese; another was, for the first time, eating blood oranges. The phrase came to mind as a title. The fruit is sweet, but it's streaked with the color of blood, which to me is a paradox. It means that the blood is real but also sweet; it means that no sweetness is ephemeral but on the contrary possesses all the life-drive seriousness of the rich black flow of blood itself. It suggests wound invading desire, desire 'containing' agony."[8] The feeling that "life-drive" contains all is resonant of Cyril's song—that all is to be accepted, that nothing (even pain) must be rejected. Hawkes's comments on the title suggest that we might not be incorrect in seeing that the novel is oxymoronic—a song against time that is yet a song in time—just as the title is suggested by an image of wound that invades desire, desire that surrounds and accepts pain.

Time and death enter Cyril's and Fiona's imaginary landscape in the person of Hugh, when he and Catherine and their three daughters blunder into the coastal paradise—for what reason, from where, we never know. Cyril and Fiona are in a ruined chapel, as is their custom, each going his separate way "to the altar of his choice" (17). The altars are "nearly opposite in color, mood, design"; Fiona displays "her girlish fixation on the altar of the dead" (18) while Cyril goes to one of white marble, flowers, a wooden Virgin—what he calls "a childish array of cheerful artifacts" (19). Ruminating, rummaging, Fiona—faunlike, graceful, very sexy, like Cyril in her love of making love—finds the skeleton of a dead child. She says " 'He's beautiful, poor thing. I'm going to kiss him, Cyril. Shall I?' " Cyril says of her, "for more than eighteen years she had been most obviously true to character . . . in the act of kissing . . . as if only by touching the world with her open lips could she make it real and bring herself to life" (20).

So we see Fiona attracted to life, as we would expect of Cyril's faun; but we also see her attracted to death, and, especially, here, a dead child. Children—she flees with Hugh's children after his death—will become important, later, as a clue to Cyril's tragedy.

While Fiona kisses the grinning skull, Cyril, at his altar, rubs the hem of the doll-like Virgin—a preoccupation which also, later, will reveal much about him and his sad end. As he says "I might have been standing in some gutted cellar of the ancient world, some pit giving onto secret viaducts packed with the old world's excrement" (21)—and we recall that Hawkes often associates excrement with death—he finds a wooden arm. At this point, Hugh and Catherine enter their ritualized, sexy, aesthetically oriented lives.

Hugh and Fiona hear sirens and the clatter of emergency; they go from the ruined chapel into the shattered-seeming coastal town—"broken tiles, the familiar cups filled with poison and set out on empty window ledges" (23)—to the edge of the canal, to see that a khaki bus has plunged into the canal. Fiona says: " 'But people commit suicide that way, baby. It has to sink' " (25). It doesn't, it is in shallow water, and the passengers—Hugh, Catherine, their three children and their dog—are rescued. But Fiona's reference to suicide will have enormous resonance when, toward the end of the novel, we learn that Hugh has killed himself. Her reference is also important because, as she was in the ruined chapel, she is attracted toward death: she mentions suicide, then decides: " 'My God, he's handsome. Just look at him!' " (30). Fiona is always attracted to death—and her attraction to Hugh should alert us that death is on its way into Illyria.

The peasants at the hilarious scene of this rescue are described as "lazy," "unskilled," "stunted," "squat," "short and fat" (23–25), and one has the sense that to Cyril—especially in comparison with him and his friends—the local people are defective in some way. Their land is seen to be as blighted as they are. In the canal is a "dark and apparently currentless flow of sewage"; the canal is filled with "waters more fetid than any waters I had ever smelled"; the bus is bogged in "the stinking depths of the timeless pestilential canal" (26). We then learn that the watching peasants "suffer from the abnormal attitudes born of the bad blood carried to this warm coast centuries before from central Europe" (27). We learn

The Blood Oranges

further that throughout this episode, in the waters of the canal, floats an orange, mentioned twice in the description of the rescue, and we must remember the blood orange of the title. The prose returns us to the canal, its "hard bed of excrement which, down through the centuries, had accumulated like lava in the bottom of the black canal" (28). Near the canal are "holes and stone gutters that fed the very smell of time." The filthy canal "had once been choked with the bodies of dead barbarians" (29).

We must remember that Hawkes accompanies the presence of death with the smell of offal. That smell, and that presence, are here in abundance—unmistakably. Also present is Hawkes's revulsion for war: dead invaders, barbarians, their assault on this paradise, the bad work their bad blood has done to the local gene pool; evidence of their onslaught is to be found, again, in the reeking canal. Death and war are linked by the smell of sewage. So, too, is the sense of invasion: as the barbarians invaded, so now does Hugh invade. He brings death with him as he emerges, like a parodistic vegetation god, from the stink of black waters. And he brings death as *time*. In describing the rescue in terms of sewage and history, Cyril has spoken of a "timeless" canal, then of excrement accumulated over centuries, in time, then of the very "smell of time." In what might be a parody of the shipwreck in *Twelfth Night*, or a parody of the conventional dramatic shipwreck in general, Hawkes brings time and death to Illyria.

Hugh has one arm, and it is not difficult to think at once that the wooden arm, the relic, in the abandoned chapel is in some way related to him: this is Illyria, and events here are magical. Furthermore, his face, not tanned like Cyril's, is "so weathered and pebbled, so grained in darkness and cold rain that it resembled stone. Gray stone" (31). In a way, then, Hugh is a monster—a handsome monster (the missing arm forces one to think of the monster Grendel, driven by rages and jealousies, bereft of his arm, pursued to the bottom of the mere). Then Cyril says: "Yet I recognized his face immediately because its exact replica, an image of Saint Peter that was perfect except for the broken ears, had been chiseled along with the head of Saint Paul into the granite arch of the entrance to the squat church" (31).

Cyril confronts a Hugh "smelling of the canal and dangling the leather cases of all his cameras" against his wet clothes. Fiona steps over to kiss "the gaunt stony cheek of this tall hero who had come to us over the same mountains once crossed by the barbarians" (34), presumably those prehistoric tribes that once in fact did ravage the shores of the Adriatic. So Hugh is associated with the barbarian invaders, and with the smell of time and death; he also is associated with Christian missionary travelers—conquerors for Christianity who invaded lands with their religion and took those lands away from their pagan inhabitants: we should consider whether Hugh brings with him the same end to paganism that the Christian fathers did. And Yeats's "The Second Coming" is suggested, with its warnings about the drowning of the ceremonies of innocence.

The remainder of the novel—told to Catherine by Cyril, although seemingly spoken to us in an occasional aside—concerns Cyril's conquest of Catherine and Fiona's unsatisfied pursuit of Hugh. When finally Hugh and Fiona do make love to her satisfaction, when Love's tapestry finally seems complete to Cyril and Fiona, Hugh hangs himself in the makeshift photography studio he has rigged in his ruined villa.

Because this discussion of *The Blood Oranges* centers about the dialectic between time and timelessness, the world and Illyria, Cyril's faith and fear, life and death, its principal focus now must be on Hugh, who represents the darkness Cyril seeks to shut out from his consciousness—who brings night to this land of eternal day.

First, Hugh is a photographer, an artist. If Cyril is a sex-singer, Hugh creates lyrics through his photographs. He is collecting sheafs of pictures of peasant nudes. Cyril says of him that he "was also a sex-singer of sorts." To Cyril, the difference between their songs is this: "But Hugh was tormented, tempestuous, unreasonable. He was capable of greed and shame and jealousy. When at last he allowed the true artistic nature of our design to seep into consciousness, for instance, he persecuted himself and begrudged me Catherine" (58).

The Blood Oranges

We witness the creation of one of Hugh's songs as he and Cyril go on one of Hugh's photographic expeditions. They see Rosella in a field—this is before Cyril knows her and, of course, long before she becomes his housekeeper—and Hugh points his stump of arm at her; Cyril calls the arm "his flipper" (58), his hand "that serpent's head." She becomes "our quarry," and in the midst of typically Hawkesian animal imagery—"the usual upright skeleton of a dog affixed to the tall stake driven through the center of the haystack" (59)—they manage to convey to Rosella that she is to pose for Hugh. (The dog's skeleton will later join with a dog's corpse to make an important thematic impact.)

Hugh photographs Rosella in a ruined barn with the "probing unblushing gaze of his high-powered cameras" (61). Here is Hugh at work: "Coming between us, pushing and inching with his dark blue contorted legs, suddenly rising to both knees so that the girl drew back, and clicking the shutter release and rewind lever and hissing eagerly between his lips which had become little more than a tight shadow, slowly Hugh approached us on his knees and then, with little more than his own intensity and the aim of the camera, moved her, repositioned the small dark head against the dark wormeaten flank of an upright beam" (63-64).

As if he were going to assault her, Hugh had preceded this picture-taking with: " 'Now let's just shove her over against the beam' " (63). The point of course is that he commits his rape through his camera. Its blunt blind snout, like the blunt end of his arm, is phallic—a substitute for his own phallus. Hugh's sex is achieved at second-hand.

When the foursome are sunbathing at dusk—when the orange light of the blood-orange sun laves their bodies—Fiona "giggled as if in a dream a small bird had alighted on her belly" (38), reminiscent of the am'rous birds of prey. Cyril, in response to this signal, rises, removes Fiona's halter so that, in the orange sunlight, "Fiona's two firm breasts suddenly became the bursting irises of a young white owl's wide open eyes." Fiona responds by saying: " 'Baby, can't we just stay here forever?' " (40).

As if in reply to Illyria's timelessness—"the preciousness of what Fiona said"—Hugh exclaims " 'That's it. All these years you've been castrating him!' " (41). His response to this "ceremony of innocence" is a Freudian declamation of interior darkness, of guilts and corruptions; woman is the enemy, man her victim. Hugh's attitude toward the idyl is "realism" which is based on fear. His attitude is that of the outside world, not Illyria, and he shows himself to be the enemy of what is essentially Illyrian.

Cyril betrays his fear—not so much of Hugh as of what the sylvan sources might intend for Illyria—by saying: "I waited, wondering if this momentary idyl would pass before the rose and golden metallic threads could begin to spin our separate anatomies forever into the sunset scene, would come to a sudden conclusion, incomplete unbalanced" (42). Again, Cyril wonders if Hugh means "to tamper with the obviously intended symmetry of our little scene on the beach? Hugh was unmusical, but I had hoped I could count on him for at least a few signs of romantic temperament. After all, how could any man love my wife and yet fail to appreciate simple harmonious arrangements of flesh, shadow, voice, hair, which were as much the result of Fiona's artistry as of mine. But perhaps I had been wrong. Perhaps Hugh had no eye for the sex-tableau" (43).

Cyril's concerns are aesthetic—"unbalanced," "simple, harmonious arrangements," "artistry," "symmetry," "tableau." Hugh's are not. For Hugh, the reality of the outside world forbids what is done in Illyria—and this includes consummation of Hugh's obvious lust for Fiona. Hugh's artistry is concerned with arrangement of "the real"—the disposition of flesh into aesthetic attitudes —at second remove: he alters the positions of bodies to capture them through technological means on paper; he obtains images. Cyril and Fiona touch the actual flesh and enjoy it at first-hand. Cyril's and Hugh's conflict is aesthetic, and the obvious moral difficulties in which Hugh finds himself are offered by Hawkes in aesthetic terms. Just as Cyril's problem in narrating the novel reveals his interior problems, so does the conflict between Hugh and Cyril reveal Hugh's interior dilemma: the world of this novel is entirely the world of art.

Later, when Cyril is out walking, he *thinks* he comes upon

The Blood Oranges

Fiona and Hugh enjoying sex together. This pleases him, for Fiona has wanted Hugh, and he knows that Hugh's pleasure in Fiona would "complete the picture," make the couplings symmetrical. As Cyril proclaims at another time: "Need I insist that the only enemy of the mature marriage is monogamy? That anything less than sexual multiplicity (body upon body, voice on voice) is naive? That our sexual selves are merely idylers in a vast wood? . . . Yes, the best of marriages are simply particular strands of pale trees sensuously stitched into the yet larger tapestry" (209).

Cyril then sees that Hugh is alone. He wonders if he is embarked "on some kind of freakish photographic experiment," or if he is reading one of "his faded erotic periodicals." And to this sense of Hugh (as virtual photographic plate that is sensitive to Freudian ills) must be added the characteristic of hiding away with erotica. But Hugh lies at Cyril's feet "like a corpse, a long fish-colored corpse, or like some fallen stone figure sandblasted, so to speak, by centuries of cruel weather. Yes, an emaciated and mutilated corpse or statue" (84). The image suggests Hugh as harbinger of death in Illyria, and his own forthcoming death; it suggests, too, the god who rose from the sea to end centuries of the ceremonies of paganism.

Hugh in fact is masturbating into the earth. Oriented to a non-Illyrian reality, his appreciation for sex effected at secondhand, afraid of woman, like a repressed Victorian gentleman in his choice of photographic subjects (peasants, the lower classes), his missing arm like a missing penis, Hugh is a Freudian nightmare in this land of sexual freedom: "He lay there on his stomach embracing not Fiona but only his clothes. . . . almost out of sight now beneath his chest, his hidden loins, his rigid outstretched white legs of the Christ" (84).

Cyril rushes to find Fiona "in time to keep her from stumbling on our sleeping and naked Saint Peter at the height of his pleasure" (85). So Hugh is the Saint, the Christ—the forces which ushered in the modern age, the death of pagan pleasures, of Illyria.

It is on this same spot of Hugh's onanistic pleasure that, later,

Cyril will help Hugh to bury Hugh's dead dog, whose death was prefigured in the skeleton near where Hugh photographed Rosella. This burial, since it is where Hugh, by showing what he preferred to Fiona, gave evidence of his failure to join Illyria, to lose time, prefigures Hugh's own death. Because Hugh is one-armed (and, symbolically, deficient in his sexual organ), Cyril must dig the grave for the dog. When he is through, he "tossed out the shovel and climbed from the grave in one slow unobtrusive motion appropriate to the man who had dug to the center of Hugh's fantasy and laid bare the wet and sandy pit of death" (221).

As happens again and again in this novel, a magical pagan figure appears from nowhere: this time he is a "typical shepherd" of whom Fiona says at once: "'Hugh, baby . . . he looks like you'" (223). Cyril muses that "even Hugh must have begun to comprehend what our unwanted intruder meant to say": "that he had slept in dark caves, that he had buried countless dead ewes, that he also knew what it was like to bury children, that only men work together in the service of death. . . . Only death mattered. He had joined us only because of the coffin" (224).

The man who looks like Hugh is the spirit of death, and of men alone: he reinforces the aura Hugh gives off—of nonsexuality, of death, and of those elements contrary to Cyril and his sense of Illyria which clearly threatens to end because of Hugh.

At another sun-bathing idyl, Hugh reveals himself as nemesis and Cyril reveals himself as very much endangered by the onslaught of time and the "real" world of Hugh. Cyril sees that Hugh is watching him watch Catherine—he makes it clear that they have already been lovers—and Cyril thinks, "how like him . . . to begrudge me Catherine's hand in the middle of the afternoon and abandon her body to me throughout the night" (90). Cyril's attitude toward Hugh is not surprising, and we might not be far from agreeing, so powerful is Cyril's rhetoric, his rush of language so engulfing. In the next instant: "And then the little invisible white goat landed among us and I rolled toward Catherine" (90). Cyril uses the pagan figure as symbol of the sylvan sources' weaving him on to a further sexuality. But Hugh becomes

The Blood Oranges

jealous and protective, and, required to attend to his small daughter, he does so while sitting on Catherine's hip, beside Cyril: "Hugh swung back his arm, reached down, and without changing his position or turning his head, fumbled briefly until his hand leapt suddenly like the small invisible white goat and, in a gesture of love or viciousness, closed on Catherine's heavy breast inside the madras halter. . . . Why could he not respect Catherine's conventional but nonetheless powerful intimacy? When would he ever respond to my omniscience and Fiona's style?" (91–92).

So accustomed is the reader to Cyril's polygamy and lack of modesty that the moment is impressive. For Cyril has assumed the outraged protectiveness which Hugh showed at the earlier beach scene; furthermore, Cyril then insisted that Hugh not shame Catherine by keeping her clothed, apart from the "obviously intended symmetry of our little scene." They have exchanged attitudes—or, more precisely, Cyril has taken on Hugh's: Hugh remains true to his own style, and Cyril here betrays his. Yet one cannot ignore that small white goat: Cyril sees it land on Catherine as Hugh's hand lands upon her breast. This is to say that Cyril, narrator, selector of detail, the novel's visionary, sees that Hugh is for an instant part of the sylvan sources' masterplan, part of the whole picture; for an instant, he and Hugh are alike. As narrator, Cyril admits this, then denies it. He once again reveals the dialectic web he has woven himself into.

At this moment, Fiona spies a baby goat—an actual creature that magically intrudes on their tableau. Cyril's reaction is one of surprising relief; not only is he delighted to see that he had guessed correctly the color of its eyes (as he had imagined them), but he is overwhelmed with relief, astonishment, and the surge of joy of the true believer at last rewarded with a sight of the word of his dreamy rhetoric made flesh: "Could it be that one of my speechless creatures of joy and sentiment had torn itself loose from the tapestry that only I could see?" (92–93).

It is important that Cyril says "one of my speechless creatures": Cyril confesses here that *he* is the author of Illyria, that the rest has been faith, hope, and the "theories" of which he has spoken; he has prayed with his language for Illyria and he takes the goat as a sign. This annunciation of love occurs several times more in the novel. Each time, an animal shows forth to convince Cyril that his faith is justified. Each time we are reminded of his fears that he may be wrong, of his paranoic sense of siege (justified finally in Hugh)—"I am a match, I hope, for the hatred of conventional enemies wherever they are" (36). Hawkes reminds us, too, of the small hint that Cyril may be mad, that Illyria may be a psychotic's vision dreamed in an insane asylum: "There are those who would deny me all my nights in Fiona's bed if they could, would strip me of silken dressing gown and fling me into some greasy white-tiled pit of naked sex-offenders. For some, love itself is a crime" (36). We may even recall Nabokov's Humbert Humbert, writing *Lolita* from an observation ward, sealing his beloved into the durable pigments of his art. And we may recall, too, Hawkes's own Nabokovian prison-and-imagination—the "pure space of psychic activity" of *The Questions*.

Cyril's art-as-narration reverses what seems obvious, makes an act sacrilege at one time, blessed at another. Cyril, when he sees the goat, suggests that "reality" supports what has been his private vision. We can think of Hugh reshaping the "reality" of the world with his lenses, his models, so as to make his private vision be true. But Cyril must win—or at least his art must triumph—for he has the last say, it seems; he tells Catherine what he wishes to be true. The final battle between these art-forms rages in his mind as he contests Illyria against time's rot.

The crucial conflict emerges when the foursome, on one of their daily outings, moves toward the breakwater that connects the nearby ruined fortress, looming like an island offshore, with the idyllic beach. Cyril calls out to Hugh, who is with Fiona, "'What's the matter . . . getting old?'" (188). The question heralds their confrontation with time and death. Hugh's stroll becomes "a compulsive quest," and the four of them move out toward the fortress. Cyril asks: "And why did I now identify that unspectacular and essentially uninteresting ruin with the dark caves of the heart? Self-imprisonment, which was what we appeared to be heading for, was hardly my own idea of pleasure" (189).

Cyril alerts the reader with his double-edged prose that *he* identifies the fortress with the human heart, that *he* will find psychic connections between prison and self. The others will too, to be sure—especially Hugh—but it is the carefree narrator who feels himself endangered, on the verge of discovering ugly things.

The tower's walls are ugly and fearful: "all four walls had been deeply and viciously scorched by some devastating blaze. . . . And everywhere the weeds and fallen pediments were encrusted with the droppings of long departed gulls" (192).

Where there is ordure there is death. And where the colors are "unnatural," Hawkes is dealing with a hellish and un-Illyrian pallet. Hugh reinforces Cyril's fear—and so we see how like Hugh Cyril becomes as the outer world takes over—when he says: "'It's just a reflection—a reflection of some fiery nightmare'" (192). Like Cyril he suggests that the fortress will be a metaphor for what is within them.

As they descend to the dungeon, with Hugh leading, Cyril detects "the unmistakable smell of human excrement" (194), and we know again that death is near. Recalling how Hugh rose from the canal smelling of excrement, hence time, we now realize that it is time into which they descend—endings, the end of Illyria. Musing on this, Cyril wonders if perhaps Hugh's true interest "was simply to bury our love in the bottom of this dismal place and in some cul-de-sac, so to speak, of his own regressive nature" (196). From what we know of Hugh, and of his contrast to the freeness of Illyria, Cyril's analysis seems astute. The point is that it is so astute: Cyril has caught Hugh, as the pagan Indians caught measles from the Christian missionaries. Later, farther down, Fiona slips, falls, cries for help. Cyril sees Hugh standing above her outstretched body and realizes that "Hugh was quite capable of attempting to transform my faunlike wife into a lifeless and sainted fixture in his mental museum" (201). And while we know this is true, we know too that Catherine hears this story from Cyril—that Cyril is transforming his wife and Hugh, offering them second-hand to Catherine through his language, and so is behaving not dissimilarly from Hugh himself.

In the deepest reaches of the fortress, in a "cold timeless space hollowed from the very roots of the sea" (203)—Cyril here again opts for timelessness—Hugh finds a medieval chastity belt in the midst of pulpy refuse. They turn and, Hugh still leading, climb back up. Cyril wonders: "But after the silence, the disbelief, the dismay, perhaps then we would move on to . . . a rendezvous of sorts with the small earthen-colored nightingale whose secret song I had recently heard not far from the villas." For he wishes to ignore "the disbelief" that may well be his. But he cannot; he continues: "Or would the strains of this day dog us into the future, disrupt our embraces, diminish the peaceful intensity of all those simple idyls I still had in mind?" (205).

Cyril rightly fears for the future; he says "dog us" because he knows that the dog was Hugh's emblem, a figure of the death that came to Illyria. He knows that "the idyls I had in mind" were just that—in his mind, further fictions, for he knows that the idyls are ended.

Later they inspect Hugh's trophy, and we begin to see that his artistry is destruction (as Cyril's, in the narration, is an exercise in repair): the chastity belt is "Hugh's destructive exhibition," an "artful relic of fear and jealousy" (207). It is the exact opposite of the Illyria Cyril has "in mind," and Illyria's days are numbered.

As he comes to Catherine's bed one night, Cyril finds that Hugh has forced her to wear the belt. Cyril goes to Hugh, they argue in the arbor behind Cyril's house, and then Cyril returns to unlock Catherine. He detects "the faint smell of Catherine's hair turning gray at the roots," reminding us of the rot he tasted in Fiona's mouth—the grindings of time. The belt is laden with death, as was the fortress—"forbidding as the cold fortress from which it had come" (255)—but Cyril can nevertheless free Catherine from the belt easily: "the single expert twist that was all it took to pick the lock of Love and unfasten the belt." Then they make tumultuous love, as if the tapestry were still being woven: "in time the fish began to flow, the birds to fly, the twin

The Blood Oranges

heavenly nudes of Love to approach through the night" (257). But Cyril's rhetoric has given him away: it all happens "in time" because Illyria now is as deep under time as the fortress dungeon was under water on the island that is opposite—dystopia burdened with death and endings—to Skipper's magical island in *Second Skin*.

Plagued now with psychological insight, because he is invaded, Cyril realizes that "Hugh's despairing use of that iron belt must have occasioned a moment more genuinely erotic than any he had known with Catherine" (257). This is true: Cyril has witnessed Hugh trying to make love to Catherine by murmuring in bed: "Don't be afraid of Daddy Bear . . . don't be afraid of Daddy Bear." He realizes Hugh's sad inadequacy and the pathos of his "nursery persona" (153). So now, Hugh, stimulated by this exercise of repression, has finally gone to Fiona's bed while Cyril is freeing Catherine, and this makes Cyril glad: "He had proven my theories, completed Love's natural structure, justified Catherine's instincts, made Fiona happy. . . . What more could I ask?" Cyril says to Fiona, " 'he can't catch up. But God knows we'll let him try" (260).

Marvell's "To His Coy Mistress" is appropriate at this point. For when Cyril picks Love's lock, despite Catherine's entreaties that she must obey Hugh, he follows Marvell's lover's advice:

> Let us roll all our Strength, and all
> Our sweetness, up into one Ball:
> And tear our pleasures with rough strife
> Through the Iron gates of Life.

What are the filigree windings of the medieval belt except those "Iron gates of Life"? And after Cyril says " 'he can't catch up. But God knows we'll let him try,' " does he not echo: "Thus, though we cannot make our Sun/Stand still, yet we will make him run."[9]

For Cyril then goes down the corridor "to the bright morning which in unaccountable silence was rushing faster than ever along the path of the sun" (260). They *have* made the sun run. The conjunction of the foursome, the coming into Illyria of Hugh, *has* made the sun run, "though we cannot make our Sun/Stand still. . . ." But the sun, the blood orange, once did stand still. From now on, when the sun sinks it will not be to a controlled "predestined death": it will sink to the end of day, and there will be enough days ending to signify years, and the ends of lives, of Illyria. After a dawn breakfast, the lovers separate, and Hugh, unable to bear his breach with his puritan repressions—unable to stand his humanness, the excess of life he has experienced with Fiona—hangs himself. (This situation parallels that of Michael Banks in *The Lime Twig* who, after his raptures with Sybilline, destroys himself and the world of dreams at Brighton.)

Fiona, fearful and missing Hugh, leads Cyril—virtually runs from him—to find Hugh's naked body hanging surrounded by his nude photographs, those symbols of "his art, as he called it, and his death" (266). Fiona unties the noose and Cyril seizes and hides from her the photograph Hugh clenches in his dead hand. We are never to know of what or whom it is, although it seems fair to surmise that it is of Rosella, who was a touchstone for Cyril during the narration, almost a talisman: if he can possess her, he can re-possess Illyria in its pre-Hugh state.

Cyril says, " 'At least it was an accident. At least he wasn't trying to kill himself' " (268). And this denial of reality, of death, is a penultimate sad signal of how Cyril, in the rhetoric of his retelling to Catherine, tries to control through the artistry of his language the real world that overwhelms him.

By the end of *The Blood Oranges*, we are accustomed to Cyril's and Fiona's *laissez-faire* attitude toward one another's comings and goings. But even when Cyril tells us that "Fiona knew her part and I knew mine" (210), we may still be struck at her departure with the three children. The sense of Cyril's double-edged rhetoric, its self-assuring qualities, forces a hard look at his certainty that Fiona, with or without the children, would return. Cyril says: "It was not certainty, of course, but that had been the tenor of our farewell. Nothing was fixed" (212). What

The Blood Oranges

he really says, in fact, is that it is very far from certain that Fiona will return. He suspects the one, but wishes to believe the other: as has been the case throughout the novel, his language works in two ways simultaneously.

It is possible that Fiona left because she blamed Cyril for Hugh's death. It is also possible that she left because of the children—and this is the more interesting possibility because it suggests a web of connections in the novel that would not otherwise be significant but that are suggested throughout.

There is, first, the fact that Fiona calls people "baby" so frequently. By itself a meaningless habit, it becomes an interesting practice when coupled with other facts. Fiona kissed the skull of the dead baby at her altar of death. Cyril explained her action in terms of a larger pattern—her need to kiss things into life. But it was a child she kissed, and it was children, not her husband, with whom she fled. Then there is the fact that Cyril often refers to Catherine's "domesticity." And, before the second sunbathing episode, we hear Cyril blurt out: "I am not opposed to domesticity . . . not at all" (88). In response, Catherine says: "'You didn't have children. That's all.'" To which Fiona replies: "'Oh, but we decided against children long ago. And now it's too late anyway. Thank God. But we love your children, Catherine. Don't we, Cyril?'" Cyril murmurs and lies beside Catherine, "listening to the epic inside Catherine's lower abdomen" (89). His attention to the organs of childbearing—his sense of childbearing as "epic" —along with Catherine's over-protestation, suggests that there is more to the couple's childlessness than meets the eye.

Turning to the penultimate section of the novel, we find Cyril studying three panels or sketches of the life of the Virgin on the wall near his altar in the ruined chapel. He muses on virginity as he studies the figure of the Virgin in her adolescence, before she became pregnant with Christ. Most of the colors are variations of yellow—"Yellow was Fiona's favorite color" (271). She wore it when, as Cyril described them, they visited their altars just before Hugh arrived—"now blond, now sandalwood, now gold, now the yellow that flows in cream. . . . The skin of the tree is yellow, the stiff gown is yellow, the bare feet" (270). In the separation of Fiona from the Virgin, Fiona's yellow from the Virgin's yellow, Fiona in yellow at the altar of the dead separated from the Virgin altar at which Cyril stood, we may see in this common denominator of color the key to Cyril's study of virginity and Fiona's flight with the children.

It is worth speculating, at least, that Fiona protested overmuch about children, kissed the child's dead skull, always spoke the word *baby*, and fled with Catherine's children because she wanted children. She was not a creature of "theories," as was Cyril; she was a creature of flesh. And she was denied children by Cyril for the reason that, in his narration, he sets the dead child's skull near the altar of the dead:[10] children mean generations, cycles of birth and death, the introduction of time into an Illyria of no-time. Cyril wanted his entire world to be virginal, and in a sense it was.

So, in Yeats's sense, was the pagan world before Christ. With His coming, the blood-dimmed tide was loosed, things fell apart, and twenty centuries of stony sleep were vexed to nightmare. A new religion of rigid ethical demands was loosed upon Illyria's paganism, and because timelessness became part of time, as God became man to die, the old joys were lost. Cyril has seen time become part of timelessness as Hugh, so often referred to as Christ-like, came to Illyria. In this case the imaginary landscape became infected with time; temporality came to eternity, and time took hold.

This has happened to Illyria. In his last section Cyril says: "The sun casts orange discs on the sea, our nights are cool" (271). We know now that the sun cannot stand still, that time now works upon him. He tells us that "from three adjacent wooden pegs on my white wall hang a dried-out flower crown, a large and sagging pair of shorts, the iron belt—and is it any coincidence that all my relics are circular. Who can tell? Everything coheres, moves forward."

The relics are a garland of flowers he has woven while babysitting with the children—relic of children, then, as much as of his bucolic pagan days; the shorts he wore while making love to Fiona—"My shorts . . . were like the bulging marble skin of a

The Blood Oranges

headless god" (75)—are suggestive of shattered statuary in the museum that his mind is becoming (Hugh's mind, he accused, was a museum in which to entomb Fiona); the iron belt which signified the end of Illyria and which, psychically, Catherine, to whom he cannot make love, wears perhaps for good.

In the face of this evidence that things are done, that time now obtains—cycles, seasons, and circles of time—Cyril can only answer "who knows" to the question of the significance of their circularity. He then denies what he knows—his double rhetoric, again—by saying "everything . . . moves forward" when it in fact no longer does: it moves like the seasons he ignores, or tries to.

He goes on to say, "I listen for footsteps" (271). They may be Catherine's, or Rosella's, or those of a returning Fiona, to be sure. But they might also be those to which Yeats refers, in "The Second Coming," when he asks "And what rough beast, its hour come round at last,/Slouches towards Bethlehem to be born?"[11]

In the teeth of time, Cyril tells Catherine—the last line of the novel—"In Illyria there are no seasons" (271). This is his final cast of rhetoric. In wooing Catherine, in wooing himself, back to Illyria, he denies what he fears to be true, then begins again. And one can see him—as if on a tapestry—telling and re-telling, forever: in a static and timeless attitude, preserved in his art but mortal in his skin. And that permanent wooing, of Catherine, of Rosella, those endless words, that unraveling tapestry, can also be seen as images on the side of an urn—a man forever pursuing a woman, silent Catherine or Rosella, "foster-child of silence and slow time":

> Bold lover, never, never canst thou kiss,
> Though winning near the goal—yet, do not grieve;
> She cannot fade, though thou hast not thy bliss,
> For ever wilt thou love, and she be fair![12]

So Cyril *will* have his eternality, but in the song he sings to convince himself that he does have it. He becomes himself an artifact; he is his own song—true or false, moral or immoral, cruel or kind: he is the song he sings, long after he ceases to be. And so *The Blood Oranges*, that savage and desperate song, is Cyril, his interior imaginative battle with himself—his language is his mace, his chains—over whether he will always be or cease, wither, disappear. This is Hawkes's most cosmic theme, his most strangely moving treatment of any theme.

Twelfth Night is a romance intended for the Christmas season—celebration of that event which to Cyril is disaster: the intersection of timelessness and time. Hawkes draws "Illyria" from the Shakespearean play, some of the character of Hugh—"'If you must know,' I said and laughed, 'she calls you Malvolio. She says she loves her Malvolio best'" (177)—and some of the character of Cyril who, it can be argued, derives from Feste in certain scenes.

Hugh's self-love and repressing spirit cast a pall over Illyria and lead to disaster. In his pinched and diseased manner—"He moaned, licked the small wispy wings of his mustache with the tip of his tongue, finally glanced up at me. 'Hand of death inside my chest, that's all'" (71)—he reminds us of the Duke and Olivia, hiding behind masks, portraying false love in the language of disease. At his overbearing and repressive worst, he seems like the worst of Malvolio. But he also rises to heights, pathetic heights, when compared to Cyril's rhetorical rushes, and he then reminds us that Malvolio can be estimable, can even at times possess a genuine sense of his own value.

The clown's songs in *Twelfth Night* are suggested by Cyril's own poetry. His wooing of Catherine, and his reference to the Marvellian birds of prey, may remind us of

> What is love? 'tis not hereafter;
> Present mirth hath present laughter;
> What's to come is still unsure:
> In delay there lies no plenty; . . .

And his confrontation with Hugh in the arbor, when Hugh has imprisoned Catherine in the chastity belt, suggests the same song. For Hugh makes a dignified, reasonable argument that Cyril must leave his wife alone; at the same time, he does threaten, with this

The Blood Oranges

argument, the perfection of four people exchanging love which Cyril strives for. Hugh is both right and, in Cyril's terms, wrong. Cyril tells him: " 'Your clenched teeth would spoil anybody's idyls. Darkness can come to Illyria' " (251). He is in fact singing a *carpe diem* song to Hugh: "Youth's a stuff will not endure." This becomes more clearly the case when Cyril returns to Catherine to remove the chastity belt and she says: " 'Hugh made me put it on. He'll have to tell me to take it off.' " Cyril realizes that "Catherine's argument was Hugh's" (254). While wooing the one he woos the other. He admits that time ends all things—this is the basis of Feste's song in Act II—and he calls, in his Janus-faced rhetoric, for Hugh and Catherine to seize the day for the sake of timelessness.

It is the final song Feste sings, at the end of Act V, which is so evocative of Cyril's final song. Saying "and thus the whirligig of time brings in his revenges," as they do in both Illyrias, the clown sings:

> A great while ago the world begun
> With hey, ho, the wind and the rain;
> But that's all one, our play is done,
> And we'll strive to please you every day.

These lines suggest regret for lost youth, for the disappearance of romance, the onslaught of reality. It is not dissimilar from Cyril's final "In Illyria there are no seasons"—if we at last understand what Cyril knows: that there are seasons in Illyria, that he is fading into them.

The Blood Oranges is a brilliant prose achievement. It becomes the song its singer chants; its structure is interior—there are no formal chapters, only section-breaks—and is derived from the tension between what the singer knows or fears, and what he wishes to be true and feels that he must claim to be true. The usual Hawkesian disregard for a sequential story is evident here, as is Hawkes's insistence upon narrative; Hawkes will purposefully scramble events, but he will not ignore them. He will tell us that Hugh dies before the end of the book, although Hugh's death *is* the end of Illyria. For that is but an event: the significance of the event is in how Cyril perceives it and, further, how he goes on to tell it. Hence his final statement—based, in part, on his experience of Hugh's death—is a more important conclusion to the novel than the death itself.

For the novel is words. As Gass described *Under the Volcano*, and as we applied that description to the Germany of *The Cannibal*, so may we apply it here: Illyria is a land of phrases, not hillsides, where chains of concepts traverse our consciousness, not a real landscape. Experience here is turned into language, and Hawkes offers words instead of representations of real birds mating on a real earth. Furthermore, he offers a Cyril who is not a real person, who is a construct of words in combat. As we study Hawkes's words about Cyril to learn "who he is," we must, further, study Cyril's words about those who experience Cyril to learn who he more intensively "is."

As the foursome waits for the dawn on a high hilltop, Cyril describes "a single line of small pungent olive trees marching, so to speak, across the soft floor of that sheltered contour" (137). That "so to speak" is important: it is our reminder that Cyril is an artist, is manufacturing this world of his "theories" in the retelling—these are made-up olive trees on a made-up ground. The experience here is of language, not vegetation.

Again, when Cyril says "I was amused at their vision of my bulky athletic figure sporting with playful aesthetic hunger among the grapes" (185), we are alerted to Hawkes's maneuverings. First, Cyril manufactures visions with his words; hence *their* vision is amusing to him, for he knows what is there to be seen: in the reconstruction he creates what is there to be seen. Second, we note how he creates his effect by offering a sense of physicality, hence tangibility: his figure is bulky, athletic, it looms in the vision. Yet it does so with a hunger that is "aesthetic." Of course, Cyril suggests that everything he does is done with a sense of the aesthetic; but it seems, here, that he goes further—that he makes the actual hunger itself an aesthetic occurrence. For noth-

The Blood Oranges

ing, finally, is purely physical as he renders his verbal artifacts. The hunger is not of the belly, but inside of words.

Again, as Hugh swims, Cyril sees "his thin legs . . . cutting imaginary paper" (229). The metaphor obviously is that the sea is like paper—suggestive that the paper of the book itself is referred to. But Cyril goes one step further: the paper itself is imaginary—a product of his mind. The sea is one of words. As if to confirm this notion, Cyril soon afterward says "in the idea as in the sea itself we snort" (230).

Cyril's disquisitions and narration are oxymoronic; he creates a sense of limitlessness while singing of limitations and then, reversing himself, uses ideas of infinity to create ideas of finitude. Thus, he defines himself most adequately when he calls himself a man who stands for "sensuous rationality" (203). His body thinks. His thoughts are his physique. His book is his body and his thoughts, his body of thoughts, his thought-up self. A more important oxymoron—it can serve as emblem for the entire novel—is Cyril's description of the path between his and Fiona's villa, and Hugh's and Catherine's: "I returned along the empty path that stretched endlessly from villa to villa" (154). The figure serves to show that the walk is long and sad, *seemingly* endless. But it also serves to give us the basic fact of Illyria: between clearly limited physical poles there is eternity. Man, to Cyril, in his world, is an infinity sandwich: an endlessness that somehow exists within finitudes. This definition can serve for the function of his art, as well. Within the limitations of the iambic sonnet there can be an infinity of suggestion; inside the flowered flatness of a Matisse there are sizes beyond measurement; and inside the skin of a man, his body of words, there can be Illyria, which goes on—so the words swear and pray—forever. This is a story of the flesh made word.

Finally, there is this to say about *The Blood Oranges:* its prose achieves heights that are shaking, as the novel goes about its business of making a man who makes a world which he narrates while simultaneously losing and retaining it. Here, for example, is Cyril watching an eagle—that showing-forth in nature which always confirms his belief in Illyria—as he and the others wait for the sun to rise: "Stark, unruffled, quite alone, a featureless image of ancient strength and unappeased appetite, certainly the distant bird was both incongruous and appropriate, at once alive and hence distracting but also sinister, a kind of totemic particle dislodged from the uninhabited hills and toneless light" (138). The prose is on-going, an organ-chord of simultaneous awe and intellection; the qualities of the sentence are of perception and of a building upon that perception—emotion and ratiocination at once. And the image itself—of a "totemic particle"—while hard to wrap the tongue around, is *right:* a high static speck of sacredness, frozen by the quality of recognition into a frieze.

And then the sun rises, and the sinister image vanishes, the day is reborn, Cyril is assured that Illyria is art and eternal: "The black and silver sky turned orange and foamed for miles behind the stationary air-borne eagle, and the purple hills dissolved, reappeared, revealed on thick green slopes a clear pattern of thistle, clay, warped trees, a few abandoned stone huts. Mist filled the valley at our feet and then lifted. The cold air grew warm, the eagle suddenly glided downward to the east and was gone, simply gone. The day was ours" (139).

Here thought is absent, the perceiver responds as we might if we saw a painting rendered on film in speeded-up motion. There is the sense of color, the sense of temperature, the sense of possession. And here we have the two Cyrils, the two moods of the novel, the two effects of the same prose which is capable of making a satyr into two beings, a novel into two statements, a thought an experience, an experience a thought—and a simple sunrise into a stunning thunderous triumph, like the book in which it occurs.

AGENDA

As Albert J. Guerard noted in his 1963 *Critique* essay on Hawkes's style: "It is hardly soon enough to engage in summaries." It still is hardly soon enough.

It is *not* hardly soon enough to say that Hawkes's works are far from ignorable. It is time, now, to say that Hawkes is a major voice in America and England (at least) and that the heft of his presence is as important to American letters as it is to the demands of literary justice. Not only is Hawkes beginning to get something approaching the readership he deserves—*The Blood Oranges* was a Book-of-the-Month Club Alternate Selection—and some of the understanding his work requires. Hawkes's readers are more and more recognizing that style is the author's intelligence, morality, and perception alive before the reader: the writer's fiction *is* how his language behaves. William Gass, Richard Gilman, and Susan Sontag, among others, have long insisted that fiction be described in terms of its language alone. Hawkes's looming public victory is, therefore, a sign that we as readers are rising to what we read. Harold Robbins and Irving Stone will continue to issue books that are called novels, of course. One cannot presume to hope for an end to that. But there is in Hawkes's growing recognition evidence that our esteem for language grows. We cannot keep pace with Hawkes—we should always be led into strange places by our writers—but we are, perhaps, beginning to want to try.

When considering our best writers—among them: Gass, Barth, Coover, Welty, Percy, Nabokov, Paul West, Updike, Mailer, Price, and Hawkes—we first consider them in terms of language. Some make characters more memorable than do others, and some approach topical concerns more directly, but all make something new of the old words. Norman Mailer's description of the artist's search for a way of dealing with the world is useful here: "The serious novel begins," he says in *Cannibals and Christians*, "from a fixed philosophical point—the desire to discover reality—and it goes to search for that reality in society, or else must embark on a trip up the upper Amazon of the inner eye."[1] While much of Mailer's concern seems societal to many readers, it reveals itself as, ultimately, verbal—

> ever see an old black man roll his eyes on a country road while some ice-green-eye redneck looks him in and out saying what black thoughts you have Sambo ass, and Mr. Black he looking back and he see Whitey the Green Eye from Texas with his ears moving in circles like old wasp wings, ZZZ, and his sharp Scotch-Irish White White White Man's Nose red as lobster is a-hovering and a-plunging like a Claw, man.[2]

—for he wants to tell us the language of our thoughts, not the philosophies of our state. Thus the rhyme ("Black" and "back"), the puns ("a Claw, man"—"Lawman"), and thus the descent from description to pure sound ("ZZZ"), as if a jazzman, trying to describe a musical passage, shifted from description to chant to imitating the instruments of which he spoke. Mailer captures here a black man's verbal music and contrasts to it the white man's analytic fearfulness ("what black thoughts you have Sambo"); he compares and contrasts two parts of a culture without *telling* us a thing: he makes the nature of our language enact the drama of our racially nagged culture. We see here how the writer is caught—pulled by—the rhythms of what he has just set down; the language dances with the play of mind, not the tug of social forces.

This is the case with Hawkes. His concerns are those of the voyager of the inner eye. He is a poet. His distortion of what one expects from a novel, his manipulation of narrators until we—who must trust them for the truth—cannot trust them, his love of the music words can make, his delight in forcing fierce verbal equivalents of deep-locked psychic history from simple events—these are the habits of the traveler into the inner eye. The reports of his voyages await us, and we need now to apply to them the tools of wit we have been blunting on the lesser sons and daughters of Wharton and Dreiser.

On the agenda should be work that follows Albert J. Guerard's lead in analyzing Hawkes's use of violence and suppressed sexuality. Especially important, it seems, is a sense of the act of writing—or telling in narrative, as a fictional character—as an act of revenge for childhood trauma. It is not difficult to think of Hawkes's wronged children—the unwanted baby in *Charivari* and the dead baby in *The Beetle Leg*, the "fox" in *The Cannibal*, Hencher the outraged son in *The Lime Twig*, the vengeful daughter Cassandra in *Second Skin*, Skipper in *Second Skin* and Edward in *The Undertaker* as horribly wronged sons, Catherine and Hugh's angry daughter in *The Blood Oranges*—and then to consider that Hawkes's characters embody his belief that the act of art is combat with personal history.

There is a need for work that concerns itself with the intrusion of a devastating past on a bleak present. The intrusion is manifest in all the works. The relationship of personal violence, the act of writing, and the cultural problem of how our past invades us (and demands analysis by us) ought to be a pressing concern for students of Hawkes.

Guerard has begun the study of Hawkes's style, and his "The Prose Style of John Hawkes" in *Critique* charts the areas of central concern. Studies of the structure of the books, their lyrical and ironic tones, will doubtless be written, along with a full-scale study of the animal imagery, which binds the works from *Charivari* to *The Blood Oranges*.

Furthermore, work is needed on the fantastic landscapes in which Hawkes sets his books. Tony Tanner's comments on these landscapes—the Germany of the mind, the verbal Brighton, Illyria —need to be followed up at considerable length.

We await studies of the relationship of the writings of Nathanael West, Djuna Barnes, and Flannery O'Connor to Hawkes's own work. Thus far, Hawkes's own comments provide the best sense of how he draws nourishment from them.

HAWKES: A Guide to His Fictions

At this writing, John Hawkes is forty-seven years old. His fiction swells in power. His style grows more controlled, and yet the visionary impulse that was with him from the beginning seems stronger. It would be premature, then, to close the case by offering ponderous summaries. It is fitting, simply, to say that further reports are clearly to come from Hawkes's unmapped worlds of the inner eye. It is just, in advance, to be grateful.

NOTES

Notes to INTRODUCTION

1. John Hawkes, "Notes on the Wild Goose Chase," *The American Novel Since World War II*, edited by Marcus Klein (New York: Fawcett Books, 1969), p. 251. This essay, first published in *The Massachusetts Review* in 1962, is also reprinted in *Studies in Second Skin*, edited by John Graham (Columbus: Charles E. Merrill, 1971), pp. 20–23.
2. *Ibid.*
3. *The Innocent Party* (New York: New Directions, 1966), p. 167.
4. *The Beetle Leg* (New York: New Directions, 1951), p. 132.
5. *The Blood Oranges* (New York: New Directions, 1971), p. 36.
6. Robert Scholes, "A Conversation on *The Blood Oranges*," *Novel: A Forum on Fiction*, V, 3 (Spring 1972), 204.
7. [John Enck,] "John Hawkes: An Interview," *Wisconsin Studies in Contemporary Literature*, VI, 2 (Summer 1964), 141–42.
8. Hawkes, "Notes on the Wild Goose Chase," *The American Novel Since World War II*, p. 250.
9. Nathanael West, *The Day of the Locust* in *Miss Lonelyhearts & The Day of the Locust* (New York: New Directions, 1962), p. 127.
10. [Enck,] "John Hawkes: An Interview," *Wisconsin Studies in Contemporary Literature*, VI, 2 (Summer 1964), 142.
11. Hawkes, "Notes on the Wild Goose Chase," *The American Novel Since World War II*, p. 249.
12. Scholes, "A Conversation on *The Blood Oranges*," *Novel: A Forum on Fiction*, V, 3 (Spring 1972), 201.
13. [Enck,] "John Hawkes: An Interview," *Wisconsin Studies in Contemporary Literature*, VI, 2 (Summer 1964), 154.
14. Samuel Johnson, *Lives of the English Poets*, edited by George Birbeck Hill (New York, 1967), I, 20.
15. Kingsley Widmer, *The Literary Rebel* (Carbondale and Edwardsdale, 1965), p. 164.
16. Webster Schott, "John Hawkes: Vision of a Nightmare," *Nation*, 193, September 2, 1961, p. 122.
17. *Ibid.*
18. Albert J. Guerard, "John Hawkes in English J," *The Harvard Advocate*, October 1970.
19. Albert J. Guerard, "Second Skin: The Light and Dark Affirmation,"

Notes

Studies in Second Skin, edited by John Graham (Columbus: Charles E. Merrill, 1971), p. 102.

Notes to Chapter One—*Charivari*

1. Page references are made to the *New Directions Eleven* (1949) imprint of the novel, pp. 365–436. Subsequent references to *Charivari* in this chapter will be given parenthetically after quotation.
2. Webster Schott, "John Hawkes: Vision of a Nightmare," *Nation,* 193, September 2, 1961, p. 122. Albert J. Guerard, "John Hawkes in English J," *The Harvard Advocate,* October 1970, writes: "I first met John Hawkes in September 1947, when he came to my Leverett House office to apply for admission to English J, 'The Writing and Criticism of Fiction.' He held out what I could see at a glance, and with some distress, was a long free verse poem. I said I would have to have a sample of his prose. Hawkes asked me, with a firmness that surprised me, to read the poem anyway. Its vision was strange, its language powerful and contorted: encouraging signs. Moreover, Hawkes did surrender some fifty pages of *Charivari.*"
3. T. S. Eliot, *The Complete Poems and Plays 1909–1950* (New York: Harcourt Brace Jovanovich, Inc., 1952), p. 41.
4. *Ibid.,* p. 6.
5. *Ibid.,* p. 7.
6. John Graham, "John Hawkes on His Novels," *The Massachusetts Review,* VII, 3 (Summer 1966), 450.
7. Robert Scholes, *The Fabulators* (New York: Oxford University Press, 1967), devotes an impressive chapter to aspects of Hawkes's work. He studies *Charivari* as a surrealistic novel, linking its hallucinatory technique to the Circe episode in Joyce's *Ulysses,* Albee's play *The American Dream,* and the satirical fantasy of Nathanael West.

Notes to Chapter Two—*The Cannibal*

1. John Graham, "John Hawkes on His Novels," *Massachusetts Review,* VII, 3 (Summer 1966), 449–50.
2. [John Enck,] "John Hawkes: An Interview," *Wisconsin Studies in Contemporary Literature,* VI, 2 (Summer 1964), 147.
3. *The Cannibal* (New York: New Directions, 1949), initial and unnumbered pages of prologue. Subsequent references to *The Cannibal* in this chapter will be given parenthetically after quotation.
4. William Gass, *Fiction and the Figures of Life* (New York: Knopf, 1970), p. 57.
5. T. S. Eliot, "Journey of the Magi," *The Complete Poems and Plays 1909–1950* (New York: Harcourt Brace Jovanovich, Inc., 1952), p. 68.
6. [Enck,] "John Hawkes: An Interview," *Wisconsin Studies in Contemporary Literature,* VI, 2 (Summer 1964), 150. Albert J. Guerard, "John Hawkes in English J," *The Harvard Advocate,* October 1970, recalls the reaction of his fiction-writing class to *The Cannibal* as Hawkes, a student in the course, brought the novel in a section at a time: "I saw that my chief function was to provide the right note of encouragement to an exceedingly lonely endeavor, and to counter

NOTES

insensitive or baffled criticism. The other students were puzzled, dismayed, and without an appropriate critical vocabulary, but they reacted with increasing enthusiasm as the year progressed. What concession could be made to the reader's longing to understand without impairing integrity or vision? I did urge Hawkes to identify the sections of *The Cannibal* according to time (1914, 1945) and ultimately suggested a narrator as an aid to the disoriented."

7. Dylan Thomas, "The Peaches," *Portrait of the Artist as a Young Dog* (New York: New Directions, 1940), p. 11.

8. *Ibid.,* p. 16.

9. We should add Tanner's provocative suggestion that "what the Duke is doing is the blackest possible parody of what Hawkes himself is doing—stalking his 'subject,' taking the carcass and trying to cut it up to fit his notion of neatness and order. That puddle of waste left behind . . . is . . . the hallmark of yet another failed artistic venture." Tony Tanner, *City of Words* (New York: Harper, 1971), p. 208. Tanner speaks of the artist's unceasing sense that he has not succeeded in doing what he intended to or should have done; he does not imply that *The Cannibal* itself fails.

Notes to Chapter Three—*The Beetle Leg*

1. *The Beetle Leg* (New York: New Directions, 1951). Subsequent references to *The Beetle Leg* in this chapter will be given parenthetically after quotation.

2. Jessie L. Weston, *From Ritual to Romance* (New York: Doubleday Anchor, 1957), p. 136.

3. *Ibid.,* p. 59.

4. *Ibid.,* p. 51.

5. James G. Frazer, *The Golden Bough* (New York: Macmillan, 1960), p. 106.

6. T. S. Eliot, *The Complete Poems and Plays 1909–1950* (New York: Harcourt Brace Jovanovich, Inc., 1952), p. 43.

7. Weston, *From Ritual to Romance*, p. 39.

8. Frazer, *The Golden Bough*, p. 815.

9. Eliot, *Complete Poems*, p. 39.

10. William Faulkner, *Collected Stories of William Faulkner* (New York: Random House, 1950), p. 8.

Notes to Chapter Four—*The Goose on the Grave*

1. *The Goose on the Grave* (New York: New Directions, 1954), p. 3. Subsequent references to *The Goose on the Grave* in this chapter will be made parenthetically after quotation. This volume also contains *The Owl*.

2. Meals, used in *The Cannibal* and here, are also important in Hawkes's related stories, "The Traveler" (1962) and "The Grandmother" (1961). The latter —both are set on the Continent and concern German characters—is about a child metaphorically devouring his family. At a meal, the boy's father, preparing to carve a roast lamb, holds the carving knife and fork above the lamb "as in some kind of feverish dying benediction." *Lunar Landscapes* (New York: New Directions, 1969), p. 15. In *The Blood Oranges* (New York: New Directions, 1970), pp. 50–53, a meal takes on the overtones of a sexual act.

3. Perhaps the consummate contemporary story of a fallen angel who is fallen

NOTES

Icarus as well—the spirit of art brought to earth—is William Gass's "In the Heart of the Heart of the Country," *In the Heart of the Heart of the Country* (New York: Harper, 1968).

4. T. S. Eliot, *The Complete Poems and Plays 1909–1950* (New York: Harcourt Brace Jovanovich, Inc., 1952), pp. 21, 23.

5. This scene is remarkably suggestive of Samuel Beckett's portrait of humanity, a mud-crawling corpse, in *How It Is*. Hawkes's book was published in 1954, while Beckett's was not published in English until 1964; as *Comment C'est* it was published in France in 1961.

6. Irving Malin, *New American Gothic* (Carbondale: Southern Illinois University Press, 1962), p. 75.

Notes to Chapter Five—The Lime Twig

1. Robert J. Edenbaum, "John Hawkes: The Lime Twig and Other Tenuous Horrors," *The Massachusetts Review*, VII, 3 (Summer 1966), 464–65.

2. [John Enck,] "John Hawkes: An Interview," *Wisconsin Studies in Contemporary Literature*, VI, 2 (Summer 1964), 150–51.

3. Albert J. Guerard, Addendum to his Introduction to *The Cannibal* (New York: New Directions, 1962), p. xviii.

4. Leslie A. Fiedler, "The Pleasures of John Hawkes," Introduction to *The Lime Twig* (New York: New Directions, 1961), pp. x–xi. Subsequent references to *The Lime Twig* in this chapter will be given parenthetically after quotation. Joan Didion echoes Fiedler, calling the novel "*Brighton Rock* [read] while in a peyote trance," in "Notes from a Helpless Reader," *The National Review*, July 15, 1961, p. 21.

5. W. M. Frohock, "John Hawkes's Vision of Violence," *Southwest Review*, L, Winter 1965, 75.

6. [Enck,] "John Hawkes: An Interview," *Wisconsin Studies in Contemporary Literature*, VI, 2 (Summer 1964), 151.

7. *Ibid*.

8. Edenbaum, "John Hawkes: The Lime Twig and Other Tenuous Horrors," *The Massachusetts Review*, VII, 3 (Summer 1966), 468.

9. Hawkes has said that he took the name of the race from Henry James and meant to imply that "Michael Banks is destroying the golden bowl of earthly pleasure at the very last moment of his life. You could say, conceivably, that the ending of that novel is redemptive." John Graham, "John Hawkes on His Novels," *The Massachusetts Review*, VII, 3. (Summer 1966), 456–57. (Hawkes's suggestion that the novel is redemptive should be borne in mind; he contradicts this idea later by stating that *Second Skin* is his first "affirmative" novel.) In *The Lime Twig* Michael sees "a dove bursting with air on a bough" as he runs to his death, thus perhaps alluding to James's *The Wings of the Dove*. Although there is little direct resemblance between the characters of Hawkes and James so far as *Dove* is concerned, there is the over-all common concern with money, illusion, a spiritually bankrupt England, repressed (and expressed) sexuality, and, most important, the transcendence of Milly into art—the habit of everyone in *Dove* of rendering others as concepts. This suggests the habit in *The Lime Twig* of shying from reality, of transmuting experience into dreams.

Notes

10. Graham Greene, *Brighton Rock* (New York: Viking, 1949), p. 291. Subsequent references to *Brighton Rock* in this chapter will be given parenthetically after quotation as *BR* and page number.

11. In [Enck,] "John Hawkes: An Interview," *Wisconsin Studies in Contemporary Literature*, VI, 2 (Summer 1964), 151.

12. In *The Fabulators* (New York: Oxford University Press, 1967), Scholes is interested in what he calls "the interconnections between cruelty and tenderness" (79) in *The Lime Twig*. He examines the scene in which Margaret is tortured, comparing it with passages in de Sade's *Justine;* he concludes that Hawkes's cruel brilliance of description is far from sadistic because his characters are imagined as people who are hurt while de Sade's victim is a mere doll that not only "says mamma but bleeds when whipped—all without in any way suggesting human life" (85).

13. "A Little Bit of the Old Slap and Tickle," *Lunar Landscapes* (New York: New Directions, 1969), pp. 26–30.

Notes to Chapter Six—Second Skin

1. John Graham, "John Hawkes on His Novels," *Massachusetts Review*, VII, 3 (Summer 1966), 459.

2. John Hawkes, *Second Skin* (New York: New Directions, 1964), p. 1. Subsequent references to *Second Skin* in this chapter will be given parenthetically after quotation.

3. *The Tempest*, Prospero, and the magic of artifice are brilliantly employed to create a character coping with his guilts and fears in Paul West's novel, *Caliban's Filibuster* (New York: Doubleday, 1971).

4. In "The Nearest Cemetery," *Lunar Landscapes* (New York: New Directions, 1969), pp. 43–50, Hawkes writes of a bewitching woman (the Princess), an island, fishermen in New England, and murder. The Barber narrates the story; he is the "final lover" of the Princess: "He loved her from afar and killed her" (43). A lighthouse dominates the island here as it does the landscape of *Second Skin*.

John Kuehl, editor of *Creative Writing & Rewriting* (New York: Appleton-Century-Crofts, 1967), copyright © 1967, by permission of Appleton-Century-Crofts, Educational Division, Meredith Corporation, cites a letter he received from John Hawkes on September 22, 1965, in which Hawkes says that he "remembered that I had published a piece called The Nearest Cemetery in the *San Francisco Review Annual* (1963) and realized that this piece is actually the preliminary vision out of which my last novel Second Skin was generated." Hawkes calls the story "a microcosmic version of a good portion of the book" (Kuehl, 265) and recalls that "The Nearest Cemetery is a compression of 20–30 handwritten pages prepared in the summer of 1960. Second Skin was written in 1962–63 and really could not have been written without the earlier microcosmic effort and the intervening two years of thought" (Kuehl, 284).

The Barber and three men are in prison; each of these men has been the Princess' lover, but none is described as having loved her as the Barber did—from afar—and so we assume that they were physical lovers, while the Barber, who narrates the story, seems not to have been. Speaking of the men in prison, the Barber says: "Each of us has his Venus . . . Venus at least in memory" (45).

NOTES

The crime was committed on Bloody Clam Shell Island, and we see a parodistic Venus—the Princess springs from her boat to the island—springing from the foam of the sea.

What she brings is language to the silent island. Hawkes ridicules New England taciturnity, as the Barber says: "The wordless life . . . none of them are talkers. They never were" (48). But "the Princess talked . . . she might have been reading aloud or singing aloud the pages of a book" (49), so magical was her effect on the men of the island.

Hawkes never reveals why the men are imprisoned, only that the inmates share a "common dream" (47) and that there is "no talking here" (48). In this silent place of violent physical prisoners—it seems little different from the island, "that prison was an island" (45)—the Barber cuts everyone's hair, dreams of the Princess and of Mildred, his wife, Calvinist conscience personified: "The Lord and Mildred deafen me" (50). In place of silence, he hears her pumping an organ and singing hymns suggesting the death of his dream—"*as a Dream dies at the opening of day*" (50) he hears Mildred singing.

Thus, tormented by his vision, haunted by a New England conscience—this is the most American story Hawkes has written—the Barber narrates his story. The act of narration makes him the only speaker in this prison of the mind, which perhaps reminds us of Kafka's Penal Colony—an island on which the condemned man did not speak the language of his captors. We recall that the Barber cuts everyone's hair, just as he is the only narrator: "my razor shapes those sideburns—they are the color of trees in gloom, the color of water at high tide" (46). If we ask who will cut the Barber's hair, we ask who will shape, with language, the Barber's dreams? Who, in fact, will understand his words? He is alone, imprisoned in himself, Prospero as his own Ariel, and it is evident that we have here not only a preparation for Hawkes's use of the New England coast for *Second Skin*, but a parable of the artist worthy of the Kafka of "A Hunger Artist" or "In the Penal Colony."

5. No matter how equal they are—and, at the novel's end, they do share in all things—Sonny and Skipper are not social equals at the start; Sonny is Skipper's "inferior" by rank. While they are companions in a journey, they are companions as Huck and Nigger Jim were, as Chingachgook and Natty Bumppo were, as those Indians were who taught Hawthorne's Chillingworth his arcane knowledge of roots and herbs, as Queequeg was to Ishmael, as Bugs was to Ad Francis in Hemingway's "The Battler," as the Negro beachcomber was to Monroe Stahr in *The Last Tycoon*, as Dilsey was to Faulkner's Compson family, as Dahfu was to Bellow's Henderson, as the Doctor was for Jake Horner in Barth's *The End of the Road*, as Shago was for Rojack in Mailer's *An American Dream*, as Skeeter was for Updike's Rabbit—these black characters are guides to their white companions, psychic guides over psychic frontiers. In grasping this thematic obsession in American writing, Hawkes again captures an American essence as, in *The Beetle Leg*, he dealt with a fundamental American landscape and concern. Leslie Fiedler is somewhere behind this note—as he is somewhere in the history of the writing of so much work on American literature.

6. Tony Tanner, in *City of Words* (New York: Harper, 1971), pp. 227–28, concludes this: the two islands of the book "define the antipodal extremes of Skipper's imaginative universe. The first is a paranoid and self-pitying projection

NOTES

of a world given totally over to the forces of negation and death. The second is a compensating and self-congratulatory version in which those forces are subsumed, rendered impotent, or transformed, and everything is in the sway of the peaceful rhythms of life. One is a nightmare of utter powerlessness; the other is a dream of pure freedom. . . . The two islands are the two necessary landscapes by which Skipper can chart the meaning of his experience, and through which Hawkes can explore the limits of his art." Lucy Frost's "Awakening Paradise," in *Studies in Second Skin*, edited by John Graham (Columbus: Charles E. Merrill, 1971), pp. 52–63, discusses these extremes in terms of Freud's Eros and its traditional antagonist, Thanatos. Frost concludes that "the chronicle Skipper writes on the sunny island is the history of his defeat."

7. Lionel Trilling, "Authenticity and the Modern Unconscious," *Commentary*, LII, 3 (September 1971), 39–50.

Notes to Chapter Seven—*The Innocent Party*

1. *The Innocent Party* (New York: New Directions, 1966). Subsequent references to *The Innocent Party* in this chapter will be given parenthetically after quotation.

2. Albert Guerard, "*Second Skin*: The Light and Dark Affirmation," *Studies in Second Skin*, edited by John Graham (Columbus: Charles E. Merrill, 1971), p. 98. Guerard cites a critical commentary written by Hawkes for *The Personal Voice*, edited by Albert J. Guerard et al. (Philadelphia: Lippincott, 1964).

Notes to Chapter Eight—*The Blood Oranges*

1. *The Blood Oranges* (New York: New Directions, 1971), Subsequent references to *The Blood Oranges* in this chapter will be given parenthetically after quotation.

2. Ford Madox Ford, *The Good Soldier: A Tale of Passion* (New York: Boni, 1927), p. 240.

3. *Ibid.*, pp. 240–41.

4. Robert Scholes, "A Conversation on *The Blood Oranges*," *Novel: A Forum on Fiction*, V, 3 (Spring 1972), 200.

5. Wayne Carver, "Fiction," *Esquire*, LXXVII, 1 (January 1972), 34.

6. *The Poems of Andrew Marvell*, edited by Hugh MacDonald (Cambridge, Mass.: Harvard University Press, 1952), p. 22.

7. Roger Sale, "What Went Wrong?" *The New York Review of Books*, XVII, 6 (October 21, 1971), 3. Contributors to *The New York Review of Books* have consistently displayed a haughty and disapproving attitude toward Hawkes's work, demanding that he give more or less or different or the-same-as—until it has become evident that, for reasons of literary or social doctrine, Hawkes will simply not be granted this journal's approbation until he stops writing like Hawkes.

8. Robert Scholes, "A Conversation on *The Blood Oranges*," *Novel: A Forum on Fiction*, V, 3 (Spring 1972), 202.

9. MacDonald, *The Poems of Andrew Marvell*.

10. When on page 18 Hawkes has Cyril speak of her "girlish fixation on the altar of the dead," we are of course reminded of Henry James's nouvelle of 1895.

NOTES

Fiona is attracted to death (as in the case of Hugh) in a sexual way; she embraces death, and she is swept away by it as is Stransom in "The Altar of the Dead." There is the possibility, too, that Cyril's alternate world becomes, as he narrates it, recollecting, a world of the dead instead of one peopled with lithe lovers; when Cyril, at the end, studies his altar of life, it can be seen to have undergone a metamorphosis into an altar of the dead. The reference to the James work suggests a world of illusions shattered by reality's harshest fact. As Hawkes made use of references to James in *The Lime Twig* as a way of suggesting the dangers—and allures—of illusion, so he apparently does here.

11. *The Collected Poems of W. B. Yeats* (New York: Macmillan, 1956), p. 185.

12. *The Poetical Works of John Keats*, edited by H. W. Garrod (London: Oxford University Press, 1956), pp. 209–10.

Notes to AGENDA

1. Norman Mailer, *Cannibals and Christians* (New York: The Dial Press, 1966), p. 128.

2. Norman Mailer, *Why Are We In Vietnam?* (New York: G. P. Putnam's Sons, 1967), p. 27.

BIBLIOGRAPHICAL NOTE

Hawkes's American publisher has always been James Laughlin's New Directions, New York City. *Charivari* appeared in *New Directions Eleven* (1949), edited, as are all the *New Directions* anthologies, by Laughlin. Hawkes made his debut in an anthology described on its dust jacket as "An Annual Exhibition Gallery of New & Divergent Trends in Modern Letters." Represented in the same issue, among other contributors, are Stephen Spender, Henry Miller, Paul Bowles, Peter Viereck, Kenneth Rexroth, William Jay Smith, May Swenson, William Carlos Williams, Tennessee Williams, Edwin Honig, and Jean Genet. The list shows not only in what company Hawkes made his initial appearance, but the breadth of Laughlin's vision and his receptiveness to experimental writing. It is probably time for a study of Laughlin's contributions to the world of letters. (See, in Chapter Five, Hawkes's description of the role Laughlin played in helping to design *The Lime Twig*.)

New Directions Eleven is in print. So are all of Hawkes's other books. Although the anthology is available in hardcover only, as is the one-volume *The Goose on the Grave* and *The Owl*, the other books are available in hardcover and paperback from New Directions. *The Owl, The Goose on the Grave*, and *Charivari* are collected in *Lunar Landscapes* (1969), which in addition collects Hawkes's short fiction from *MSS 1, New Directions Twelve, Seventeen* and *Eighteen, The Noble Savage, San Francisco Review,* and *San Francisco Review Annual;* the stories are "Death of An Airman" (1950), "The Grandmother" (1961), "A Little Bit of the Old Slap and Tickle" (1962), "The Traveler" (1962), "A Song Outside" (1962), and "The Nearest Cemetery" (1963).

Useful interviews with Hawkes are those conducted by John Enck, "John Hawkes: An Interview," *Wisconsin Studies in Comparative Literature*, VI, 2 (Summer 1964), 141–55; John Graham, "John

BIBLIOGRAPHICAL NOTE

Hawkes On His Novels," *Massachusetts Review*, VII, 3 (Summer 1966), 449–61; and Robert Scholes, "A Conversation on *The Blood Oranges*," *Novel*, V, 3 (Spring 1972). For excerpts from correspondence from Hawkes, see also *Creative Writing and Rewriting*, edited by John Kuehl (New York: Appleton-Century-Crofts, 1967), pp. 265, 284–87. In *The Harvard Advocate*, CIV, 2 (October 1970), 6, 34–35, two small interviews—"Talks With John Hawkes"—though highly impressionistic, are worth looking at for the sense they give of Hawkes the man.

Hawkes's critical writings, small in number, are informative about his own fictive cast of mind. He speaks of Nathanael West and Flannery O'Connor in "Flannery O'Connor's Devil," *Sewanee Review*, LXX, Summer 1962, 395–407. In "Notes on *The Wild Goose Chase*," originally published in *The Massachusetts Review* in 1962, now collected in *The American Novel Since World War II*, edited by Marcus Klein (New York: Fawcett Books, 1969), p. 251, and in *Studies in Second Skin*, edited by John Graham (Columbus: Charles E. Merrill, 1971), p. 20, Hawkes writes on Rex Warner and experimental fiction in general. His remarks here echo his three-paragraph introduction to "The Lodging House Fires," an excerpt from *The Lime Twig*, which was published in *Audience*, VII, Spring 1960, 60–77; the remarks are entitled "Notes On Violence." In a college text, *The Personal Voice* (Philadelphia: Lippincott, 1964), of which Hawkes and Albert J. Guerard are, with others, the editors, Hawkes writes of the Freudian origins of literary images.

The most recently published bibliography is by Jackson R. Bryer, *Critique*, VI, 2 (Fall 1963), 89–94; Marshall C. Olds's unpublished bibliography supersedes Bryer's.

Chapters on Hawkes are to be found in Tony Tanner, *City of Words* (New York: Harper, 1971); Richard Pearce, *Stages of the Clown* (Carbondale: Southern Illinois University Press, 1970); and Robert Scholes, *The Fabulators* (New York: Oxford University Press, 1967). Hawkes is discussed in Kingsley Widmer, *The Literary Rebel* (Carbondale: Southern Illinois University Press, 1965); Irving Malin, *New American Gothic* (Carbondale: Southern Illinois University Press, 1962); and in Ihab Hassan, *Radical Innocence* (Princeton: Princeton University Press, 1961).

The only book devoted wholly to Hawkes is the compilation by John Graham, *Studies in Second Skin*. This important and useful book, with an instructive Preface, offers some contemporary reviews of *Second Skin*, the Enck and Graham interviews with Hawkes, the text of "The Nearest Cemetery," Hawkes's "Notes on *The Wild Goose Chase*," and six excellent critical essays on *Second Skin*, each by a different author.

There have been many intelligent reviews of Hawkes's books (each decrying his status as "writer's writer," each calling for a reassessment of him as a more important author than he has seemed to be). Stanley Kauffmann writes of Hawkes's break with the traditional novel in "Further Adventures of the Novel," *The New Republic*, CL., June 6, 1964, 19, as does Susan Sontag in *The New York Times Book Review*, April 5, 1964, p. 5. Joan Didion, in "Notes From a Helpless Reader," *National Review*, July 15, 1961, p. 21, and F. W. Dupee, in "An Imaginary Island," *The Reporter*, July 20, 1961, p. 56, both herald Hawkes's "arrival." Claire Rosenfield's review of *The Lime Twig*, "John Hawks: Nightmares of the Real," *Minnesota Review*, VI, 2 (Winter 1962), 249, provides an excellent evaluation of Hawkes's earlier work. In his review of *Lunar Landscapes* in *The New York Times Book Review*, July 13, 1969, p. 4, Robert Scholes continues to explore the theme of cruelty in Hawkes's work and calls for his widespread acceptance. The novelist Thomas McGuane, calling Hawkes "feasibly our best writer," does the same in his review of *The Blood Oranges* in *The New York Times Book Review*, September 19, 1971, p. 1. Charles Moran's "John Hawkes: Paradise Gaining," *Massachusetts Review*, XII, 4 (Autumn 1971), 840, is the most useful review of *The Blood Oranges*. Webster Schott has written several reviews of Hawkes's work and was an early defender. His longest review (with the most biographical data) is "John Hawkes, An American Original," *The New York Times Book Review*, May 29, 1966, p. 4. Interesting British reviews are "Into the Atmosphere," *The Times Literary Supplement*, August 29, 1968, p. 929, and "Improvisations and Rituals," *The Times Literary Supplement*, January 4, 1968, p. 15; the reviews are of, respectively, *The Lime Twig* and *The Innocent Party*, both published by Chatto and Windus.

Albert J. Guerard, Hawkes's teacher and champion from the start, writes of Hawkes as a young writer in "John Hawkes in English J," *The Harvard Advocate*, CIV, 2 (October 1970), 10. His essay, "*Second Skin*: The Light and Dark Affirmation," originally a paper read at the 1968 Conference of the Pennsylvania Council of Teachers of

English, is an outstanding piece in *Studies in Second Skin*. His "The Prose Style of John Hawkes," *Critique*, VI, 2 (Fall 1963), 19, is indispensable. See also his "Illuminating Distortion," *Novel*, V, 2 (Winter, 1972), 101, in which he alludes to overtones of homosexuality in *Second Skin* and relates them to the novel's violence.

Good starting-points for further study of Hawkes are also to be found in Earl Rovit, "The Fiction of John Hawkes: An Introductory View," *Modern Fiction Studies*, XI, 2 (Summer 1964), 150; W. M. Frohock, "John Hawkes's Vision of Violence," *Southwest Review*, L, Winter 1965, 69; Robert I. Edenbaum, "*The Lime Twig* and Other Tenuous Horrors," *The Massachusetts Review*, VII, 3 (Summer 1966), 462. Anthony C. Santore's "Narrative Unreliability and the Structure of *Second Skin*," in *Studies in Second Skin*, although a specialized article, is nevertheless a good introduction to Hawkes's general tactic of making his narrator unreliable—of forcing the reader to work through and around what the narrative voice claims the facts of the case (often wrongly) to be.

INDEX

Absalom, Absalom: xvii, 125
Actor's Workshop, 123
Ada, xvi
Adeppi: 109; *see also* Chapter 4, Animal imagery
Adrian. *See The Questions*
Albatross, 115
Albee, Edward, 123, 176
Alligator, 46
America, 124–25
American West: mythical treatment of, 110; *see also* Chapter 3
An American Dream, 102
An American Tragedy, 102
Anderson, Chester, x
Andrewes, Lancelot, 33
Animal imagery: xvi, xx, 1–4, 58, 85, 105; as analog, 81, 89; and death, 43, 94; genitals, 50; metaphorical transfer of characteristics, 9–11, 13, 18, 20–21, 37, 46, 51, 53–54, 59, 62, 107–108, 118–22, 144ff; mythic quality, 48–49; narrator of, 63, 80; unity of, 132ff; worlds of characters, 7–8, 25–26, 30, 41, 49, 65, 83, 85–86, 98, 114–15, 121, 127–28; *see also* specific animals, Chapter 8
Ant, 21, 82
Antonina. *See* Chapter 4
Apocalypse, 82
The Armies of the Night, xvi
Arsella. *See* Chapter 4
Art: Cyril's concept of, 145, 154, 162; *see also* Tapestry, Photography
Artificial insemination, 113, 117–18
Assassin, 25

Assassins, 102
Atmosphere. *See* Narrative
Balamir. *See* Chapter 2
Banks, Margaret: 109; *see also* Chapter 5
Banks, Michael: 109, 126, 162, 178*n*; *see also* Chapter 5
Barabo, Signor. *See* Chapter 4
"Barn Burning," 60
Barnes, Djuna: xviii, 88, 122; influence on Hawkes, xvii
Barth, John, ix
Bat, 6, 109, 132
Beatrix. *See The Innocent Party*
Bech: A Book, xvi
Beckett, Samuel: 123, 130; characters, xi, 178*n*
Bees, 7, 110
The Beetle Leg: xii, 62, 65, 68, 78, 81, 84, 110–11, 120–21, 124, 127; locale of, xi; *see also* Chapter 3
Beetle, 48, 111
Benito Cereno, 125, 129
Bestiality. *See* Animal imagery
Bingo. *See The Wax Museum*
Bird: xvii, 7, 9, 23–27, 32, 34, 43, 51, 55–56, 66, 70, 73–74, 81, 84–85, 91, 98, 114, 144–46, 153, 160; *see also* Chapter 8
Blau, Herbert, on *The Innocent Party,* 123–24, 134
The Blood Oranges: xi, xii, xix, 4, 124, 129, 135; excerpted, xxi; *see also* Chapter 8
Boar, 65
Bohn, Harry. *See* Chapter 3

Brighton: 162; *see also* Chapter 5
Brighton Rock, 88, 101–103
Brother Bolo. *See* Chapter 4
Brother Dolce. *See* Chapter 4
Buck, 24
Bull, 144
Burgess, Anthony, 102
Butterfly, 4

Camper. *See* Chapter 3
The Cannibal: xvi, 43, 58, 62–63, 77–78, 81, 100, 109, 120–21, 131, 143, 168; *see also* Chapter 2
Cannibals and Christians, xv, 172
Carver, Wayne, on *The Blood Oranges,* 141
Cassandra. *See* Chapter 6
Cat, xx, 5, 12–13, 44, 65, 74–75, 89, 92, 95
Catherine. *See* Chapter 8
Cello, 118, 122, 135
The Centaur, xvi
Centipede, 1, 127–28, 137
Characterization: and narration, 60; nature of Hawkes's, ix, xi, xii, 1, 11, 37, 61, 85–86; stereotyped, 17; *see also* Animal imagery, Language
Charivari: 35–37, 58, 60, 85, 95, 124, 127; language of, 59, 120–21; *see also* Chapter 1
Chicken, 24, 31–32, 56, 118
Children in Hawkes's fictions, 173
Christ: 27–30, 71, 81, 155, 164; symbol, 63, 68, 82, 84; *see also* Chapter 4
Christianity, 49, 58, 61
Circe, 7, 97
Clam, 119
Cock. *See* Rooster
Cocoon, 28
Contessa. *See* Chapter 4
Couples, xiv
Cow, 9, 11–12, 21, 31, 52–53, 77, 79, 85, 111, 113, 116–18, 120
Cowboy myth: 58, 60; *see also* Chapter 3
Cowles. *See* Chapter 5
Cricket, 116
Critics, on Hawkes, xxi

Cromwell, *See* Chapter 2
Crow, 67, 85
Crucifixion: 28–29, 33; *see also* Christianity
Cyril: xi; narrator, xii, 134; on sexuality, 144–45; *see also* Chapter 8

The Day of the Locust, 69
Death: 3, 8, 13, 19, 21, 23–24, 26–28, 30, 65, 83–84, 95, 109–10, 112, 116–19, 122, 135–38, 159–60; animal imagery, 43, 54, 94, 98–100, 148; Stella kills fowl, 31–32; suicide, 57, 134, 136, 141; time, 149ff, 168–69; *see also* Stench, Chapter 8
Deer, 68
Detail of Hawkes's language, 32, 127–28
Divining rod, 51
Dog, 2, 8, 21, 26, 29–30, 43, 45–46, 49, 56, 58, 67, 70, 72, 76–77, 81–83, 89–90, 99, 111, 114, 118, 139, 156, 159
Donkey, 21, 56, 65, 72, 81, 83
Dolphin, 25
Dora. *See* Chapter 5
Dove, 6, 72–73, 178n
Dream, in Hawkes's fictions, xii, 15, 25, 34, 79, 92, 94, 98–100, 119, 126–27, 131–33, 135–36, 153, 158
Dreiser, Theodore, 102
Duck, 24
The Duke. *See* Chapter 2

Eagle, 25, 83, 169–70
Edenbaum, Robert, on *The Lime Twig,* 87, 99
Edouard, *See* Chapter 4
Edward: 132; *see also The Innocent Party, The Undertaker*
Eel, 48, 76
Egg, 111–12, 120, 126
Eliot, T. S.: influence on Hawkes, xvii, 3, 33, 41, 47, 49–51, 59, 72; *see also Gerontion, Magi, Prufrock, The Waste Land*
Enck, John, Hawkes interviewer, xv
Epiphany, 33

INDEX

Ernst. See Chapter 2
Evil: 62–63, 141; see also Death

Fatima, 47
Faulkner, William: 126–27; characters of, 60; influence on Hawkes, xvii, 125
Fernandez. See Chapter 6
Fertility myth: 58, 71; see also Chapter 3
Feste, and Cyril, 166–67
Fiedler, Leslie: 180n; on *The Lime Twig*, 88; support of Hawkes, xxi
The Finn. See Chapter 3
Fiona. See Chapter 8
Fish: 8–9, 22, 65, 68, 118, 126, 155, 160; see also Chapter 3
Fisher King, 39–41, 48, 51, 53, 55–56, 58
Fishermen, 115
Fishing, xii, xv, xix, 7–8, 46, 48–50, 53, 55, 118
Fishook, xii, xiii, 137
Flea, 26
Ford, Ford Madox: 139–41; influence on Hawkes, xvii; see also Chapter 8
Form, Hawkes's novels: xvi; see also Narrative
Fox, xx, 23, 35–36, 65, 71, 131
Frank. See *The Wax Museum*
Frazer, James G., 40
Freud, Sigmund, 13, 122
Frohock, W. M., on *The Lime Twig*, 88–89

Gander. See Goose
Gass, William, on *Under the Volcano*, 19, 168, 178
A Generous Man, xvi
Gentleness: 52; see also Cow
Germany. See Chapter 2
Gerontion, 59, 72
George. See *The Wax Museum*
Gertrude. See Chapter 6
Goat, 22, 79, 156–57
The Good Soldier: 139; see also Chapter 8
Goose, 21, 68, 71, 79–80

The Goose on the Grave: 19, 33, 72–86, 105, 109; see also Chapter 4
Graham, John, xxii
"The Grandmother," 177n
Greene, Graham: 101, 104; see also Chapter 5
Grotesqueries, in Hawkes's fictions, xvii, 1, 18, 22, 64
Guerard, Albert J.: x, 171; on *The Cannibal*, 176–77n; on dreams, 95; Hawkes's teacher, xiii, xxi, 1, 176n; on Hawkes's characters, 88, 173; on *Second Skin*, 134
Il Gufo. See Chapter 4
Guinea hen, 74
Gull, 115, 159

Hallucination: 11, 14–15; Hawkes on, 17; use of in narrative, 1–2; see also Dream
Hangman: 67; see also Chapter 4
Hawkes, John: as dramatist, 123, 134; background of, xiii, xiv; on *The Blood Oranges*, 139–40; on *The Cannibal*, 17, 35–36; on Céline, xvi; fascination with England, 28; on Faulkner, xvii; on fiction, xv, xvi; on Hencher, 90, 94–95; importance of, xvi; on *The Lime Twig*, 87–88, 178n; nature of prose, xviii–xix, 59; on parody of novel, 102; preoccupation with war, 109, see also Chapter 2; on *Second Skin*, 107, 179n; on title for *The Blood Oranges*, 148–49; on writing, xii, xviii–xix, 134
Hencher, William. See Chapter 5
Historical investigation: 23; see also Time
Homosexuality. See Sexuality
Horse: 15, 21, 25, 27, 29, 34, 63, 75, 85; symbol of death, 94, 131; symbol of suffering, 32; see also Chapter 5
How It Is, xi, 178n
Hugh. See Chapter 8, Photography
Hummingbird, 10, 107–108, 122

Iguana, 108, 116, 120
Illyria: 130; see also Chapter 8, Time

189

INDEX

Imagistic power, Hawkes's, 28, 31, 58
"In the Penal Colony," 14, 180n
Incest: 126–27, 131; see also Sexuality
The Innocent Party: xvi, 124–29, 132; see also Chapter 7
Insane asylum, 18, 32, 158
Insect, 10, 13, 46, 55, 69, 82, 109, 111
Irony, Hawkes's use of, 8, 147
Irving, Jules, 123
Italy. See Chapter 4

Jackal, 66
Jackdaw, 1, 121
Jacop. See Chapter 4
James, Henry, 122, 178n, 181–82n
Jane. See The Innocent Party
Jellyfish, 126
Jonah, 54
Journey to the End of the Night, Hawkes on, xvi
Jutta: 109; see also Chapter 2

Kafka, Franz, 11, 14, 180n
Kate, Catalina. See Chapter 6
Kinter, William, x
Kuehl, John, on Hawkes, 179–80n

Lamb, 82
Lampson, Luke. See Chapter 3, Death
Lampson, Ma. See Chapter 3, Animal imagery
Lampson, Mulge: 84; see also Chapter 3
Language: The Blood Oranges, 140, 163–64, 167–70; The Cannibal, 18, 32; Charivari, 1, 15; critics on fictional, 171; The Lime Twig, 105; narrative, 73–74; nature of Hawkes's, xx, xxi, 172–73; poetic quality, 59; Second Skin, 120–22
Larry. See Chapter 5
The Last Gentleman, xiv
Last Supper, parody of, 68–69
Laughlin, James, 88, 183
Laval, Sybilline: 115, 162; see also Chapter 5
Leech, Cap. See Chapter 3
Leevey. See Chapter 2
The Lime Twig: 19, 29, 85, 109, 115,

119–20, 126, 131, 144, 162; Hawkes on, 87–88; see also Chapter 5
Lion, 24, 115
Lizard: xx, 108, 110–11; see also Chapter 6
Locust, 111, 116
Lolita, xiv, 158
London. See Chapter 5
A Long and Happy Life, xiv
Lou. See Chapter 3
Lowry, Malcolm, 19, 117, 131
Lyricism, 59, 141ff

Madonna. See Mary, Virgin
Magi, 33, 55
Magic Mountain, 27
Mailer, Norman: xiv, 102; as interviewer, xv; language of, 172
"The Man." See The Questions
Mandan, 44
Marvell, Andrew, 145, 161, 166
Mary, Virgin: 62, 65–68, 71, 74, 76, 79, 163–64; see also Chapter 4
Melville, Herman, 125
"The Merchant." See Chapter 2
The Metamorphosis, 11
Metaphoric worlds, of Hawkes's fictions: xi, 2, 4, 7, 31; dancer, 12; murder, 32; narrative tapestry, 4, 80; see also Animal imagery
Miranda. See Chapter 6
Mistletoe, 44, 46
Mollusk, 118
Monco, 70
Monica. See Chapter 5
Monkey, 22–23, 31–32, 67
Monologue, interior: 59; see also Language
Moses, 54
Mosley, Nicholas, 102
Moth, 22
Mouse, 3, 76, 114, 118
The Moviegoer, xiv
Mule. See Donkey
Mussel, 119
Myth: 60; animal, 41, 48, 50; Christian, 52; fertility, 58; water god, 39; women, 43; see also Chapter 3

INDEX

Nabokov, Vladimir: xiv, 158; influence on Hawkes, xix
Narrative: change of focus, 77, 85; cyclical, 122; discussion of line, 35–36; tapestry, 140; unity of, 80, 124; see also Time, Language, Animal imagery
Narrators: xvi; see also Chapter 8
Native Son, 102
The Nativity, 79
Nazism: 18; see also Chapter 2
"The Nearest Cemetery," 179–80n
Negro, 108, 125, 128, 133, 135–36
Nightmare. See Dream
Nino. See Chapter 4

O'Connor, Flannery, influence on Hawkes, xvii, 122
Oedipus, 57, 82
Olds, Marshall, ix
Orpheus, 121, 135
Oven tit, 99
Owl: 85; see also Chapter 4
The Owl: 19, 61–72, 74, 77–78, 89, 105; see also Chapter 4
Ox, 21, 67

Pagan: 156; see also Chapter 8
Parody, Hawkes's use of: 1, 28, 42, 135, 138; Christian, 68–69; of Eliot, 33; of Hamlet, 108; of Indians, 56; of novel, 102; of Renaissance romances, 129; of Twelfth Night, 151
Peacock, 109
Pearls, 99
Pentecost, 67–68, 71
Percy, Walker, xiv
Phoebe. See The Innocent Party
Photography, 132, 135, 152–53, 162
Pig, 77, 111
Pinter, Harold, 123
Pipistrello. See Chapter 4
Pixie. See Chapter 6
Pnin, xiv
Price, Reynolds, xiv
Prometheus, 128
Prose style, Hawkes's. See Language

Prufrock, The Love Song of J. Alfred, 7–10, 59, 126
Pucento. See Chapter 4
Pynchon, Thomas, 102

Quail, xvi
The Questions, 123, 130–34, 158

Rabbit, 31
Rat, 31, 80, 109
Raven, 65
Reader response to Hawkes: xiii, xxi, 11, 43, 90, 170; see also Chapter 8
Red Devils: 111; see also Chapter 3
Reptile: 47, 120; see also Lizard, Iguana
Rock Castle. See Chapter 5
Rook, 67, 85
Rooster, 2, 55, 72
Rosella. See Chapter 8
Royal Canadian Mounted Policeman, 129

Sale, Roger, 147–49
Sally Ann. See The Wax Museum
Sardine, 74
Sasso Fetore. See Chapter 4
Satan, 58
Satyr: xx, 141; see also Chapter 8
Scholes, Robert, on Charivari, 176n
Scorpion, 19
Seal, 115
"The Second Coming," 152, 165
Second Skin: xi, 52, 85, 106, 124, 130, 132, 134–35, 139, 144, 161; critical study of, xxi, xxii; see also Chapter 6
Selvaggia. See Chapter 2
Serpent. See Snake
Sexuality: 8, 13, 15, 49–50, 52, 65–66, 70, 85, 98–99, 112, 115–16, 118, 124, 131; homosexuality, 73, 76, 108, 117; singer of, 143; see especially Chapter 8
Shark, 25, 128
Sheep, 21
Sheriff. See Chapter 3
Sisyphus, 82, 127
Skipper: xi, 132, 134, 139, 161, 180n; see also Chapter 6

191

INDEX

Slyter, Sidney. *See* Chapter 5
Snake: 13–14, 37, 46, 59, 65, 93, 111–13, 144, 153; *see also* Chapter 6
Snow, Herr. *See* Chapter 2
Snow, Madame Stella: 43, 100; *see also* Chapter 2
Sonny: 180*n; see also* Chapter 6
Sosostris, Madame, 47
The Sound and the Fury, 108
Sparrow. *See* Chapter 5
Speer, Albert, 20
Spider, 20, 53, 83
Squid, 115
Stags, 8
Stench: 9, 13, 20–21, 23–24, 30, 118–19, 125, 151, 159; *see also* Death
Stenger, Harold L., Jr., x
Stintz, Herr. *See* Chapter 2
Suicide. *See* Death
Surrealism: 11, 89; of fables, 62; *see also* Dream
Swine, 67, 99
Sylvan sources: 134, 145–46, 156; *see also* Chapter 8

Tammuz, 40, 42, 51
Tanner, Tony: on *The Cannibal,* 177*n;* on Hawkes's landscapes, 173; on *Second Skin,* 180–81*n*
Tantalus, 128
Tapestry: 4, 141, 146, 148, 155, 157, 165; *see also* Chapter 8
Tattoo, 109, 132
Tayler, Edward, x
The Tempest, 41
Thegna. *See* Chapter 3
Thick. *See* Chapter 5
Thomas, Dylan, 37
Tiger, 21
Time: 23, 26, 77–78, 113, 115, 124, 130, 135, 137–38, 164, 167; dialectic,

143; warp, 46, 62, 99, 117; *see also* Chapter 8
"To His Coy Mistress," 145, 161
"The Traveler," 177*n*
Tremor of Intent, 102
Trilling, Lionel, 122
Turkey, 115
Twelfth Night, and *The Blood Oranges,* 140, 151, 166

Under the Volcano, 19, 117, 131, 168
The Undertaker, xii, 134–38
Updike, John, xiv

V, 102
Van, Emily: 95; *see also* Chapter 1
Van, Henry. *See* Chapter 1
Visual images, Hawkes on, xix
Wade. *See* Chapter 3
Wandering Jew, 58
Wasp, 114
The Waste Land, 3, 8, 35, 41, 59
Water-god myth, 39, 44, 50–51, 53
The Wax Museum, 129–30
West, Nathanael: influences on Hawkes, 69; techniques of, xvi, xvii
Weston, Jessie L., 39
Whale, 54, 126
Why Are We in Vietnam? xiv
Williams, Tennessee, 123, 125
The Wings of the Dove, 178*n*
Wolf, 51, 65, 76, 79
Wolfhound, 74
Worm, 22, 111, 115, 127
Womb, 6
Wright, Richard, 102, 133
"Writer's writer," discussion of, xiii

Yeats, William Butler, 152, 164–65
"The Young Girl." *See The Questions*

Zizendorf: 143; *see also* Chapter 2